Educational Vision *of* Mahatma Gandhi

2025

Educational Vision *of* Mahatma Gandhi

Dr. Rajesh Verma
Lecturer, School of Education
Nalanda Open University, Patna

ABD PUBLISHERS
Jaipur New Delhi

ABD PUBLISHERS

Regd. Off. "Bony Residency", Gate No. 2
Opp. Tilak Public School, Vishweswariya Nagar,
Gopalpura Road, Jaipur - 302018, India
Ph: 0141 - 2761280, Telefax: 2761381
Email: abdpublishersjpr@gmail.com

Delhi Office: 102, 1st Floor, Satyam House,
4327/3, Ansari Road, Darya Ganj,
New Delhi - 110002, India
Ph: 011-45652440

visit us: www.oxfordbookcompany.com

Published in India, 2023

ISBN: 9788183762373

Typeset by Shivangi Computer, Jaipur

Printed and bound in India by Thomson Press Ltd.,
New Delhi

Contents

Preface

Given Gandhi's values and his vision of what constituted a truly civilized and free India, it was not surprising that he developed firm views on education. Education not only moulds the new generation, but reflects a society's fundamental assumptions about itself and the individuals which compose it. His experience in South Africa not only changed his outlook on politics but also helped him to see the role education played in that struggle. He was aware that he had been a beneficiary of Western education and for a number of years while he was in South Africa he still tried to persuade Indians to take advantage of it. However, it was not until the early years of this century, when he was in his middle thirties, that he became so opposed to English education that he could write about 'the rottenness of this education' and that 'to give millions a knowledge of English is to enslave them ... that, by receiving English education, we have enslaved the nation'. He was enraged that he had to speak of Home Rule or Independence in what was clearly a foreign tongue, that he could not practice in court in his mother tongue, that all official documents were in English as were all the best newspapers and that education was carried out in English for the chosen few. He did not blame the colonial powers for this. He saw that it was quite logical that they would want an elite of native Indians to become like their rulers in both manners and values. In this way, the Empire could be consolidated. Gandhi blamed his fellow Indians for accepting the situation. Later in his life he was to declare that 'real freedom will come only when we free ourselves of the domination of Western education, Western culture and Western way of living which have been ingrained in us .. . Emancipation from this culture would mean real freedom for us'.

As we have seen, Gandhi had not only rejected colonial education but also put forward a radical alternative. So what was this alternative? What was so radical about it? Gandhi's proposal intended to stand the education system on its head. The social philosophy and the curriculum of what he called 'basic education' thus favoured the child belonging to the lowest stratum of society in such a way it implied a programme of social transformation. It sought to alter the symbolic meaning of 'education' and to change the established structure of opportunities for education.

This book presents Gandhian educational thought in pros and cons. Certainly, this book will help the readers to systematize their ideas about Gandhi's educational thought and provide them the glimpses of the original ideas and thinking about various aspects of education, which are definitely products of his creative genius.

—*Rajesh Verma*

1

Medium of Instruction

Mother Tongue Fundamental

I must cling to my mother tongue as to my mother's breast, in spite of its shortcomings. It alone can give me the life-giving milk. *(Harijan, 25 August 1946 (CW 85, p. 88))*

Medium of Instruction: Mother Tongue

I am hoping that this University will see to it that the youths who come to it will receive their instruction through the medium of their vernaculars. Our language is the reflection of ourselves, and if you tell me that our languages are too poor to express the best thought, then I say that the sooner we are wiped out of existence the better for us. Is there a man who dreams that English can ever become the national language of India? (Cries of 'Never') Why this handicap on the nation? Just consider for one moment what an unequal race our lads have to run with every English lad. I had the privilege of a close conversation with some Poona professors.

They assured me that every Indian youth, because he reached his knowledge through the English language, lost at least six precious years of life. Multiply that by the number of students turned out by our schools and colleges and find out for yourselves how many thousand years have been lost to the nation. The charge against us is, that we have no initiative. How can we have any if we are to devote the precious years of our life to the mastery of a foreign tongue? We fail in this attempt also.... I have heard it said that after all it is English-educated India which is leading and which is doing everything for the nation.

It would be monstrous if it were otherwise. The only education we receive is English education. Surely we must show something for it. But suppose that we had been receiving during the past fifty years education through our vernaculars, what should we have today? We should have today a free India, we should have our educated men, not as if they were foreigners in their own land, but speaking to the heart of the nation; they would be working amongst the poorest of the poor, and whatever they would have gained during the past fifty years would be a heritage for the nation (Applause). Today even our wives are not sharers in our best thought. Look at Professor Bose and Professor Ray and their brilliant researches. Is it not a shame that their researches are not the common property of the masses? *(Speech at Banaras Hindu University, 6 February 1916 – Speeches and Writings of Mahatma Gandhi, pp.318–20 (CW 13, pp. 211–12))*

Foreign Medium

The foreign medium has caused brain fag, put an undue strain upon the nerves of our children, made them crammers and imitators, unfitted them for original work and thought, and disabled them for filtrating their learning to the family or the masses. The foreign medium has made our children practically foreigners in their own land. It is the greatest tragedy of the existing system. The foreign medium has prevented the growth of our vernaculars. If I had the powers of a despot, I would today stop the tuition of our boys and girls through a foreign medium, and require all the teachers and professors on pain of dismissal to introduce the change forthwith. I would not wait for the preparation of textbooks. They will follow the change. It is an evil that needs a summary remedy. *(Young India, 1 September 1921 (CW 21, p. 40))*

Vernacular versus Foreign Medium

But for the fact that the only higher education, the only education worth the name has been received by us through the English medium, there would be no need to prove such a self-evident proposition that the youth of a nation to remain a nation must receive all instruction including the highest in its own vernacular or vernaculars. Surely, it is a self-demonstrated proposition that the youth of a nation cannot keep or establish a living contact with the masses unless their knowledge is received and assimilated through a medium understood by the people.

Who can calculate the immeasurable loss sustained by the nation owing to thousands of its young men having been obliged to waste years in mastering a foreign language and its idiom of which in their daily life they have the least use and in learning which they had to neglect their own mother tongue and their own literature? There never was a greater superstition than that a particular language can be incapable of expansion or expressing abstruse or scientific ideas. A language is an exact reflection of the character and growth of its speakers.

Among the many evils of foreign rule this blighting imposition of a foreign medium upon the youth of the country will be counted by history as one of the greatest. It has sapped the energy of the nation, it has shortened the lives of the pupils, it has estranged them from the masses, it has made education unnecessarily expensive. If this process is still persisted in, it bids fair to rob the nation of its soul. The sooner therefore educated India shakes itself free from the hypnotic spell of the foreign medium, the better it would be for them and the people. *(Young India, 5 July 1928 (CW 37, p. 22))*

De-Indianizing Education

I find daily proof of the increasing and continuing wrong being done to the millions by our false de-Indianizing education. These graduates who are my valued associates themselves flounder when they have to give expression to their innermost thoughts. They are strangers in their own homes. Their vocabulary in the mother tongue is so limited that they cannot always finish their speech without having recourse to English words and even sentences. Nor can they exist without English books. They often write to one another in English. I cite the case of my companions to show how deep the evil has gone. For we have made a conscious effort to mend ourselves.

It has been argued that the wastage that occurs in our colleges need not worry us if, out of the collegians, one Jagadish Bose can be produced by them. I should freely subscribe to the argument, if the wastage was unavoidable. I hope I have shown that it was and is even now avoidable. Moreover the creation of a Bose does not help the argument. For Bose was not a product of the present education. He rose in spite of the terrible handicaps under which he had to labour. And his knowledge became almost intransmissible to the masses. We seem to have come to think that no one can hope to be like a Bose unless he knows English. I cannot conceive a grosser superstition than this. No Japanese feels so helpless as we seem to do.

The medium of instruction should be altered at once and at any cost, the provincial languages being given their rightful place. I would prefer temporary chaos in higher education to the criminal waste that is daily accumulating.

In order to enhance the status and the market-value of the provincial languages, I would have the language of the law courts to be the language of the province where the court is situated. The proceedings of the provincial legislatures must be in the language, or even the languages of the province where a province has more than one language within its borders. I suggest to the legislators that they could, by enough application, inside of a month understand the languages of their provinces. There is nothing to prevent a Tamilian from easily learning the simple grammar and a few hundred words of Telugu, Malayalam, and Kanarese all allied to Tamil. At the centre Hindustani must rule supreme.

In my opinion this is not a question to be decided by academicians. They cannot decide through what language the boys and girls of a place are to be educated. That question is already decided for them in every free country. Nor can they decide the subjects to be taught. That depends upon the wants of the country to which they belong. Theirs is a privilege of enforcing the nation's will in the best manner possible. When this country becomes really free the question of medium will be settled only one way. The academicians will frame the syllabus and prepare textbooks accordingly. And the products of the education of a free

India will answer the requirements of the country as today they answer those of the foreign ruler. So long as we the educated classes play with this question, I very much fear we shall not produce the free and healthy India of our dream. We have to grow by strenuous effort out of our bondage, whether it is Educational, Economical, Social or Political. The effort itself is three-fourths of the battle. *(Harijan, 9 July 1938 (CW 67, pp. 162–63))*

State Languages

If the medium is changed at once and not gradually, in an incredibly short time we shall find textbooks and teachers coming into being to supply the want. And if we mean business, in a year's time we shall find that we need never have been party to the tragic waste of the nation's time and energy in trying to learn the essentials of culture through a foreign medium. The condition of success is undoubtedly that provincial languages are introduced at once in Government offices and courts, if the Provincial Governments have the power or the influence over the courts. If we believe in the necessity of the reform, we can achieve it in no time. *(Harijan, 30 July 1938 (CW 67, p. 212))*

Richness of Dialects

Gandhiji deprecated the suggestion that it would need a lot of research and preparation to enable them to impart technical education through the medium of the mother tongue. Those who argued like that, were unaware of the rich treasure of expressions and idioms that were buried in the dialects of our villages. In Gandhiji's opinion there was no need to go to Sanskrit or Persian in search for many expressions. He had been in Champaran and he had found that the village folk there, could fully express themselves with ease and without the help of a single foreign expression or idiom. As an illustration of their resourcefulness, he mentioned the word *hava gadi* which they had coined to denote a motor car. *(Harijan, 18 August 1946 (CW 85, p. 144))*

National Language

It behoves us to devote attention to a consideration of a national language, as we have done to that of the medium of instruction. If English is to become a national language, it ought to be treated as a compulsory subject. Can English become the national language? Some learned patriots contend that even to raise the question betrays ignorance. In their opinion, English already occupies that place. His Excellency the Viceroy in his recent utterance has merely expressed a hope that English will occupy that place. His enthusiasm does not take him as far as that of the former. His Excellency believes that English will day after day command a larger place, will permeate the family circle, and at last rise to the status of a national language. A superficial consideration will support the viceregal contention. The condition of our educated classes gives one the impression that all our activities would come to a standstill if we stop the use of English. And yet deeper thought will show that English can never and ought not to become the national language of India. What is the test of national language?

1. For the official class it should be easy to learn.
2. The religious, commercial and political activity throughout India should be possible in that language.
3. It should be the speech of the majority of the inhabitants of India.
4. For the whole of the country it should be easy to learn.
5. In considering the question, weight ought not to be put upon momentary of shortlived conditions.

The English language does not fulfil any of the conditions above-named. The first ought to have been the last, but I have purposely given it the first place, because that condition alone gives it the appearance of being applicable to the English language. But upon further consideration we should find that for the officials even at the present moment it is not an easy language to learn. In our scheme of administration, it is assumed that the number of English officials will progressively decrease, so that in the end only the Viceroy and others whom one may count on one's finger-tips will be English. The majority are of Indian nationality today, and their number must increase.

And every one will admit that for them, English is more difficult to be learnt than any Indian language. Upon an examination of the second condition, we find that until the public at large can speak English, religious activity through that tongue is an impossibility. And a spread of English to that extent among the masses seems also impossible. English cannot satisfy the third condition, because the majority in India do not speak it. The fourth, too, cannot be satisfied by English, because it is not an easy language to learn for the whole of India.

Considering the last condition we observe that the position that English occupies today is momentary. The permanent condition is that there will be little necessity for English in national affairs. It will certainly be required for imperial affairs. That, therefore, it will be an imperial language, the language of diplomacy, is a different question. For that purpose its knowledge is a necessity. We are not jealous of English. All that is contended for is, that it ought not to be allowed to go beyond its proper sphere. And as it will be the imperial language, we shall compel our Malaviyajis, our Shastriars and our Banerjees to learn it. And we shall feel assured that they will advertise the greatness of India in other parts of the world. But English cannot become the national language of India. To give it that place is like an attempt to introduce Esperanto. In my opinion, it is unmanly even to think that English can become our national language. The attempt to introduce Esperanto merely betrays ignorance. Then which is the language that satisfies all the five conditions? We shall be obliged to admit that Hindi satisfies all those conditions.

I call that language Hindi which Hindus and Mohammedans in the North speak and write, either in the Devanagari or the Urdu character. Exception has been taken to this definition. It seems to be argued that Hindi and Urdu are different languages. This is not a valid argument. In the Northern parts of India, Musalmans and Hindus speak the same language. The literate classes have created a division. The learned Hindus have Sanskritized Hindi. The Musalmans, therefore, cannot understand it. The Moslems of Lucknow have Persianized their speech and made it unintelligible to the Hindus. These represent two excesses of the same language. They find no common place in the speech of the masses. I have lived in the North. I have freely mixed with Hindus and Mohammedans and although I have but a poor knowledge of Hindi, I have never found any difficulty in holding communion with them. Call the language of the North what you will, Urdu or Hindi, it is the same. If you write it in the Urdu character, you may know it as Urdu. Write the same thing in the Nagari character and it is Hindi.

There, therefore, remains a difference about the script. For the time being Mohammedan children will certainly write in the Urdu character, and Hindus will mostly write in the Devanagari. I say mostly, because thousands of Hindus use the Urdu character, and some do not even know the Nagari character. But when Hindus and Mohammedans come to regard one another without suspicion, when the causes begetting suspicion are removed, that script which has greater vitality will be more universally used, and therefore, become the national script. Meanwhile those Hindus and Mohammedans who desire to write their petitions in the Urdu character, should be free to do so and should have the right of having them accepted at the seat of the National Government.

There is not another language capable of competing with Hindi in satisfying the five conditions. Bengali comes next to Hindi. But the Bengalis themselves make use of Hindi outside Bengal. No one wonders to see a Hindi-speaking man making use of Hindi, no matter where he goes. Hindu preachers and Mohammedan Moulvis deliver their religious discourses throughout India in Hindi and Urdu and even the illiterate masses follow them. Even the unlettered Gujarati going to the North, attempts to use a few Hindi words whereas a gatekeeper from the North declines to speak in Gujarati even to his employer, who has on that account to speak to him in broken Hindi. I have heard Hindi spoken even in the Dravid country.

It is not true to say that in Madras one can go on with English. Even there I have employed Hindi with effect. In the trains I have heard Madras passengers undoubtedly use Hindi. It is worthy of note that Mohammedans throughout India speak Urdu and they are to be found in large numbers in every Province. Thus Hindi is destined to be the national language. We have made use of it as such in times gone by. The rise of Urdu itself is due to that fact. The Mohammedan kings were unable to make Persian or Arabic the national language. They accepted the Hindi grammar but employed the Urdu character and Persian words in their speeches.

They could not, however, carry on their intercourse with the masses through a foreign tongue. All this is not unknown to the English. Those who know anything of the sepoys, know that for them military terms have had to be prepared in Hindi or Urdu.

Thus we see that Hindi alone can become the national language. It presents some difficulty in the case of the learned classes in Madras. For men from the Deccan, Gujarat, Sind and Bengal it is easy enough. In a few months they can acquire sufficient command over Hindi to enable them to carry on national intercourse in that tongue. It is not so for the Tamils. The Dravidian languages are distinct from their Sanskrit sister in structure and grammar. The only thing common to the two groups is their Sanskrit vocabulary to an extent. But the difficulty is confined to the learned class alone. We have a right to appeal to their patriotic spirit and expect them to put forth sufficient effort in order to learn Hindi. For in future when Hindi has received State recognition, it will be introduced as a compulsory language in Madras as in other Provinces, and intercourse between Madras and them will then increase. English has not permeated the Dravidian masses. Hindi, however, will take no time. *(Speeches and Writings of Mahatma Gandhi, pp. 395-99)*

Hindustani

Do not consider for one moment that you can possibly make English a common medium of expression between the masses. Twenty-two crores of Indians know Hindustani—they do not know any other language. And if you want to steal into their hearts Hindustani is the only language open to you. *(Young India, 2 February 1921 (CW 19, p. 314))*

Richness of the Hindi Language

You talk of the poverty of Hindi literature—you talk of the poverty of today's Hindi, but if you dive deep into the pages of Tulsidas, probably you will share my opinion that there is no other book that stands equal to it in the literature of the world in modern languages. That one book has given me faith and hope which no other book has given. I think that it is a book which can stand any criticism and any scrutiny, alike in literary grace, in metaphor and in religious fervour. *(Young India, 9 February 1921 (CW 19, p. 322))*

National Languages Vs. State Languages

A fear had been expressed, observed Gandhiji, that the propagation of Rashtrabhasha or the national tongue would prove inimical to the provincial languages. That fear was rooted in ignorance. Provincial tongues provided the sure foundation on which the edifice of the national tongue should rest. The two were intended to complement, not supplant each other. *(Harijan, 18 August 1946 (Towards New Education, p. 74))*

Place of English

I do not dislike English; its riches are infinite. It is the language of administration and is rich with the wealth of knowledge. All this notwithstanding, I hold that it is not necessary for every Indian to learn it. But of this, I do not wish to speak more here. Students have been learning English and they have no option but to do so till some other system is devised and the present schools undergo a revolution. I shall, therefore, end this all-important subject of the mother tongue here, merely saying in conclusion that in their dealings with one another, and whenever possible, people should use only their mother tongue and that others, besides students, who are present here should strive their utmost to make the mother tongue the medium of education. *(Speech at Bihar Students Conference, Bhagalpur – 17 July 1917 (CW 14, p. 133))*

English versus Mother Tongue

English is a language of international commerce, it is the language of diplomacy, and it contains many a rich literary treasure, it gives us an introduction to Western thought and culture. For a few of us, therefore, a knowledge of English is necessary. They can carry on the departments of national commerce and international diplomacy, and for giving to the nation the best of Western literature, thought, and science. That would be the legitimate use of English, whereas today English has usurped the dearest place in our hearts and dethroned our mother tongues. It is an unnatural place due to our unequal relations with Englishmen. The highest development of the Indian mind must be possible without a knowledge of English. It is doing violence to the manhood and specially the womanhood of India to encourage our boys and girls to think that an entry into the best society is impossible without a knowledge of English. It is too humiliating a thought to be bearable. To get rid of the infatuation for English is one of the essentials of Swaraj. *(Young India, 2 February 1921 (CW 19, pp. 314–15))*

English: Language and Culture

My uncompromising opposition to the foreign medium has resulted in an unwarranted charge being levelled against me of being hostile to foreign culture or the learning of the English language. No reader of *Young India* could have missed the statement often made by me in these pages, that I regard English as the language of international commerce and diplomacy and therefore consider its knowledge on the part of some of us as essential. As it contains some of the richest treasures of thought and literature, I would certainly encourage its careful study among them who have linguistic talents and expect them to translate those treasures for the nation in its vernaculars. *(Young India, 1 September 1921 (CW 21, p. 40))*

English versus Hindi

I know this tussle between English and Hindi is almost an eternal tussle. Whenever I have addressed student audiences, I have been surprised by the demand for English. You know, or ought to know, that I am a lover of the English language. But I do believe that the students of India, who are expected to throw in their lot with the teeming millions and to serve them, will be better qualified if they pay more attention to Hindi than to English. I do not say that you should not learn English; learn it by all means. But, so far as I can see, it cannot be the language of the millions of Indian homes. It will be confined to thousands or tens of thousands, but it will not reach the millions. *(Harijan, 17 November 1933 (Towards New Education, p. 80))*

Literary Treasure in English

I must not be understood to decry English or its noble literature. The columns of the *Harijan* are sufficient evidence of my love of English. But the nobility of its literature cannot avail the Indian nation any more than the temperate climate or the scenery of

England can avail her. India has to flourish in her own climate, and scenery, and her own literature, even though all the three may be inferior to the English climate, scenery and literature. We and our children must build on our own heritage. If we borrow another, we impoverish our own. We can never grow on foreign victuals. I want the nation to have the treasures contained in that language and, for that matter, in other languages of the world, through its own vernaculars. I do not need to learn Bengali in order to know the beauties of Rabindranath's matchless productions. I get them through good translations. Gujarati boys and girls do not need to learn Russian to appreciate Tolstoy's short stories. They learn them through good translations. It is the boast of Englishmen that the best of the world's literary output is in the hands of that nation in simple English inside of a week of its publication. Why need I learn English to get at the best of what Shakespeare and Milton thought and wrote? *(Harijan, 9 July 1938 (CW 67, p. 161))*

English as an Optional Language

English is today admittedly the world language. I would therefore accord it a place as a second, optional language, not in the school but in the university course. That can only be for the select few—not for the millions. Today when we have not the means to introduce even free compulsory primary education, how can we make provision for teaching English? Russia has achieved all her scientific progress without English. It is our mental slavery that makes us feel that we cannot do without English. I can never subscribe to that defeatist creed. *(Harijan, 25 August 1946)*

Sanskrit and Education

For the purpose of marriage ceremonies, *sandhya, yajna* rituals and prayers, Sanskrit verses are used in our age. The verses are recited by the person officiating on these occasions and those who have engaged him join him in reciting the verses without understanding their meaning. Sanskrit is no longer our mother tongue. Many institutions ask the people to use that language for prayers, *sandhya, yajna* rituals, etc. But the people do not understand the language. How, then, can they concentrate attention on what is being recited? Sanskrit, moreover, is a difficult language. Learning the verses by heart and remembering their meanings seems to me, therefore, a double burden. When Sanskrit was people's mother tongue, all their work was done in it and that was but right. That is no longer the position now. It helps people to use their mother tongue for all their work, but our present practice is different. The religious ceremonies mentioned above are performed in Sanskrit among the general public.

My view is that Sanskrit should be used in all Hindu religious ceremonies. However good a translation, it cannot give us the meaning which lies in the sounds of certain words in the original. Moreover, by translating into regional languages, and remaining content with such translations, verses which belong to a language which has acquired a certain refinement over thousands of years and in which those verses have always been recited, we diminish the air of solemnity which attaches to them. But I have no doubt at all in my mind that the meaning of every verse and every step in the ceremony should be explained in their own language to the people for whose benefit they are being recited or performed.

It is also my view that the education of every Hindu is incomplete without an elementary knowledge of Sanskrit. I simply cannot conceive the continued existence of Hinduism without a widespread knowledge of Sanskrit. The language has been made difficult by the type of curriculum we follow in teaching it, in itself it is not difficult at all. Even if it is, the practice of dharma is still more difficult and, therefore, to those who wish to follow it in life the means of doing so should seem easy, however difficult they may actually be. *(Navajivan, 28 March 1926 (CW 30, p. 195) (Translated from Gujarati))*

Sanskrit and Other Languages

"It is the duty of every Indian student to learn Sanskrit—the duty not only of the Hindus but also of the Muslims, because, after all, Rama and Krishna were as much their ancestors as of the Hindus, and to understand them they must learn Sanskrit. But it is equally the duty of the Hindus to learn the language of the Muslims in order to keep in touch and communicate with them. Today we run away from each other's language because we have turned mad. Be sure that an institution which preaches hate and fear is not, cannot be, national." *(Speech at National Educational Conference, Hardwar – 20 March 1927 (CW 33, p. 170))*

Sanskrit Scriptures

And remember that since you are in a vast majority, the responsibility rests on your shoulders to make Jaffna, and through Jaffna Ceylon also perfectly dry. Hinduism does not permit you to drink. And if the board of education will do its duty, you will encourage Sanskrit study in your schools. I regard the education of any Hindu child as incomplete unless he has some knowledge of Sanskrit. And so far as I have been able to see we have in Hinduism no book so compact and so acceptable all round as the *Bhagavad Gita*. If you will, therefore, saturate your children and yourselves with the spirit of Hinduism, you will endeavour to understand the spirit of the teachings of the *Gita*. You should also cultivate a common knowledge of the *Mahabharata* and the *Ramayana*. *(Speech to Ceylon Hindus, Jaffna, 27 November 1927 (CW 35, p. 337))*

Sanskrit versus State Languages

Do you know that the Patna University has practically tabooed the study of Sanskrit? Do you approve of the step? If you do not, will you express your opinion in *Harijan*?

I do not know what the Patna University has done. But I quite agree with you that the study of Sanskrit is being sadly neglected. I belong to a generation which believed in the study of the ancient languages. I do not believe that such a study is a waste of time and effort. I believe it is an aid to the study of modern languages. This is truer of Sanskrit than of any other ancient language so far as India is concerned, and every nationalist should study it because it makes a study of the provincial languages easier than otherwise. It is the language in which our forefathers thought and wrote. No Hindu boy or girl should be without a knowledge of the rudiments of Sanskrit, if he will imbibe the spirit of his religion. Thus the Gayatri is untranslatable. No translation can give the music of the original which I hold has a meaning all its own. The Gayatri is but one example of what I have said. *(Harijan, 23 March 1940 (CW 71, p. 346))*

Pronunciation

By all means study Sanskrit. The effort made for learning correct pronunciation will not be wasted. Chaste pronunciation is a requisite for [learning] any language. But perhaps for Sanskrit accuracy of pronunciation is imperative. It is not at all necessary for you to study English. Assimilate the knowledge you already have and add to it. *(Letter to Balvant Sinha, 21 October 1944 (CW 78, p. 217))*

Languages versus Composite Culture

Every cultured Indian should know in addition to his own provincial language, if a Hindu, Sanskrit; if a Mohammedan, Arabic; if a Parsee, Persian; and all, Hindi. Some Hindus should know Arabic and Persian; some Mohammedans and Parsees, Sanskrit. Several Northerners and Westerners should learn Tamil. A universal language for India should be Hindi, with the option of writing it in Persian or Nagari characters. In order that the Hindus and Mohammedans may have closer relations, it is necessary to know both the characters. *(Hind Swaraj, p. 107)*

Language Chasm

Our love of the English language in preference to our own mother tongue has caused a deep chasm between the educated and politically-minded classes and the masses. The languages of India have suffered impoverishment. We flounder when we make the vain attempt to express abstruse thought in the mother tongue. There are no equivalents for scientific terms. The result has been disastrous. The masses remain cut off from the modern mind. We are too near our own times correctly to measure the disservice caused to India by this neglect of its great languages. It is easy enough to understand that unless we undo the mischief the mass mind must remain imprisoned. The masses can make no solid contribution to the construction of swaraj. It is inherent in swaraj based on nonviolence that every individual makes his own direct contribution to the Independence movement. The masses cannot do this fully unless they understand every step with all its implications. This is impossible unless every step is explained in their own languages. *((CW 75, p. 156-57))*

Place for Languages in Curriculum

It is now my opinion that in all Indian curricula of higher education there should be a place for Hindi, Sanskrit, Persian, Arabic and English, besides of course the vernacular. This big list need not frighten anyone. If our education were more systematic, and the boys free from the burden of having to learn their subjects through a foreign medium, I am sure learning all these languages would not be an irksome task, but a perfect pleasure. A scientific knowledge of one language makes a knowledge of other languages comparatively easy. *(Autobiography, p. 30)*

Multiplicity of Scripts

If we are to make good our claim as one nation, we must have several things common. We have a common culture running through a variety of creeds and sub-creeds. We have common disabilities. I am endeavouring to show that a common material for our dress is not only desirable but necessary. We need also a common language not in suppression of the vernaculars, but in addition to them. It is generally agreed that medium should be Hindustani—a resultant of Hindi and Urdu, neither highly Sanskritized, nor highly Persianized or Arabianized. The greatest obstacle in the way are the numerous scripts we have for the vernaculars. If it is possible to adopt a common script, we should remove a great hindrance in the way of realizing the dream, which at present it is, of having a common language.

A variety of scripts is an obstacle in more ways than one. It constitutes an effectual barrier against the acquisition of knowledge. The Aryan languages have so much in common that, if a great deal of time had not to be wasted in mastering the different scripts, we should all know several languages without much difficulty; for instance, most people who have a little knowledge of Sanskrit would have no difficulty in understanding the matchless creation of Rabindranath Tagore, if it was all printed in Devanagari script. But the Bengali script is a notice to the non-Bengalis—"hands off". Conversely, if the Bengalis knew the Devanagari script, they would at once be able to enjoy the marvellous beauty and spirituality of Tulsidas and a host of other Hindustani writers. When I returned to India in 1905, I had a communication from a society whose headquarters were, I believe, in Calcutta, and whose object was to advocate a common script for all India. I do not know the activities of that society, but its object is worthy, and a great deal of substantial work can be done by a few earnest workers in this direction.

There are obvious limitations. A common script for all India is a distant ideal. A common script for all those who speak the Indo-Sanskrit languages, including the Southern stock, is a practical ideal, if we can but shed our provincialisms. There is little virtue, for instance, in a Gujarati clinging to the Gujarati script. A provincial patriotism is good where it feeds the larger stream of all-India patriotism, as the latter is good to the extent that it serves the still larger end of the universe.

But a provincial patriotism that says "India is nothing, Gujarat is all", is wickedness. I have selected Gujarat because it is the halfway house, and because I am myself a Gujarati. In Gujarat, somewhat fortunately those who settled the principles of primary education, decided to make Devanagari script compulsory. Every Gujarati boy or girl, who has passed through a school, therefore knows both the Gujarati and the Devanagari scripts. If the committee had decided upon purely Devanagari script, it would have been better still. No doubt, the research scholars would still have learnt the Gujarati script for deciphering old manuscripts, but the Gujarati boy's energy would have been spared for more useful labour, if he had to learn only one instead of two scripts. The committee that settled the education scheme for Maharashtra, was more enlightened, and it simply required the Devanagari script.

The result is that a Mahratta reads, so far as mere reading is concerned, Tulsidas with as much facility as he reads Tukaram, and Gujaratis and Hindustanis read Tukaram with equal facility. The committee in Bengal, on the other hand, ruled otherwise, with the result we all know and many of us deplore. The treasures of the richest Indian vernacular have been rendered most difficult of access as if by design. That Devanagari should be the common script, I suppose, does not need any demonstration—the deciding factor being that it is the script known to the largest part of India.

These reflections arise, because, I was called upon to solve, during my visit to Cuttack, a practical question. There is a tribe wedged between the Hindi-speaking people in Bihar and Uriya-speaking people of Orissa. What was to be done for the education of its children? Were they to be taught through Uriya or through Hindi? Or were they to be taught their own dialect, and if they were, was the script to be Devanagari or a new invention? The first thought of the Utkal Friends was to absorb the tribe amongst the Uriyas.

The Biharis would think of absorbing them in Bihar, and if the elders of the tribe were consulted, they would most probably and naturally say that their dialect was just as good as the Uriya or the Bihari, and that it should be reduced to writing. And for them it would be a toss whether the script to be adopted should be Devanagari or Uriya, if not even a newly invented script, as has happened in modern times in at least two instances I know. Endeavouring to think in terms of all-India I suggested to my friends that, whilst it was proper for them to strengthen the Uriya language among the Uriya-speaking people, the children of this tribe should be taught Hindi and naturally the script should be Devanagari. A spirit that is so exclusive and narrow as to want every form of speech to be perpetuated and developed, is anti-national and anti-universal.

All undeveloped and unwritten dialects should, in my humble opinion, be sacrificed and merged in the great Hindustani stream. It would be a sacrifice only to be nobler, not a suicide. If we are to have a common language for cultured India, we must arrest the growth of any process of disintegration or multiplication of languages and scripts. We must promote a common language.

The beginning must naturally be made with the script, and until the Hindu–Muslim question is solved, confined perhaps to Hindu India. If I could have my way, I would make the learning of Devanagari script and Urdu script, in addition to the established provincial script, compulsory in all the provinces and I would print in Devanagari chief books in the different vernaculars with a literal translation in Hindustani. *(Young India, 27 August 1925 (CW 26, pp. 119–22))*

One Script, Many Languages

Although it is my firm conviction that there should be one script for all the Indian languages, and that script can only be Devanagari, I could not follow the correspondent's advice for the reasons stated in my note in *Navajivan,* and which I need not reiterate here. But there is no doubt that we ought to seize the opportunity that the great national awakening gives us, of not merely popularizing the idea but of doing something concrete in that direction. The Hindu–Muslim madness no doubt stands in the way of a thorough reform. But before the acceptance of Devanagari script becomes a universal fact in India, Hindu India has got to be converted to the idea of one script for all the languages derived from Sanskrit and the Dravidian stock.

At the present moment we have Bengali script in Bengal, Gurmukhi in the Punjab, Sindhi in Sind, Oriya in Utkal, Gujarati in Gujarat, Telugu in Andhradesha, Tamil in Tamil Nadu, Malayalam in Kerala, Kanarese in Karnataka, not to speak of Kaithi in Bihar and Modi in the Deccan. If all these scripts could be replaced by Devanagari for all practical and national purposes, it would mean a tremendous step forward. It will help to solidify Hindu India and bring the different provinces in closer touch. Anyone who has any knowledge of the different Indian languages and scripts knows to his cost what time it takes to master a new script. For the love of his country, no doubt, nothing is difficult, and time spent in mastering the different scripts, some of which are very beautiful, is in no way idly spent.

But this spirit of abandon is not to be expected of millions. National leaders have to make things easy for them. Therefore, we must have an easily adaptable universal script for all India, and there is nothing so adaptable and readymade as Devanagari script. There is, or there used to be, an all-India organization for this very purpose. I do not know what its activities are at present. But if the work has to be done, either the original association should be strengthened, or a new one formed for this purpose. The movement should in no way be confused with the spread of Hindi or Hindustani as the lingua franca. The latter work is going on very slowly, but steadily. Use of one script will facilitate the spread of one language.

But the functions of the two run parallel only up to a point. Hindi or Hindustani is not designed to replace the provincial languages, but is intended to supplement them, and to be used for interprovincial contact. And till the Hindu–Muslim tension lasts it takes the form either of Urdu written in the Persian script, and containing preponderance of Persian or Arabic words, or Hindi written in Devanagari and containing a preponderance of Sanskrit words. When the hearts of the two meet, the two forms of the same language will be fused together, and we shall have a resultant of the two, containing as many Sanskrit, Persians, Arabic or other words as may be necessary for its full growth and full expression. But one script is undoubtedly designed to displace all the different scripts so as to render it easy for people belonging to different provinces to learn provincial languages. The best way of achieving the purpose is first to make the learning of Devanagari script compulsory at least for Hindus in all the schools, as it is in Gujarat, and secondly to print the important literature in different Indian languages in Devanagari script.

Such effort has already been made to a certain extent. I have seen *Gitanjali* printed in Devanagari script. But the effort requires to be made on a large scale, and there should be propaganda carried on for the spread of such books. *(Young India, 14 July 1927 (CW 34, pp. 168–69))*

Devanagari and National Unity

The object of this conference is to collect gems from all provincial literatures and to make them available through Hindi. For this purpose I would make an appeal to you. Of course everyone must know his own language thoroughly well, and he should also know the great literature of other Indian languages through Hindi. But it is also the object of this conference to stimulate in our people the desire to know languages of other provinces, *e.g.*, Gujaratis should know Tamil, Bengalis should know Gujarati and so on. And I tell you from experience that it is not at all difficult to pick up another Indian language. But to this end a common script is quite essential.

It is not difficult to achieve in Tamil Nadu. For look at this simple fact: over 90 per cent our people are illiterate. We have to start with a clean slate with them. Why should we not start making them literate by means of a common script? In Europe they have tried the experiment of a common script quite successfully. Some people even go the length of saying that we might adopt the Roman script from Europe. After a good deal of controversy there is a consensus of opinion that the common script can be Devanagari and none else. Urdu is claimed as a rival, but I think neither Urdu nor Roman has the perfection and phonetic capacity of Devanagari. Please remember that I say nothing against your languages.

Tamil, Telugu, Malayalam, Kannada must be there and will be there. But why not teach the illiterate in these parts these languages through the Devanagari script. In the interest of the national unity we desire to achieve, the adoption of Devanagari as a common script is so essential. Here it is a question of just shedding our provincialism and narrowness, there are no difficulties at all. *(The Hindu, 27 March 1937 (CW 65, p. 27))*

Universalising Devanagari

I understand that some of the tribes in Assam are being taught to read and write through the Roman script instead of Devanagari. I have already expressed my opinion that the only script that is ever likely to be universal in India is Devanagari, either reformed or as it is. Urdu or Persian will go hand in hand unless Muslims, of their own free will, acknowledge the superiority of Devanagari from a purely scientific and national standpoint. But this is irrelevant to the present problem. The Roman cannot go hand in hand with the other two scripts. Protagonists of the Roman script would displace both. But sentiment and science alike are against the Roman script. Its sole merit is its convenience for printing and typing purpose. But that is nothing compared to the strain its learning would put upon millions.

It can be of no help to the millions who have to read their own literature either in their own provincial scripts or in Devanagari. Devanagari is easier for the millions of Hindus and even Muslims to learn, because the provincial scripts are mostly derived from Devanagari. I have included Muslims advisedly. The mother tongue of Bengali Muslims, for instance, is Bengali as is Tamil of Tamil Muslims. The present movement for the propagation of Urdu will, as it should, result in Muslims all over India learning Urdu in addition to their mother tongue. They must, in any case, know Arabic for the purpose of learning the Holy Koran.

But the millions whether Hindus or Muslims will never need the Roman script except when they wish to learn English. Similarly, Hindus who want to read their scriptures in the original have to and do learn the Devanagari script. The movement for universalizing the Devanagari script has thus a sound basis. The introduction of the Roman script is a superimposition which can never become popular. And all superimpositions will be swept out of existence when the true mass awakening comes, as it is coming, much sooner than anyone of us can expect from known causes. Yet the awakening of millions does take time. It cannot be manufactured. It comes or seems to come mysteriously. National workers can merely hasten the process by anticipating the mass mind. *(Harijan, 11February 1939 (CW 68, pp. 380–81))*

One Script for Sister Languages

The question of having one script for the Indian languages which are daughters of Sanskrit by birth or adoption has been before the public for a number of years. Yet in these days of aggressive provincialism, perhaps, any plea for one script will be regarded as an impertinence. But the literacy campaigns raging all over the country should compel a hearing for the advocates of one script. I have been one such for years. I remember having even adopted in South Africa Devanagari script for my Indian correspondence with Gujaratis in select cases. Interprovincial intercourse will be much facilitated by such adoption, and the learning of the various provincial languages will be made infinitely easier than it is today.

If the educated people of the land were to put their heads together and decide upon one script, its universal adoption should be an easy thing. To the millions who are illiterate it is a matter of indifference what script is prescribed to them. If the happy consummation comes to pass, there will be only two scripts in India—Devanagari and Urdu, and every nationalist will deem it his duty to master the two scripts. I am a lover of all Indian languages. I have tried to learn as many scripts as possible. And if only I had the time, even at the age of seventy I have energy enough to learn more Indian languages. That would be a recreation for me. But in spite of all my love for the languages I must confess that I have not learnt all the scripts.

But if the sister languages were written in one script, I should pick up a workable knowledge of the principal languages of the provinces in very little time. And Devanagari has nothing to be ashamed of in point of symmetry or beauty. I hope that those who are engaged in the literacy campaigns will give a passing thought to my suggestion. If they will adopt Devanagari script, they will save for the future generations tons of labour and time and earn their blessings. *(Harijan, 5 August 1939 (CW 70, pp. 46–47))*

National versus International Language

Where is the need for a national language? Will not the mother tongue and an international language suffice? And then why not the Roman script for both?

Your question surprises me. English no doubt is the international language. But can it ever be our national language? The latter must be the common property of millions of our people. How can they sustain the burden of learning the English tongue? Hindustani is the natural national language, for it is already understood by 21 crores. The remainder of the population can also easily understand it. But English may be said to be the mother tongue of a mere handful—say, a lac at the most. If India is a nation, it must have a national language. English will appropriately remain the international language with the Roman script. But the latter can never be the script of the national language. *(Harijan, 26 April 1942 (CW 76, p. 49))*

Religious Education

The question of religious education is very difficult. Yet we cannot do without it. India will never be godless. Rank atheism cannot flourish in this land. The task is indeed difficult. My head begins to turn as I think of religious education. Our religious teachers are hypocritical and selfish; they will have to be approached. The Mullas, the Dasturs and the Brahmins hold the key in their hands, but if they will not have the good sense, the energy that we have derived from English education will have to be devoted to religious education. This is not very difficult. Only the fringe of the ocean has been polluted, and it is those who are within the fringe who alone need cleaning. We who come under this category can even cleanse ourselves, because my remarks do not apply to the millions. In order to restore India to its pristine condition, we have to return to it. *(Hind Swaraj, p.107)*

2

Religious Education

Dharma and Scriptures

This brings me to the subject of dharma. Where there is no dharma, there can be neither knowledge nor wealth, nor health, nor anything else. Where there is no dharma, life is devoid of all joy, is mere emptiness. We have had to go without instruction in dharma; we are in much the same position as the bridegroom's party at a wedding without the bridegroom. Students cannot have innocent joy without a knowledge of dharma. That they may have such joy, it is necessary for them to study the Shastras, to reflect over their teaching and bring their conduct in comformity with their ideals. Smoking a cigarette the first thing in the morning or idle gossip does good to nobody. Nazir has said that, even the sparrows as they twitter, sing the name of the Lord morning and evening, when we are still lying in our beds full-length.

It is the duty of every student to acquire the knowledge of dharma in any manner he can. Whether or not dharma is taught in schools, it is my prayer to students who have assembled here that they introduce its essential principles in their life. What exactly is dharma? In what manner can instruction in religion be imparted? This is not the place for a discussion of this subject. But I shall give you this practical advice, based on my own experience, that you should take to the *Ramacharitamanasa* [of Tulsidas] and the *Bhagavad Gita* in love and reverence. You have a real jewel in the latter; seize it. But see that you study these two books in order to learn the secret of dharma. The seers who wrote these works did not set out to write history but only to teach dharma and morals. Millions of people read these books and lead pure lives. They read them with a guileless heart and live in this world full of innocent joy. It never occurs to them even in a dream to ask whether or not Ravana was a historical figure or whether they might not kill their enemies as Rama killed Ravana. Even when face to face with enemies, they pray for Ramachandra's protection and ramain unafraid. Tulsidas, the author of the *Ramayana,* had nothing but compassion by way of a weapon. He desired to kill none. He who creates, destroys.

Rama was God; He had created Ravana and so had the right to kill him. When any of us becomes God; he may consider whether he is fit to have the power to destroy. I have ventured to say this by way of introduction to these great books. I was, myself, a sceptic once and lived in fear of being destroyed. I have grown out of that stage and become a believer. I have thought it fit here to describe the influence which these books have had on me. For Muslim students, the *Koran* is the best book in this respect. I would counsel them as well that they study this book in a spirit of devotion. They should understand its true message. I feel, too, that both Hindus and Muslims should study each other's religious scriptures with due respect and try to understand them. *(CW 14, pp. 136–37)*

State versus Religious Instruction

If India is not to declare spiritual bankruptcy, religious instruction of its youth must be held to be at least as necessary as secular instruction. It is true that knowledge of religious books is no equivalent of that of religion. But if we cannot have religion, we must be satisfied with providing out boys and girls with what is next best. And whether there is such instruction given in the schools or not, grown-up students must cultivate the art of self-help about matters religious as about others. They may start their own class just as they have their debating, and now, spinners' clubs.

I do not believe that the State can concern itself or cope with religious education. I believe that religious education must be the sole concern of religious associations. Do not mix up religion and ethics. I believe that fundamental ethics is common to all religions. Teaching of fundamental ethics is undoubtedly a function of the State. By religion I have not in mind fundamental ethics but what goes by the name of denominationalism. We have suffered enough from State-aided religion and a State Church. A society or a group, which depends partly or wholly on State aid for the existence of its religion, does not deserve, or, better still, does not have any religion worth the name.

Religious Education and the Teacher

You have rightly found place for religious instruction. I have experimented with quite a number of boys in order to understand how best to impart religious instruction and whilst I found that book instruction was somewhat of an aid, by itself it was useless. Religious instruction, I discovered, was imparted by teachers living the religion themselves. I have found that boys imbibe more from the teachers' own lives than they do from the books that they read to them, or the lectures that they deliver to them with their lips. I have discovered to my great joy that boys and girls have unconsciously a faculty of penetration whereby they read the thoughts of their teachers. Woe to the teacher who teaches one thing with his lips, and carries another in his breast. *(24 November 1927 (CW 35, p. 306))*

Liberal Education

I shall say to the 75 per cent Hindus receiving instruction in this College that your lives will be incomplete unless you reverently study the teaching of Jesus. I have come to the conclusion, in my own experience, that those who, no matter to what faith they belong, reverently study the teaching of other faiths broaden their own, instead of slackening their hearts. Personally, I do not regard any of the great religions of the world as false. All have served in embellishing mankind and are even now serving their purpose. A liberal education to all should include, as I have put it, a reverent study of other faiths, but I do not want to labour this point, nor have I the time to do so. *(The Hindu, 2 December 1927 (CW 35, p. 343))*

Religious Instruction

The other day, in the course of a conversation, a missionary friend asked me, if India was really a spiritually advanced country, why it was that he found only a few students having any knowledge of their own religion, even of the *Bhagavad Gita*. In support of the statement, the friend who is himself an educationist told me that he had made it a point to ask the students he met whether they had any knowledge of their religion or of the *Bhagavad Gita*. A vast majority of them were found to be innocent of any such knowledge.

I do not propose to take up at the present moment the inference that because certain students had no knowledge of their own religion, India was not a spiritually advanced country, beyond saying that the ignorance on the part of the students of religious books did not necessarily mean absence of all religious life or want of spirituality among the people to which the students belonged. But there is no doubt that the vast majority of students who pass through the Government educational institutions are devoid of any religious instruction. The remark of the missionary had reference to the Mysore students, and I was somewhat pained to observe that even the students of Mysore had no religious instruction in the State schools. I know that there is a school of thought which believes in only secular instruction being given in public schools. I know also that in a country like India, where there are most religions of the world represented and where there are so many denominations in the same religion, there must be difficulty about making provision for religious instruction.

Addressing the Collegiate High School students at Shimoga, I found upon enquiry at the meeting that out of a hundred or more Hindu boys, there were hardly eight who had read the *Bhagavad Gita*. None raised his hand in answer to the question, whether of the few who had read the *Gita* there was any who understood it. Out of five or six Musalman boys all raised their hands as having read the Koran. But only one could say that he knew its meaning. The *Gita* is, in my opinion, a very easy book to understand. It does present some fundamental problems which are no doubt difficult of solution. But the general trend of the *Gita* is in my opinion unmistakable. It is accepted by all Hindu sects as authoritative. It is free from any form of dogma.

In a short compass it gives a complete reasoned moral code. It satisfies both the intellect and the heart. It is thus both philosophical and devotional. Its appeal is universal. The language is incredibly simple. But I nevertheless think that there should be an authoritative version in each vernacular, and the translations should be so prepared as to avoid technicalities and in a manner that would make the teaching of the *Gita* intelligible to the average man. The suggestion is not intended in any way to supplement the original. For I reiterate my opinion that every Hindu boy and girl should know Sanskrit. But for a long time to come, there will be millions without any knowledge of Sanskrit. It would be suicidal to keep them deprived of the teachings of the *Bhagavad Gita* because they do not know Sanskrit. *(Young India, 25 August 1927 (CW 34, pp. 394–95))*

Religious versus Fundamental Virtues

To me religion means Truth and *ahimsa* or rather Truth alone, because Truth includes *ahimsa, ahimsa* being the necessary and indispensable means for its discovery. Therefore, anything that promotes the practice of these virtues is a means for imparting religious education and the best way to do this, in my opinion, is for the teachers rigorously to practise these virtues in their own person. Their very association with the boys, whether on the playground or in the classroom, will then give the pupils a fine training in these fundamental virtues.

So much for instruction in the universal essentials of religion. A curriculum of religious instruction should include a study of the tenets of faiths other than one's own. For this purpose the students should be trained to cultivate the habit of understanding and appreciating the doctrines of various great religions of the world in a spirit of reverence and broad-minded tolerance. This if properly done would help to give them a spiritual assurance and a better appreciation of their own religion.

There is one rule, however, which should always be kept in mind while studying all great religions and that is that one should study them only through the writings of known votaries of the respective religions. For instance, if one wants to study the *Bhagavata* one should do so not through a translation of it made by a hostile critic but one prepared by a lover of the *Bhagavata.* Similarly to study the Bible one should study it through the commentaries of devoted Christians. This study of other religions besides one's own will give one a grasp of the rock-bottom unity of all religions and afford a glimpse also of that universal and absolute Truth which lies beyond the 'dust of creeds and faiths'.

Let no one even for a moment entertain, the fear that a reverent study of other religions is likely to weaken or shake one's faith in one's own. The Hindu system of philosophy regards all religions as containing the elements of truth in them and enjoins an attitude of respect and reverence towards them all. This of course presupposes regard for one's own religion. Study and appreciation of other religions need not cause a weakening of that regard; it should mean extension of that regard to other religions.

In this respect religion stands on the same footing as culture. Just as preservation of one's own culture does not mean contempt for that of others, but requires assimilation of the best that there may be in all other cultures, even so should be the case with religion. Our present fears and apprehensions are a result of the poisonous atmosphere that has been generated in the country, the atmosphere of mutual hatred, ill-will and distrust. We are constantly labouring under a nightmare of fear lest some one should stealthily undermine our faith or the faith of those who are dear and near to us. But this unnatural state will cease when we have learnt to cultivate respect and tolerance towards other religions and their votaries. *(Young India, 6 December 1928 (True Education, pp. 127-28))*

Religious Instruction Framework

Teachers who teach under a common administrative system have no right to impart religious instruction according to their own viewpoint.

As in the case of other subjects, religious instruction too must be given in accordance with the scheme provided by the administrative authorities. Every teacher will have his own method of teaching within that framework; however, such instruction may be imparted only in accordance with the ideals that have been laid down by the authorities with regard to religion. It is true that instruction in other subjects can be imparted by one who has read certain books on these subjects. That is not the case of religious instruction. It is never given through books. The method of imparting this instruction is quite different from that followed in the case of other subjects. Whereas the latter is communicated through the intellect, the former can proceed from one's heart alone. Hence so long as the teacher is not steeped in religion, he should not impart religious instruction. Although in this manner the means of imparting religious instruction are different, nevertheless it is necessary to have a certain amount of understanding about the way in which it is to be done. In other words, one cannot impart education which would encourage violence where nonviolence has been accepted as the supreme dharma. Or, instruction antagonistic to other religions cannot be imparted where the ideal of love, tolerance and compassion towards all religions has been accepted as the ideal. In short, there can be no place for a state of anarchy with regard to religious instruction where its necessity has already been accepted. *(Navajivan, 10 June 1928 (CW 36, pp. 383–84) (Translated from Gujarati))*

Satsang

It is true that we lack religious education in the country. Religious instruction can only be imparted through the practice of religion, not by exhibiting mere learning. That's why someone has said: What is there that *Satsang* cannot do for a man? Who does not know the emphasis Tulsidas laid on the importance of *Satsang*? This does not mean that there is no need to read and understand religious books. But the need for books, etc., arises only after a man has had *Satsang* and has purified himself to a certain extent. If one starts studying religious books before this stage then instead of bringing peace this study could hinder the growth. This means that an intelligent man should put his religion into practice straightaway instead of worrying himself with all manner of questions. Then according to the maxim "as with the individual so with the world", one is bound to influence the other. If each one of us was to take care of one's self, nobody would need to worry about the others. *(Navajivan, 15 August 1929 (CW 41, p. 291) (Translated from Hindi))*

Ethical Teaching in Schools

Should religious instruction form part of the school curriculum as approved by the State? Do you favour separate schools for children belonging to different denominations for facility of religious instruction? Or should religious instruction be left in the hands of private bodies? If so, do you think it is right for the State to subsidize such bodies? I do not believe in State religion even though the whole community has one religion. The State interference would probably always be unwelcome. Religion is purely a personal matter. There are in reality as many religions as minds. Each mind has a different conception of God from that of the other. I am also opposed to State aid, partly or wholly, to religious bodies. For I know that an institution or group which does not manage to finance its own religious teaching, is a stranger to true religion. This does not mean that the State schools would not give ethical teaching. The fundamental ethics are common to all religions. *(Harijan, 16 March 1947)*

Ethics and Religion

Regarding religious education Dr. Zakir Hussain thought that facilities should be provided for and time apportioned for religious education in our schools so as to enable those, who understood religion, to come and teach. More than that the Government should not undertake, if it wanted to avoid the appearance of undue interference. Gandhiji said in reply, "You should talk it over with Maulana Saheb. I do not agree that the Government should provide religious education. If there are some people who want to give religious education of the wrong type, you cannot prevent it. If you try to do so, the result can only be bad. Those who want to give religious education may do so on their own, so long as it is not subversive of law and order or morals. The Governments can only teach ethics based on the main principles common to all religions and agreed to by all parties. In fact ours is a secular State." *(Harijan, 9 November 1947 (Basic Education, p. 120))*

Fundamental Ethics

Religious instruction in the sense of denominational religion has been deliberately omitted. Unless there is a State religion it is very difficult, if not impossible, to provide religious instruction as it would mean providing for every denomination. Such instruction is best given at home. The State should allow enough time for every child to receive such instruction at home or otherwise. It is also conceivable that the State should provide facilities for private tuition by those denominations which may wish to instruct their children at school provided that such instruction is paid for by such denominations.

As to the necessity of teaching equal regard for all religions, I personally hold strong views. Till we reach that happy state, I see no prospect of real unity among all the different communities. I regard it as fatal to the growth of a friendly spirit among the children belonging to the different faiths if they are taught either that their religion is superior to every other or that it is the only true religion. If that exclusive spirit is to pervade the nation, the necessary corollary would be that there should be separate schools for every denomination with freedom to each to decry every other, or that the mention of religion must be entirely prohibited.

The result of such a policy is too dreadful to contemplate. Fundamental principles of ethics are common to all religions. These should certainly be taught to the children and that should be regarded as adequate religious instruction so far as the schools under the Wardha scheme are concerned. *(Harijan, 16 July 1938 (CW 67, p. 175))*

3

Adult and Women Education

Adult Franchise

Considering the minutes of the proposal, I feel that while extending the franchise, it is not at all proper to confine it to literates. It is possible that an educated young man of 21 may not at all be fit to exercise his franchise, whereas an illiterate man of 50, experienced and sensible, may realize the value of his vote and his vote will have its own significance. It has been daily happening that way.

There are many things taken for granted even in the Congress advocacy of adult franchise. I am firmly convinced that the deaf and dumb, known idiots, lunatics, persons indulging in secret crimes and those suffering from incurable diseases cannot enjoy the right to vote even if they have attained the prescribed age.

Moreover, there is no reason to believe that those who have learnt to read and write have achieved something great. I am not prepared to say that those who have not been able so far to get educated are themselves responsible for their ignorance. It is indeed the indifference of the middle-class people that is responsible for the ignorance of the masses. The number of illiterate people in India has remained so large because these people have not discharged their duty.

Hence, in my view it is a double crime to give franchise to those who, by the favour of the Government, have become educated and to deny it to those who, because of the Government's indifference, received no education. It becomes the duty of those in power to arrange for early education of those illiterates who are entitled to exercise their votes. Thus, on the one hand, it would mean atonement for not giving franchise to those who should have had it from the beginning, and, on the other, it would encourage efforts to educate the electorate so that voters can exercise their franchise intelligently. *(Harijanbandhu, 3 October 1937 (CW 66, p. 198) (Translated from Gujarati))*

Mass Illiteracy

In our schemes for adult education should the aim be to promote the spread of literacy or to impart useful knowledge? What about the education of women?

The primary need of those who are come of age and are following an avocation, is to know how to read and write. Mass illiteracy is India's sin and shame and must be liquidated. Of course, the literacy campaign must not begin and end with mere knowledge of the alphabet. It must go hand in hand with the spread of useful knowledge. But municipal bodies should beware of trying to ride two horses at a time, or else they are sure to come a cropper.

As for illiteracy among the women, its cause is not mere laziness and inertia as in the case of men. A more potent cause is the status of inferiority with which an immemorial tradition has unjustly branded her. Man has converted her into a domestic drudge and an instrument of his pleasure, instead of regarding here as his helpmate and 'better half!' The result is a semi-paralysis of our society. Woman has rightly been called the mother of the race. We owe it to her and to ourselves to undo the great wrong that we have done her. *(Harijan, 18 February 1939 (CW 68, p. 341))*

Adult Education

In my opinion what we have reason to deplore and be ashamed of is not so much illiteracy as ignorance. Therefore adult education, too, should have an intensive programme of driving out ignorance through carefully selected teachers with an equally carefully selected syllabus according to which they would educate the adult villagers' mind. This is not to say that I would not give them a knowledge of the alphabet. I value it too much to despise or even belittle its merit as a vehicle of education. I appreciate Prof. Laubach's immense labours in the way of making the alphabet easy and Prof. Bhagwat's great and practical contribution in the same direction. Indeed I have invited the latter to come to Segaon whenever he chooses and try his art on the men, women and even children of Segaon. *(Harijan, 5 June 1937 (CW 65, pp. 234–35))*

Education for Life

As to adult education, Gandhiji observed that it had become clear to him that the scope of basic education had to be extended. It should include the education of everybody at every stage of life.

A basic school teacher must consider himself a universal teacher. As soon as he comes in contact with anybody, man or woman, young or old, he should say to himself: 'Now, what can I give to this person?'

Won't that be supererogation on his part?

No. Supposing I come across an old man who is dirty and ignorant. His village is his universe. It would be my job to teach him cleanliness, to remove his ignorance and widen his mental horizon. I need not tell him that I am to be his teacher. I will try to establish a living contact with his mind and win his confidence. He may reject my advances. I won't accept defeat, but continue my effort till I succeed in making friends with him. Once that is achieved, the rest must follow. Again, I must have my eye on the children right from their birth. I will go a step further and say that the work of the educationist begins even before that. For instance, if a woman becomes pregnant, Ashadevi will go to her and tell her: 'I am a mother as you will be. I can tell you from my experience what you should do to ensure the health of your unborn baby and your own.' She will tell the husband what his duty towards his wife is and about his share in the care of their expected baby. Thus the basic school teacher will cover the entire span of life. Naturally, his activity will cover adult education.

Some work for adult education is being done in many places. It is mostly concentrated among mill-hands and the like in big cities. No one has really touched the village. Mere three R's and lectures on politics won't satisfy me. Adult education of my conception must make men and women better citizens all round. To work out the syllabus and to organize the work of adult education is a more difficult task than preparation of the seven years' course for children. The common central feature of both will be the imparting of education through village crafts. Agriculture will play an important part in adult education under the basic scheme. Literary instruction must be there. Much information will be given orally. There will be books more for the teachers than the taught. We must teach the majority how to behave towards the minority and vice versa. The right type of adult education should teach good neighbourliness and cut at the very root of untouchability and communal problem.

The particular industry which is to serve as the medium of instruction will be determined by local conditions in each place. For instance, people in a village might tell you that they are interested in agriculture, but they are not interested in the spinning-wheel. In that case, you will choose the former as the medium of instruction. You could make a beginning by taking a census of its cattle. For instance, I find that almost everyone in Sevagram has a bullock and a bullock-cart.

It seems wasteful. The villagers should be taught cooperation. Again, we must inculcate in them the right principles of relationship between men and women. Men get almost double the women's wages for identical work. Sometimes men sit lazily at home and smoke while the women toil the whole day. People should be made to realize that this is doubly wrong and ought to go. If you agree with me that the scope of basic education should be extended, you might have to change your constitution. *(The Hindu, 29 October 1944 (CW 78, pp. 237–38))*

Functional Literacy

The dry knowledge of three R's is not even now, it can never be, permanent part of the villagers' life. They must have knowledge given to them which they must use daily. It must not be thrust upon them. They should have the appetite for it. What they have today is something they neither want nor appreciate. Give the villagers village arithmetic, village geography, village history, and the literacy knowledge that they must use daily, *i.e.*, reading and writing letters, etc. They will treasure such knowledge and pass on to the other stages. They have no use for books which give them nothing of daily use. *(Harijan, 22 June 1940 (CW 72, pp. 180–81))*

Self-supporting Adult Education

It is my firm belief that if Nayee Taleem cannot become self-supporting, then the teachers do not understand what it is. In my view, amongst other characteristics self-reliance is the most important characteristic of Nayee Taleem.

If this is so for the education of boys and girls, then adult education must also be self-supporting. If we believe that it is difficult to convince adults about the value of education, then I have to say that this is nothing but an old illusion. And the teaching of the three R's in adult education is not part of our Nayee Taleem. The meaning of adult education is that we will give them, through their own language, all-round education of a pure and socially useful life. And if they do not easily become self-supporting, in my view there is some serious defect in that education. We should not also forget that complete cooperation should be the basis from the very beginning. Those who know the full meaning of cooperation will raise no doubts about self-reliance. *(Khadi Jagat, November 1945 (CW 82, pp. 143–44))*

Knowledge of Alphabet

In the consideration of public education, knowledge of the alphabet takes subordinate place. It can be said that knowledge of the alphabet has no place at all among the important aspects of life. *Moksha* is for us the final state to be desired. Who will deny that knowledge of the alphabet is not necessary for *moksha* here and hereafter? If we have to wait until crores of people have gained a knowledge of the alphabet in order to win swaraj, attainment of the latter will become almost an impossibility. Moreover, no one has claimed that the great teachers of the world like Jesus Christ had this knowledge.

Knowledge of the alphabet has been given the least important place in this series of articles. It is a means and not an end. It is a well-known fact that as a means it is very useful. However, when considering the type of knowledge that is required for crores of farmers who are engaged in their occupations and have reached a mature age, we find that there is much else that they should be taught before being given a knowledge of the alphabet. *(Navajivan, 15 December 1929 (CW 42, p. 281) (Translated from Gujarati))*

Women's Education

That India is very backward in the education of women is a fact that cannot be denied. But by admitting this, we do not mean to suggest that Indian women fail in their duty. We believe that, as there are in world few men of any class who can compete with the Indians considered from all points of view, so are there few women anywhere in the world who can compare with Indian women. But this position can no longer be kept up in the present squalid, low and helpless state of India. The modern age is such that it does not allow anyone to remain in the same position. Those who do not want to go forward, or do not do so, must fall behind. In so far as this is true, we can see that Indian men have deliberately kept their women backward. Those who pose as reformers as also other well-to-do Indians, whether Hindu or Muslim, Parsi or Christian, either treat their women as if they were playthings or use them as they fancy for self-indulgence, with the result that they themselves become weak and help only to produce weaklings.

And in this way they lead irreligious lives and still say, 'It is God's will that prevails.' If this state of affairs continues, India will remain in its present abominable condition even if she were to secure all her rights from the British Government. In all countries where the people live a decent life, there is no disparity in the condition of men and women. It is easy to see how much the real wealth of India would be attenuated, if one half of her human beings remained ignorant and existed only as playthings of the others. *(Indian Opinion, 19 January 1907 (CW 6, pp. 282–83))*

Yusuf Ali on Women's Education

Mr. Yusuf Ali's book on conditions prevailing in India is widely read. His views on the education of women as expressed therein are worth noting. He says that so long as Indian women do not get proper education, the condition of India is not likely to improve. Woman is known as the better half of man. If a half of one's body ceases to function, we call it paralysis and the person becomes unfit for any activity. Thus, if women in India are not employed as they should be, it can be said that the entire country suffers from paralysis. How is it surprising then that India is not able to keep pace with other countries? All parents should think of this in regard to their daughters, and all Indians should do likewise with regard to the womenfolk of India. We badly need thousands of women who can compare with Mirabai and Rabia Bibi. *(Indian Opinion, 22 June 1907 (CW 7, p. 51) (Translated from Gujarati))*

Equality of Rights for Women

We shall accept equality of rights for women, but I think their education should differ from men's as their nature and functions do. In progressive countries, women receive the very highest education but, after it is over, they do not have to perform the same duties as men and in our country women have never to compete with men for a livelihood. *(Prajabandhu, 27 February 1916 (CW 13, p. 246) (Translated from Gujarati))*

Educated Women's Role

The women whom this message reaches are likely to have had some measure of education. I wish, therefore, to consider one thing. What should educated women do for their illiterate sisters? This is a very important issue. Beyond question, if women choose... they can attain a far greater measure of success in this field than men can ever do. At present, we do not find many women taking to this work. That is, I believe, not their fault but that of their education. The first thing, therefore, which educated women must do is to try and see that their sisters do not fall a victim to it. Modern education fails utterly to prepare women for their distinctive role; this is not questioned by anyone. I do not wish here to examine the shortcomings of modern education or to bother you with the question how they may be overcome. All that I desire is that educated women should make this question their own and that those of them with some experience should dedicate their all to rouse Gujarat over it and focus attention on the right lines [of reform].

Educated women have no contact with those not educated; often, they don't welcome such contacts. This disease must be cured. It is necessary that educated women are made conscious of their most obvious duty. Men also are not free from faults of this kind, but women need not follow in their footsteps. They have the power, denied to men, of creating new ideals and translating them into action. By comparison, man is thoughtless, impatient and given to the pursuit of novelty. *(Gujarati, 2 November 1917 (CW 14, pp. 86–87) (Translated from Gujarati))*

Men versus Women's Education

The education of women is as faulty as that of men. They have not given any thought to the relations obtaining between men and women, or to the place woman occupies in India society.

It may be admitted that for the most part preliminary teaching of both boys and girls would be much the same. Barring that, there is great dissimilarity. There is need for similar distinction between the education of males and females as has been made between them by Mother Nature herself. True, they are equals. But there is a difference in the work they are ordained to do. It is woman's right to rule inside the home. Man is master outside it. Man is the earner of livelihood, woman saves and spends. Woman brings up children. She is their mother. She is responsible for building up their character. She is their educator, and hence the *mother* of the race. Man is not, in that sense, the father of the race. After a certain age a father ceases to influence his son, but not so the mother. The son, even after attaining manhood, behaves like a child in the presence of his mother. He cannot, however, do this with his father.

If this arrangement is considered natural and right a woman should not have to earn her living. A society in which women have to work as telegraph clerks, typists or compositors is, I think, not well-organized. It is a symptom of moral and economic bankruptcy and is an indication that they, *i.e.*, the people belonging to that society, have begun to live on their capital. Hence, just as it is wrong to keep women in ignorance and under suppression on the one hand, it is wrong, on the other hand, to entrust them with the work which is ordinarily done by men; for this is a sign of weakness and is tantamount to oppression.

Therefore, after a certain age, there must be arrangements to provide women with a kind of education different to that of men. Women should be taught the management of the home, the things they should or should not do during pregnancy, and the nursing and care of children. It is difficult to make suitable arrangements for providing such teaching as the idea is a new one. The right course under the circumstances would be to constitute a committee of enlightened and experienced men and women of good character who would then explore the problem, come to the right decision, and produce a suitable plan for the purpose.

This committee should find out how best to impart the necessary education to girls after they have completed the period of childhood and enter on that of womanhood. But, unfortunately, there are a large number of girls in our country who get married even while they are in their childhood. Besides, the number goes on increasing. And once they are married, they just disappear from social life. I have expressed my views about them fully in my foreword contributed to the first book of the "Bhagini Pustak-mala" series. I reproduce them here:

> *"We cannot achieve the education of women merely by educating girls. Claimed by the monster of child-marriage, thousands of girls disappear from view at the early age of twelve. From girls they change into house-wives at one stroke. As long as this wicked custom continues, the only alternative is that men must learn to act as teachers to women. A great many of our hopes in regard to the education of women rest on how men discharge their duty in this respect. Women must cease to be our servants and objects of enjoyment as they are at present, and become, instead, our life-companions, equal partners in the battle of life, sharers in our happiness and unhappiness. All our efforts seem utterly futile as long as this is not accomplished. There are some men who regard their women as beasts. For this sad state some of the Sanskrit sayings and the following well-known doha of Tulsidas may be held responsible. Tulsidas says at one place in*

his Ramayana: "The drum, the fool, the Shudra and the woman – all these are fit objects to beat." I hold Tulasidasji in high esteem, but my worship is not blind. Either this couplet is an interpolation, or, if it is his, he must have written it without thought – as reflecting the prevailing views of the then society. As to the saying in Sanskrit, people seem to be labouring under the impression that every shloka written is, as it were, a scriptural precept. We must fight this impression and eradicate from its very root the custom of regarding women as inferior beings. On the other hand, blinded by passion many among us adore women and decorate them with ornaments just as we decorate idols. We must keep away from this evil also. Our ultimate goal, however, will not be achieved until our women become to us what Parvati was to Mahadeva, Sita to Rama, Damayanti to Nala. Then, they will participate in our discussions, argue things with us on an equal basis, understand through their wonderful insight born of sympathy, be partners in our fight for resolving them and become for us, when we need it, the givers of the most soothing peace. This goal cannot be achieved merely by starting girls' schools. As long as we have around our necks the noose of child-marriage, men must be the teachers of their womenfolk. And this education which men will give to women will not be merely literacy; it will be extended to cover social reform and politics. Literacy must be only a preliminary to the teaching of the other subjects mentioned above. These may be taught even without it. A man who undertakes to teach his wife in this manner will have to change his attitude towards her. A man will himself be a student with his wife and will observe complete celibacy in his relation with her until she attains maturity. In no case will he subject a girl of twelve to fifteen years of age to the agony of bearing children to him. One ought to shudder at the very thought of it. If this is done we will not be crushed under the weight of inertia as we are at present.

"Classes are being started for married women and lecturers arranged for them. All this is good as far as it goes. Those who are engaged in this work are sacrificing their time and energy for a good cause. This is quite creditable. But simultaneously men must also undertake to discharge the duty indicated above,

because in its absence all these efforts will not bear much result. On deeper reflection, I am sure that what I have said is self-evident." (Speech at Second Gujarat Educational Conference, 20 October 1917 (CW 14, pp. 31–33))

Woman, like Man, Needs Education

Though much good and useful work can be done without a knowledge of reading and writing, yet I believe that such knowledge is necessary, for one can hardly do without it these days. Reading of good books develops the intellect and that, in its turn, increases our capacity for service to our people and our country. I do not over-estimate the value of this knowledge, but I should like to give it its due place in the scheme of things. I have pointed out on several occasions that lack of education among women should not be made the reason for men to deprive them of their due human rights.

But proper education is essential in order that they may use those rights well, adorn them and spread them amongst our masses. Without proper education and the knowledge acquired through such education, millions cannot acquire the true knowledge of the Self. Without education, the inexhaustible fund of innocent pleasure which lies in various books is also closed to us. It is no exaggeration but a statement of fact that a man without learning is not far removed from an animal.

Thus, a woman, like man, needs education. Not that a woman should get the same kind of education as given to a man. In the first place, the education that is being given us by the Government is, to a great extent, faulty and harmful. It should therefore be eschewed by both men and women. Even if its defects were removed I would not consider it proper for women. Men and women are equal in status, but they are not the same in physical or mental make-up. They are a unique pair. They complement each other and are absolutely necessary to each other, so much so that one cannot exist without the other. It follows as a corollary from these facts that anything that will impair the status of either of them will involve the ruin of both, in equal measure.

Those who draw up plans for the education of women must remember this. Man rules the outer circle of the life of a married pair. Therefore he must have the greater knowledge of all those activities of life which constitute his sphere. The woman, on the other hand, is dominant in the inner or domestic circle of their life. She must have special knowledge of the management of the home, care of children, their education, etc. It is not suggested that either men or women should be forbidden from acquiring a knowledge of what belongs specially to the province of the other. But unless courses of instruction are based on a discriminating appreciation of these ideas, both men and women would be deprived of the opportunity of achieving perfection in their respective spheres.

A few words are also necessary about the question as to whether or not women need to know English. I feel that generally speaking, knowledge of English is not necessary either for men or for women. Men might require it for earning their livelihood or for taking part in political work. But I do not believe in women working for a living or undertaking commercial enterprises. Therefore, only a few women would need to learn English. And those who want to may well learn it in the schools for men.

Introducing English in all schools for women will only lead to a prolongation of the period of our helplessness. I have often heard people say that the rich treasures of English literature should be as easily available to women as they are to men. I humbly submit that this is an erroneous view even though the error may not be evident. No one says that the treasures of English literature should be open to men but closed to women. He who loves literature may well explore the literature of the whole world. None will, or can, stop him from doing so, if he has the necessary will. But, since we are concerned with formulating a plan to suit the needs of our people in general, we cannot attend to the special needs of a few lovers of literature.

For them there will have to be—when we are sufficiently advanced and prosperous—separate institutions for learning and research as there are in Europe. When there is a general spread of education, when most of our men and women start getting educated, we may be sure that numerous writers will rise from amongst us who will make available to us the joy of the literatures of other languages. If we continue to derive pleasure only from

English literature alone, our language will always remain poor. This means that we as a people will also remain mentally poor. I would even say, if you will forgive me for the simile, that the habit of deriving joy from the literature of another language is like that of a thief who derives joy from stolen property.

The English poet Pope presented to his people, in his beautiful English, whatever joy he tasted in *Iliad;* in the same way, Fitzgerald embodied the joy he derived from the poetry of Omar Khayyam in such attractive English that millions of Englishmen love and treasure his translation of the poetry of Khayyam like their own Bible. Edwin Arnold tasted the nectar of our *Bhagavad Gita.* He did not ask his people to learn Sanskrit to experience the joy that he had experienced in that book. On the other hand, he made it available to the people in English which is as beautiful as the original Sanskrit and in which besides he has succeeded in pouring out his very soul as it were. Seeing that we are still backward in this respect, we must pay more attention to the work of translating. But it will be possible only when we have made our plan of education along the lines I have indicated and implement it. If we give up being fascinated by English and our distrust of the power of our own language, this will not be difficult to achieve.

It is not necessary for any man or woman to spend his or her time learning English in order to appreciate good literature. I do not say this merely to be a wet blanket. But because I want the pleasure, which the English-educated people derive with great difficulty, made easily available to all of us through translations. The languages of the world are full of many a invaluable gem. And not all the gems of literature are in English. I want all these gems to be brought within the reach of our people. The only way to achieve this end is for those of us who have a flair for languages to learn them and then present the foreign literary classics in our own. Presidential speech on the occasion of the Second Annual Conference of the Bombay Bhagini Samaj, 1918 (*CW* 14, pp. 207-09)

Higher Education for Women

After primary education, a girl gets another four to five years of secondary education. Expressing his views on the question as to whether in this period she should be taught through English or the mother tongue, Gandhiji said: "I feel that teaching English to them under the circumstances would be like killing them. It will never be possible for hundreds of thousands of women to think or express their thoughts in English; and even if it were possible, it would be undesirable.

> *"If the women for whom we are drawing up this plan are imparted higher education through the mother tongue, they could make their homes as bright and beautiful as gold. Not only that, they could also exert their good influence on their uneducated sisters and thus render valuable service to them as well." (True Education, pp. 157–58)*

Modern Girls' Education

I was really surprised to see the stride that education among girls had taken in the State of Travancore. It was a perfect eye-opener to me. The question has always occurred to me: "What will India do with its modern girls?" I call you modern girls of India. The education that we are receiving in these institutions, in my opinion, does not correspond with the life around us, and, when I say life around us, I do not mean the life around us in the cities but the life around us in the villages. Perhaps some of you girls, if not all of you, know that real India is to be found not here in the very few cities but in the seven hundred thousand villages covering a surface of 1,900 miles long and 1,500 miles broad. The question is whether you have any message for your sisters in the villages. Men do not need the message perhaps so much as the women, and I have long before come to the conclusion that unless women of India work side by side with men, there is no salvation for India, salvation in more senses than one. I mean political salvation in the broadest sense, and I mean economic salvation and spiritual salvation also. *(Speech at Women's College, Madras, 24 March 1925 (CW 26, pp. 395–96))*

Curriculum for Girls' Education

Women must learn as part of elementary education at least their own mother tongue, Hindi if it is not their mother tongue, enough Sanskrit to be able to understand the drift of the *Bhagavad Gita*, elementary arithmetic, elementary composition, elementary music and child-care. Along with this, I think they should know well the processes up to the weaving from cotton. When a woman receives this education she should have an environment that will shape her character and enable her to see clearly the evils in society and to avoid them. I have not mentioned religious education separately as it is acquired by practice and would be covered by general reading. Truly speaking, it is a part of the elevating company of a teacher. This is about girls. The education of a widow or a married woman is of course a different matter. *(Letter to Aanandibai, 22 August 1927 (CW 34, p. 384) (Translated from Gujarati))*

Education to Women

Today we have assembled for the opening of a girls' school. I have made a thorough study of child education. I could say the same thing about girls' education. But how can experts accepts this? Today, even I cannot make that claim. In the prevailing state of affairs it is not easy to talk about girls' education. Everyone may well claim that he is capable of giving education to girls. I will however ask him whether he has imparted true education to his daughter or his wife.

How can he who has not observed his dharma towards his wife, sister, mother or mother-in-law, set out to teach the daughters or sisters of others? They may well become B.As. or M.As. but I shall put them to the same test. I should like to know what kind of husbands and fathers those who write books on girls' education are. *(Speech at Inauguration of Vithal Kanya Vidyalaya, Nadiad, 31 May 1935 (CW 61, p. 118))*

Coeducation

In theory, we are quite in favour of boys and girls receiving education together. But, in practice, it is impossible to ignore deep-rooted habits or prejudices. Experience has shown that Indian parents, as a rule, will not allow their daughters to mingle with boys at a school or elsewhere. And, whenever a forcible mixture takes place, the result is ludicrous in the extreme. Both the boys and girls feel awkward. "Let them", shouts the unthinking reformer. "They will soon be at home, if left alone." But the parents will not wait for the process. They are not reformers and they will not allow experiments to be made at their children's expense. *(Indian Opinion, 19 August 1911 (CW 11, p. 145))*

Coeducation not Compulsory

As for coeducation, the Zakir Hussain Committee has not made it compulsory. Where there is a demand for a separate school for girls, the State will have to make provision. The question of coeducation has been left open. It will regulate itself according to the time-spirit. So far as I am aware the members of the Committee were not all of one mind. Personally I have an open mind. I think that there are just as valid reasons for as against coeducation. And I would not oppose the experiment wherever it is made. *(Harijan, 16 July 1938 (CW 67, p. 175))*

Coeducation in Training Schools

Shri Avinashilingam, the Education Minister of Madras, felt that the coeducation policy of the Talimi Sangh was not suitable to Madras. He had no objection to coeducation among children and among grown-ups, when they knew their own minds. But he was not in favour of coeducation at the impressionable age of 15 or 16 when most of the girls came to training schools. Gandhiji, however, disagreed. "If you keep coeducation in your schools but not in your training-schools, the children will think there is something wrong somewhere. I should allow my children to run the risk. We shall have to rid ourselves one day of this sex mentality. We should not seek for examples from the West. Even in training-schools, if the teachers are intelligent, pure and filled with the spirit of Nayee Taleem, there is no danger. Supposing if some accidents do take place, we should not be frightened by them. They would take place anywhere. Although I speak thus boldly, I am not unaware of the attendant risks. You, as a responsible Minister, should think for yourself and act accordingly." *(Harijan, 9 November 1947 (CW 89, pp. 332–33))*

Sex Education

May I invite you to discuss in the columns of *Harijanbandhu* a question which you have so far left more or less untouched, I mean the question of imparting sex instruction to young people?

Should sex education be included in the educational curricula of our children? Who should impart it? What would be the necessary qualification for the task? Should this subject be taught in a matter-of-fact manner to all and sundry just like geography or arithmetic? Or is there any limit? And if so, who is to draw the line and where? Again should the aim of sex education be to combat the onset of libido or simply to recognize it as an inevitable fact of nature which has to be accepted and submitted to?

What place has instruction in sexual science in our educational system, or has it any place there at all? Sexual science is of two kinds, that which is used for controlling or overcoming the sexual passion and that which is used to stimulate and feed it. Instruction in the former is as necessary a part of a child's education as the latter is harmful and dangerous and fit therefore only to be shunned. All great religions have rightly regarded 'Kama' as the archenemy of man; anger or hatred coming only in the second place. According to the Gita, the latter is an offspring of the former. The Gita of course uses the word 'Kama' in its wider sense of desire. But the same holds good of the narrow sense in which it is used here.

This, however, still leaves unanswered the question, *i.e.*, whether it is desirable to impart to young pupils a knowledge about the use and function of generative organs. It seems to me that it is necessary to impart such knowledge to a certain extent. At present they are often left to pick up such knowledge anyhow with the result that they are misled into abusive practices. We cannot properly control or conquer the sexual passion by turning a blind eye to it. I am therefore strongly in favour of teaching young boys and girls the significance and right use of their generative organs. And in my own way I have tried to impart this knowledge to young children of both sexes for whose training I was responsible.

But the sex education that I stand for must have for its object the conquest and sublimation of the sex passion. Such education should automatically serve to bring home to children the essential distinction between man and brute, to make them realize that it is man's special privilege and pride to be gifted with the faculties of head and heart both; that he is a thinking no less than a feeling animal, as the very derivation of the word Yktknazk; (man) shows, and to renounce the sovereignty of reason over the blind instincts is therefore to renounce a man's estate. In man reason quickens and guides the feeling, in brute the soul lies ever dormant. To awaken the heart is to awaken the dormant soul, to awaken reason, to inculcate discrimination between good and evil.

Who should teach this true science of sex? Clearly, he who has attained mastery over his passions. To teach astronomy and kindred sciences we have teachers who have gone through a course of training in them and are masters of their art. Even so must we have as teachers of sexual science, *i.e.*, the science of sex control, those who have studied it and have acquired mastery over self. Even a lofty utterance, that has not the backing of sincerity and experience, will be inert and lifeless, and will utterly fail to penetrate and quicken the hearts of men, while the speech that springs from self-realization and genuine experience is always fruitful.

Today our entire environment—our reading, our thinking, our social behaviour—is generally calculated to subserve and cater for the sex urge. To break through its coils is no easy task. But it is a task worthy of our highest endeavour. Even if there are a handful of teachers endowed with practical experience, who accept the ideal of attaining self-control as the highest duty of man, and are fired by a genuine and undying faith in their mission, and are sleeplessly vigilant and active, their labour will light the path of the children of Gujarat, save the unwary from falling into the mire of sexuality and rescue those who might be already engulfed in it. *(Harijan, 22 November 1936 (CW 64, pp. 59-62))*

4

Gandhi on Various Aspects of Education

An Ideal Hostel

Since a Hostels' Conference is to be held this month in this city, I was asked to express my views as to what would be an ideal hostel. I have been running students' hostels since 1904 according to my lights. I am therefore inclined to claim that I have some knowledge and experience of how hostels should be run and managed. Here, we would do well to take a wider sense of the term "hostel". Every person who is learning anything is a student; and the place where more than one such student live I consider a students' hostel.

The first and the most important condition for the success of such hostels is that the superintendents must be men of good character.

A hostel should never be allowed to degenerate into a mere boarding house, that is, a place where students live together for the sake of obtaining their meals.

Students should cultivate a family feeling towards one another, and the superintendent should take the place of a father. He should take an interest in them, take part in their social life and also have his meals with them.

An ideal hostel would be almost more important to the student than school. In fact, the hostel is the real school. In schools or colleges the students get only verbal knowledge while in the hostels they get all kinds of knowledge. An ideal hostel should not be a separate institution from the school; hence, both should be under the same management, and teachers and students should live together. Thus, we should make the hostels like home, and create in them ideal conditions for growth and development such as do not obtain even in real homes. Therefore, the thing to do would be to turn the hostels into *gurukulas*.

There are many defects in our hostels. The reason lies in the fact that students lack a sense of belonging to a family group, and those who run them do not enter fully into the life of the students.

Then, these hostels should be outside the city limits, and all the reforms which are considered necessary for the villages or cities should be carried out in them, that is, there must be the necessary arrangements for hygienic and sanitary living and the rules of such living should be strictly followed. An ideal hostel cannot be set up in a rented building. There should be good bathrooms and latrines. The building should be well-ventilated and have a garden attached to it.

An ideal hostel should be *Swadeshi* in all respects—in the way the building is constructed, furnished and decorated. There should be too a reflection of village arts and crafts and way of life. The building itself should be in keeping with our need and our means, considering the poverty of India. Thus, hostels—as built in properous and affluent Western countries cannot serve as models for ours. Climate conditions abroad and here differ. Hence, the type of building put up must be in accordance with prevailing conditions.

There must be nothing in the ideal hostel which might encourage indolence and delicacy, or lead to waywardness. Therefore, the food served there should be simple—as becomes the life of seekers of knowledge. There should be regular prayers, and rules governing work, rest and sleep.

An ideal hostel will be a *brahmacharyashram*, *i.e.*, a colony of students living the life of *brahmacharis*. The word student is of recent origin—a modern word. The old word for a student—*Brahmachari*—is richer in meaning and connotes the ideal of student life more truly. *Brahmacharya* or spiritual discipline—control of the senses, purity of body and mind, and devotion to studies with a view to attaining the Ultimate Reality—is absolutely necessary during the period of study. In the rather topsy-turvy conditions obtaining today, I would like married students also, if admitted into the hostel, to observe *Brahmacharya* until the completion of their studies. This means, among other things, that during this period they should live away from their wives.

The readers should remember that I have described what would be an ideal hostel. It is understandable that all hostels may not be able to realize this goal. But, if the ideal described above is accepted as the standard, then every hostel should strive to reach it, and assess their achievement by comparison with it. *(Navajivan, 3 March 1929 (CW 40, pp. 72–73))*

True Prayer

As feed food is necessary for the body, prayer is necessary for the soul. A man may be able to do without food for a number of days,—as Mac Swiney did for over 70 days—but believing in God, man cannot, should not, live a moment without prayer. You will say that we see lots of people living without prayer. I dare say they do, but it is the existence of the brute which, for man, is worse than death. I have not the shadow of a doubt that the strife and quarrels with which our atmosphere is so full today are due to the absence of the spirit of true prayer. You will demur to the statement, I know, and contend that millions of Hindus, Musalmans and Christians do offer their prayers.

It is because I had thought you would raise this objection that I sued the words 'true prayers'. The fact is we have been offering our prayers with the lips but hardly ever with our hearts, and it is to escape, if possible, the hypocrisy of the lip-prayer, that we in the Ashram repeat every evening the last verses of the second chapter of the Bhagavad Gita. The condition of the 'Equable in Spirit' that is described in those verses, if we contemplate them daily, is bound slowly to turn our hearts towards God. If you students would base your education on the true foundation of a pure character and pure heart there is nothing so helpful as to offer your prayers every day truly and religiously. *(Speech at Students' Meeting, Berhampur Young India, 15 December 1927 (CW 35, p. 361))*

Prayer Meetings

Here is a letter written by a student to the Principal of a national institution asking to be excused from attending its prayer meetings:

> *I beg to state that I have no belief in prayer, as I do not believe in anything known as God to whom I should pray. I never feel any necessity of supposing a god for myself. What do I lose if do not care for Him and calmly and sincerely work my own schemes?*

So far as congregational prayer is concerned, it is of no use. Can such a huge mass of men enter into any mental concentration upon a thing, however trifling it may be? Are the little and ignorant children expected to fix their fickle attention on the subtlest ideas of our great scriptures, God and soul and equality of all men and many other high-sounding phrases? This great performance is required to be done at a particular time at the command of a particular man. Can love for the so-called Lord take its root in the hearts of boys by any such mechanical function? Nothing can be more repugnant to reason than to expect the same behaviour from men of every temperament. Therefore, prayer should not be a compulsion. Let those pray who have a taste for it and those avoid who dislike it. Anything done without conviction is an immoral and degrading action.

Let us first examine the worth of the last idea. Is it an immoral and degrading act to submit to discipline before one beings to have conviction about its necessity? Is it immoral and degrading to study subjects according to the school syllabus if one has no conviction about its utility? May a boy be excused from studying his vernacular if he has persuaded himself that it is useless?

Is it not truer to say that a school boy has no conviction about the things he has to learn or the discipline he has to go through? His choice is exhausted if he had it, when he elected to belong to an institution. His joining one means that he will willingly submit to its rules and regulations. It is open to him to leave it, but he may not choose what or how he will learn.

It is for teachers to make attractive and intelligible what to the pupils may at first appear repulsive or uninteresting.

It is easy enough to say, 'I do not believe in God.' For God permits all things to be said of Him with impunity. He looks at our acts. And any breach of His law carried with it, not its vindictive, but its purifying, compelling, punishment. God's existence cannot be, does cannot be, does not need to be, proved. God is. If He is not felt, so much the worse for us. The absence of feeling is a disease which we shall some day throw off nolens volens.

But a boy may not argue. He must, out of a sense of discipline, attend prayer meetings if the institution to which he belongs requires such attendance. He may respectfully put his doubts before his teachers. He need not believe what does not appeal to him. But if he has respect for his teachers, he will do without believing what he is asked to do, not out of fear, not out of churlishness, but with the knowledge that it is right for him so to do and with the hope that what is dark to him today will some day be made clear to him.

Prayer is not an asking. It is a longing of the soul. It is a daily admission of one's weakness. The tallest among us has a perpetual reminder of his nothingness before death, disease, old age, accidents, etc. We are living in the midst of death. What is the value of "working for our own schemes" when they might be reduced to naught in the twinkling of an eye, or when we may be equally swiftly and unawares be taken away from them? But we may feel strong as a rock, if we could truthfully say: "We work for God and his schemes." Then all is as clear as day-light. Then nothing perishes. All perishing is then only what seems. Death and destruction have then, but only then, no reality about them. For death or destruction is then but a change. An artist destroys his picture for creating a better one. A watchmaker throws away a bad spring to put in a new and useful one.

A congregational prayer is a mighty thing. What we do not often do alone, we do together. Boys do not need conviction. If they merely attend in obedience to the call to prayer without inward resistance, they feel the exaltation. But many do not. They are even mischievous. All the same the unconscious effect cannot be resisted. Are there not boys who at the commencement of their career were scoffers but who subsequently became mighty believers in the efficacy of congregational prayer?

It is a common experience for men who have no robust faith to seek the comfort for congregational prayer. All who flock to churches, temples, or mosques are not scoffers or humbugs. They are honest men and women. For them congregational prayer is like a daily bath, a necessity, of their existence. These places of worship are not a mere idle superstition to be swept away at the first opportunity. They have survived all attacks up to now and are likely to persist to the end of time. *(Young India, 23 September 1926 (CW 31, pp. 439–41))*

Essence of Prayer

I am glad that you all want me to speak to you on the meaning of and the necessity for prayer. I believe that prayer is the very soul and essence of religion, and therefore prayer must be the very core of the life of man, for no man can live without religion. There are some who in the egotism of their reason declare that they have nothing to do with religion. But it is like a man saying that he breathes but that he has no nose. Whether by reason, or by instinct, or by superstition, man acknowledges some sort of relationship with the divine.

The rankest agnostic or atheist does acknowledge the need of a moral principle, and associates something good with its observance and something bad with its non-observance. Bradlaugh, whose atheism is well known, always insisted on proclaiming his innermost conviction. He had to suffer a lot for thus speaking the truth, but he delighted in it and said that truth is its own reward. Not that he was quite insensible to the joy resulting from the observance of truth. This joy however is not at all worldly, but springs out of communion with the divine. That is why I have said that even a man who disowns religion cannot and does not live without religion.

Now I come to the next thing, *viz.*, that prayer is the very core of man's life, as it is the most vital part of religion. Prayer is either petitional or in its wider sense is inward communion. In either case the ultimate result is the same. Even when it is petitional, the petition should be for the cleansing and purification of the soul, for freeing it from the layers of ignorance and darkness that envelop it. He therefore who hungers for the awakening of the divine in him must fall back on prayer.

But prayer is no mere exercise of words or of the ears, it is no mere repetition of empty formula. Any amount of repetition of Ramanama is futile if it fails to stir the soul. It is better in prayer to have a heart without word than words without a heart. It must be in clear response to the spirit which hungers for it. And even as a hungry man relishes a hearty meal, a hungry soul will relish a heartfelt prayer. And I am giving you a bit of my experience and that of my companions when I say that he who has experienced the magic of prayer may do without food for days together but not a single moment without prayer. For without prayer there is no inward peace.

If that is the case, someone will say, we should be offering our prayers every minute of our lives. There is no doubt about it, but we erring mortals, who find it difficult to retire within ourselves for inward communion even for a single moment will find it impossible to remain perpetually in communion with the divine. We therefore fix some hours when we make a serious effort to throw off the attachments of the world for a while, we make a serious endeavour to remain, so to say, out of the flesh. You have heard Surdas's hymn. It is the passionate cry of a soul hungry for union with the divine. According to our standards he was a saint, but according to his own he was a proclaimed sinner. Spiritually he was miles ahead of us, but he felt the separation from the divine so keenly that he has uttered that anguished cry in loathing and despair.

I have talked of the necessity for prayer, and therethrough I have dealt with the essence of prayer. We are born to serve our fellowmen, and we cannot properly do so unless we are wide awake. There is an eternal struggle raging in man's breast between the powers of darkness and of light, and he who has not the sheet-anchor of prayer to rely upon will be a victim to the powers of darkness.

The man of prayer will be at peace with himself and with the whole world, the man who goes about the affairs of the world without a prayerful heart will be miserable and will make the world also miserable. Apart therefore from its bearing on man's condition after death, prayer has incalculable value for man in this world of the living. Prayer is the only means of bringing about orderliness and peace and repose in our daily acts. We inmates of the Ashram who came here in search of truth and for insistence on truth professed to believe in the efficacy of prayer, but had never up to now made it a matter of vital concern. We did not bestow on it the care that we did on other matters. I awoke from my slumbers one day and realized that I had been woefully negligent of my duty in the matter. I have therefore suggested measures of stern discipline and far from being any the worse, I hope we are the better for it. For it is so obvious. Take care of the vital thing and other things will take care of themselves. Rectify one angle of a square, and then other angles will be automatically right.

Begin therefore your day with prayer, and make it so soulful that it may remain with you until the evening. Close the day with prayer so that you may have a peaceful night free from dreams and nightmares. Do not worry about the form of prayer. Let it be any form, it should be such as can put us into communion with the divine. Only, whatever be the form, let not the spirit wander while the words of prayer run on out of your mouth.

If what I have said has gone home to you, you will not be at peace until you have compelled your hostel superintendents to interest themselves in your prayer and to make it obligatory. Restraint self-imposed is no compulsion. A man, who chooses the path of freedom from restraint, *i.e.*, of self-indulgence, will be a bondslave of passions, whilst the man who binds himself to rules and restraints releases himself. All things in the universe, including the sun and the moon and the stars, obey certain laws. Without the restraining influence of these laws the world would not go on for a single moment. You, whose mission in life is service of your fellowmen, will go to pieces if you do not impose on yourselves some sort of discipline, and prayer is a necessary spiritual discipline. It is discipline and restraint that separates us from the brute. If we will be men walking with our heads erect and not walking on all fours, let us understand and put ourselves under voluntary discipline and restraint. *(Speech at Prayer Meeting, Sabarmati Ashram, 17 January 1930 (CW 42, pp. 411–13))*

Sound Mind in a Sound Body

Exercise is just as essential to mankind as are air, water and food, though it is true that man cannot get on for a long time without air, water and food as he can without exercise. It is a fact of common experience, however, that one cannot enjoy really good health without exercise. We have to interpret exercise in the same way that we did "food". Exercise does not necessarily mean *moidanda* football, cricket or going out for a walk. Exercise means physical and mental activity. Just as food is necessary for the mind as much as for bones and flesh, so also is exercise necessary both for body and mind. If the body has no exercise, it is sickly and, if the mind has none, it is dull. Stupidity should also be regarded only as a kind of illness. It betrays sheer ignorance to describe as healthy a wrestler who, though adept at wrestling, is mentally a boor. There is a saying in English that he alone is healthy who has a sound mind in a sound body.

What is this exercise? Nature has so arranged things for us that we can be continuously taking exercise in one way or another. If we but think calmly enough, we shall see that a majority of people in the world live on agriculture. All members in a farmer's family have some form of exercise. It is only if they work eight, ten or even more hours every day in the fields or elsewhere that they can get their daily bread. They need no separate exercise for the mind. A farmer cannot work without applying his mind. He must be able to test the nature of his soil, must watch changes of weather, must know how to manipulate his plough skilfully and be generally familiar with the movements of the stars, the sun and the moon. However clever a city-dweller may be, every time he goes to a farmer's house, he feels altogether out of his element.

The farmer can say how seed should be sown; he is familiar with all the by-ways in the vicinity and knows all the men in the neighbourhood. By looking at the stars he can judge the direction even at night. He can make certain deductions from the voice and speed of birds; for instance, when certain birds cluster or sing together, he sees in it a sign of the approach of the monsoon or some other similar phenomenon. Thus, the farmer knows enough of astronomy, geography and geology to serve his needs. He has to feed his children and has, therefore, some idea of the duties of man, and, residing as he does in the vast open spaces of this earth, he naturally becomes aware of the greatness of God. Physically, it goes without saying, he is always sturdy. He is his own physician, when ill. Thus, we can see, he does have an educated mind.

But all men are not going to be farmers. Moreover, these chapters are not being written for the benefit of farmers. The question is, what should those who have gone into business or some similar profession do in this regard? The farmer's life has been described at some length in order that we may find a rational answer to this problem, that we who are not farmers can arrange our way of life somewhat on the pattern of his and that we may realize that, in so far as our manner of living differs from the farmer's, we would enjoy poorer health. We can conclude from a farmer's way of living that a man should do physical work for eight hours a day and that of a kind that would stimulate our mental powers in the very process of doing it.

Now, merchants and others certainly obtain mental exercise in the course of their work, but this is one-sided. A businessman does not know astronomy or geography or history, as the farmer does. He may be able to judge about movements of prices and may be proficient in the art of salesmanship, but this is not enough to exercise fully his mental faculties. In this type of work, the body does perform some movements now and then, but they are too slight to be of any account.

In the West, they have invented games like cricket for such people. Another way is to observe some days in the year as holidays, when more games are played, and to do some light reading by way of mental exercise. This is one method which we may consider. To be sure, spending time in sports does give some exercise to the body, but exercise of this kind does nothing to improve the mind. We can see the truth of this from numerous instances. What proportion of men of high intellectual calibre shall we find among those who regularly play cricket or from among the large number who play football? In India, what do we observe as regards the mental development of the princes who give their time to sports? Again, how many of those with well-developed intellectual powers are sportsmen? Experience shows that highly intellectual men are seldom sportsmen as well.

The British nowadays are very much given to sports. Their own poet, Kipling has described these sportsmen as enemies of the mind, and adds that they will also prove themselves enemies to their country. In India, our intellectuals seem to have found a different way. They provide exercise for their minds but relatively very little or none for their bodies. These people are lost to us. Their bodies are enfeebled by excessive intellectual work. They are continually pursued by some ailment or other and just when they have gained enough experience to be of real use to the country, they pass away. From this we may conclude that neither exercising the brain alone nor the body alone is enough and also that exercise which serves no useful purpose, namely, that derived from sports, has little meaning. Real exercise is that which trains, continuously, both mind and body alike. He alone who takes such exercise can preserve good health. The farmer is the only such person.

Then, what are those to do who are not farmers? The exercise obtained from sports such as cricket leaves much to be desired. We must, therefore, think of a form of exercise something like what the farmer gets. Businessmen and others similarly placed can make a garden round their house and regularly spend two to four hours a day digging there. Hawkers get exercise from their own work itself. If we are living in a rented room, we should not raise any difficulty about working in another's land, for that would indicate a small mind. We would derive nothing but benefit from working on land, whosoever's it might be. The appearance of our house would be improved and we would have the satisfaction of having looked after another's land.

It is necessary to say a few words for those who cannot find an opportunity to work on land or who do not favour such work in any circumstances. Apart from working on land, the best form of exercise is walking. It has been truly described as the king of physical exercises. Our *fakirs* and *sadhus* are very healthy. One reason for this is that they do not use horses, carriages or other vehicles. Their journeys are always performed on foot. There has been a famous American writer named Thoreau who has written a highly thought-provoking book on the subject of walking. According to him, the writings of one who refuses to leave his house on the excuse of lack of time and who undertakes no physical activity, are bound to be anaemic like himself. Speaking of his own experience, he says that when he wrote his best books he was doing his longest walking. He thought nothing of walking four or five hours at a stretch. Just as we cannot work when we are hungry, so it should be with exercise. We do not know how to measure mental work, therefore, we are not able to realize that mental work done unaccompanied by physical exercise will inevitably be dull and ineffectual.

Walking results in rapid circulation of blood in all the parts of the body, promotes movements in every organ and strengthens it. One should remember that the arms move during walking. We obtain fresh air by going for a walk and behold the beauties of Nature. One should not take walks always in the same place or in narrow lanes but go out into fields and groves. We will then be able to appreciate in some measure the beauty of Nature. A walk of a mile or two can scarcely be called walking. A walk, to be worth the name, should cover ten or twelve miles. Those who cannot do this regularly can take long walks on Sundays. A certain patient, who used to suffer from indigestion, went one day to an experienced *vaidya* for some pills.

The *vaidya* advised him to take short but regular walks. The patient protested that he was too weak. The *vaidya* realized that he was, in fact, a timid man. He thereupon took the patient with him in his carriage. On the way he purposely dropped his whip. The patient, out of politeness, had to get out to pick it up. The *vaidya* immediately drove off. The poor patient had to follow, panting hard for breath. The *vaidya* having made sure that the former had covered a fairly long distance, turned the carriage back, picked him up and told him that, since walking was the only medicine for him, he—the *vaidya*—had forced him to walk even at the risk of appearing cruel. By this time, however, the patient was ravenously hungry and had forgotten all about the whip episode. He thanked the doctor, went home and ate his fill. Those who are not in the habit of walking and suffer from indigestion and its accompanying ills should try the experiment. *(Indian Opinion, 12 April 1913 (Translated from Gujarati) (CW 12, pp. 22-27))*

Walking is the Best Exercise

We are as careless about exercise as about diet. To stroll one or two miles at a leisurely pace is no exercise. To hit a billiard ball one or two hundred times with a cue is also no exercise. When exercise is taken in this manner in a room with foul-smelling air, the effect is bound to harmful. In our predicament, when no other form of exercise is convenient, walking is the best exercise. But exercise is worth the name only if one can walk six miles at a stretch in the morning and again in the evening. The walking should be done briskly, at a speed of four miles an hour. Thoreau used to walk for eight hours daily when he wrote his best book. Tolstoy testifies to the fact that while writing his best books he never used to sit at his desk before he had plenty of exercise.

He always used to work on a farm. [Some people say]: "I cannot spare a minute from the client's work or from public work, and take exercise." Such talk is sheer vanity. It would seem to proceed from a belief that but for us public work would go to the dogs. The Grand Old Man of India, Dadabhai has been observing all the general rules of hygiene and has never departed from his routine of exercise, etc. Hence, we see him alive to this day, and it would in no way be surprising if this rishi were to live a hundred years like those of old times. *(Prajabandhu, 23 April 1916 (CW 13, p. 270) (Translated from Gujarati))*

Indigenous Games

They have included various games, etc. in physical training. But, in this sphere too, nobody seems to have realized their true meaning and purpose, and our indigenous games have been left out. Tennis, cricket and football have gained in popularity. Admittedly, these three games are enjoyable. But if we had not been carried away by enthusiasm for these Western forms of sport, we would not have given up our inexpensive but equally interesting indigenous games like *gend-balla, gilli-danda, kho-kho, sat-tali, kabaddi,* etc. The old *akhadas,* which provided training in wrestling and various Indian forms of bodily exercise, have nearly gone out of existence for want of use. I think that the only western item in this field we may well copy is 'drill'. A friend once remarked that we do not know how to walk—particularly when there are more than one, and we have to walk in step. We totally lack the ability to walk quietly and regularly, to the accompaniment of *tal,* in formation of twos and fours, when there are hundreds or thousands of us.

It is not that such drilling is useful only in actual battle. It may prove quite useful in many acts of service also. For example, in extinguishing fire, in rescuing people from drowning, in carrying the sick and disabled in *doli,* etc. previous practice in drill is a valuable aid. Thus, it is necessary to introduce in our schools indigenous games, exercise and the Western type of drill. Speech at Second Gujarat Educational Conference, Broach, 20 October 1917. *(CW 14, pp. 30–31)*

Inexpensive Exercises

Many students feel that it is not necessary to make any special effort for health. However, regular exercise is absolutely necessary for the body. What can be expected of a student who is not well-equipped in health? Just as milk cannot be held in a paper container, so also education is not likely to remain for long in the paper-like bodies of our students. The body is the abode of the spirit and, therefore, holy like a place of pilgrimage. We must see that it is well protected.

Walking regularly and energetically for an hour and a half in the morning and for the same period in the evening in open air keeps it healthy and the mind fresh. The time thus spent is not wasted. Such exercise, coupled with rest, will invigorate both the body and the intellect, enabling one to learn things more quickly. I think games like cricket have no place in a poor country like India. We have a number of inexpensive games of our own which afford innocent joy. *(CW 14, pp. 135–36)*

Ancient Indian Asanas

In my opinion the physical training for our students should follow the old Indian system—that of *pranayam, asanas,* etc. I believe that the system of physical education developed by Muller and others in the West, who have written on this subject and also demonstrated the efficacy of their system through practical results, has its roots in the old Indian system. What these writers have done is to set it out in modern scientific language and perhaps to improve it in places. I am conscious that we have done very little work in this direction. Having gone through a course of training according to this old system, those who further want to learn the present day wrestling, etc. may be given the facilities to do so. But training *lathi* and sword, etc. should not be considered necessary. I do not think that it is necessary to give lathi-training, etc. to the boys. Lathi does not seem to have much to do with the toning up of the body or with the development of its different parts. It is not therefore a part of the physical training but a part of the training useful in one's defence or similar purposes.

Compulsory Physical Training

I was glad to hear that physical training and games have been made compulsory. Let us make compulsory for ourselves all that is good. Gujarati and Sanskrit, etc. we consider good and necessary and therefore prescribe them as compulsory subjects. We did not consider physical training and games equally necessary and had left them to the choice of the students. Now that we have made them compulsory it means that we consider them as necessary as Gujarati. Restraints imposed upon us against our will tend to make slaves of us, but restraints willingly accepted augment our true independence.

Brahmacharya and Ahimsa

'You know,' said he, 'that I am a man conscious of my limitations and it is not in my nature to have more things than I can attend to. But I could not resist Dr. Patwardhan's request. I was glad to be told that this gymnasium was open to Hindus and Musalmans alike, and that not only Musalman but 'untouchable' youths are members of it. I rejoice to see that the institution is thus free from communalism. 'Our Shastras say that a boy who would keep his body fit and strong and make the best use of it should observe *Brahmacharya.* I have travelled all over the country and one of the most deplorable things I have noticed is the rickety bodies of young men. So long as we labour under the curse of child marriage, and so long as many members of our society are children of such marriages, so long much bodily exercise is an impossibility. Who will recommend physical exercise to consumptives? We should therefore lay the axe at the root of this curse, if we would see our young men and women strong and healthy and India on the path of vigorous and healthy growth. Manu has laid down that a student should observe *Brahmacharya* up to his 25th year at least. All physical exercise will be futile so long as these conditions are not satisfied.

'But there is another thing to which I should like to draw your attention. You know that I am pledged to have nothing to do with things even remotely connected with violence. Whatever others may say, I am convinced that the way of nonviolence is the only way and the highest and permanent religion for me. How is it then, some one might ask, that an avowed votary of nonviolence like me has at all associated himself with an institution like this? The reason is clear. *Ahimsa* or nonviolence means the renunciation of the capacity to use violence. He who has not that capacity is therefore incapable of exercising nonviolence.

Nonviolence is a mighty spiritual force, but its votary should have the power to use physical force and should consciously and deliberately refuse to exercise that force. Not that physical training is a *sine qua non* for acquiring capacity for violence, but we may not encourage our youths to have feeble physiques in order to be capable of *ahimsa.* You cannot make a man nonviolent by depriving him of arms. One of the many crimes of the British rule in India is that we have been forcibly deprived of our arms—not indeed with a view to making us nonviolent even if such a thing was possible but to emasculating us. I want India to be strong and free to exercise its strength and yet to renounce it.

'Thus I like institutions like these for physical training. But let me utter a word of warning. No institution that has as its object the subjection of a community, whether Hindu, Musalman, Parsi or Christian, can have my blessings.

Only that institution can have my blessings which aims at the growth of the physical culture of all communities, of all the youths of the nation, to whatever creed or community they belong. I should not have come here, did I not know that the gymnasium I have opened belonged to the latter type. Congratulating you once more I wish and pray that you may all be true and pure, and your lives may be consecrated to the service of our nation and of our religions.' *(Speech at Vyayam Mandir, Amaraoti, Young India, 30 December 1926 True Education, pp. 108-109))*

Physical versus Spiritual Strength

I install this image of Maruti here, not merely because Maruti had the strength of a giant. Even Ravana had that strength. But Maruti had the strength of soul, and his physical strength was only a manifestation of his spiritual strength which in its turn was the direct fruit of his exclusive devotion to Rama and his *Brahmacharya.* May you therefore be like Maruti of matchless valour born out of your *Brahmacharya* and may that valour be dedicated to the service of the Motherland. *(Speech at Vaisya Vidyashram Gymnasium, Young India, 17 March 1927 (CW 33, p. 143))*

Time for Exercise

'But you do not even go out for walks,' said I. 'Is it surprising that you should be always ailing? Should public work leave no time for physical exercise?'

'When do you ever find me free to go out for a walk?' He replied.

I had such a great regard for Gokhale that I never strove with him. Though this reply was far from satisfying me, I remained silent. I believed then and I believe even now, that no matter what amount of work one has, one should always find some time for exercise, just as one does for one's meals. It is my humble opinion that, far from taking away from one's capacity for work, it adds to it. *(An Autobiography, Vol. I, p. 348 (CW 39, pp. 188–9))*

Mass Drill

The object of mass drill is to enable large bodies of people to perform any movement rhythmically and swiftly and with absolute precision. What a saving in national time and energy it would mean if we could do that in our public meetings and functions! There is a silent music in disciplined movement of masses of men and women. Just now I asked you to move a little towards me so that my low voice may reach you. Had you advanced far enough in your drill, you would have been able to perform that movement with ease without any noise or confusion.

There is a rhythm and music in drill that makes action effortless and eliminates fatigue. If the whole nation of 300 millions could be drilled so as to move together and act together and if necessary to die together as one man, we should attain independence without striking a blow and set an example of a peaceful revolution for the whole world to emulate. *(Speech at Scouts Rally Segaon, 22 December 1938 (CW 68, pp. 232-3))*

Right to Punish

> *"I believe that corporal punishment does not improve anyone If, in spite of my belief, I still punish the students of my class, would it be regarded as violence on my part on not? Again, if I do not punish them myself and send a boy who is mischievous or dull to the Headmaster knowing that he will award him physical punishment, would I be deemed to be guilty of violence or not?"*

There is certainly violence in punishing the students – whether one punishes them oneself, or sends them to the Headmaster to be punished by him. The question whether a teacher may at all punish any student has not been explicitly asked, but it is implied in the original question. I can imagine a situation when it may be one's duty to punish even a young boy if he has committed a wrong and is conscious of it. Every teacher must decide for himself what course of action to take. But, as a general rule, a teacher should never inflict corporal punishment on students.

The right to punish them belongs to the parents, if at all. A punishment is just only if it is accepted by the student himself.

Such occasions, however, do not often arise. Even when they arise, punishment should never be inflicted if there is any doubt about its justness. Lastly, no punishment should be inflicted in anger. *(Navajivan, 27 September 1925 (CW 28, p. 242))*

Teaching sans Punishment

A teacher in a *Vinaya Mandir* (national high school) asks:

1. Is there any justification for corporal punishment being meted out to boys in schools, especially in national schools?
2. Some teachers opine: "We may not punish boys who fail to fulfil the assignments given them; but there would be nothing wrong in punishing them if they commit mischief or moral offence?" Is this opinion correct?
3. Some friends say that they punish boys at times in order to improve them, but they are also sorry for having done so afterwards and no blame, therefore, attaches to them. Could we excuse the teacher who punishes his pupils and makes this plea afterwards?
4. What other forms of punishment, besides the corporal, should be prohibited in national schools?
5. What forms of punishment will imply a breach of the pledge of nonviolence on the part of the teacher in a national school?

The above questions have not been put to you through idle curiosity. The teachers of this school have been discussing them for some time past, and the arguments which I have quoted were actually used by some of them.

Because they are of practical importance, your considered opinion on them will provide guidance to a large number of teachers. You may answer them in the columns of the *Harijan* – if you will be so kind.

I hold the view that it is wrong to inflict punishment on the boys in any form whatsoever. It diminishes the love for, and pride in, their students which teachers should have. The old system of punishing students in order to teach them is fast disappearing in modern educational methods. I know that occasions crop up when even the best teachers cannot help punishing the offender among students. But, fortunately, such occasions are few, and, in any case, it would not be right to justify them. If a teacher feels compelled to resort to punishment it should be taken as implying a deficiency, to that extent, in his profession. Educationists like Spencer have held as improper every form of punishment, though he could not always stick by his precept.

After giving the above answer, it does not seem necessary to reply the other questions in detail. As a general rule, nonviolence and punishment cannot go together. I can certainly imagine cases in which punishment would not be punishment. But such examples would not be useful to teachers. For instance, if a father is very sad over his son's misconduct and, unable to bear the grief, beats him, his beating the boy might well be regarded as the punishment of love. The boy would also not consider it violence. Those who nurse a patient in delirium have, at times, to slap him in order to control him. This would also be not violence, but nonviolence. But such examples are worthless to teachers. They must acquire the art of disciplining students and of teaching them without punishing them. There are examples of teachers who have never used punishment. Other forms of punishment, besides corporal punishment, are: to make the students get down from their seat, to make them do the stand-and-sit exercise, to abuse them, etc. According to me, the teacher should not punish students at all.

To punish the boys first for improving them and then be sorry for it is no true penitence. Besides, if the teachers adopt this practice and act on it, it will ultimately become a behaviour pattern of people in our society. Punishment has led us to believe in the illusion that improvement can be brought about through the use of violence. I hold the view that a teacher, who deliberately uses punishment, commits a breach of his pledge in regard to non violence. *(Navajivan, 21 October 1928 (CW 37, pp. 399–400))*

Spare the Rod

I am a teacher. I try to follow the principle of nonviolence in dealing with my schoolboys and my own children. I am successful to a great extent in case of the school children, excepting a bully whom I would send to the Head Master. But in case of my own children I often feel like beating, though I successfully restrain myself. I find that these are readily obedient to my uncle who, unlike me, believes in the old saying 'Spare the rod, spoil the child.' What should I do with my own children? How should a nonviolent Head Master deal with a bully?

I am quite clear that you must not inflict corporal or other punishment on your children or pupils. You can punish yourself, if you like and are qualified, in order to melt your children's or pupils' hearts. Many mothers are known to have corrected their children in this manner. I have on many occasions. I had to deal with wild boys in South Africa—Muslims, Christians, Hindus and Parsis. With one exception; I do not remember ever having punished a single boy. The nonviolent method invariably succeeded. When a bond is established between a teacher and his pupils, the latter will generally yield before their teachers' suffering for their sake. In the case of your 'bully' if he has no respect for you, you can non-co-operate with him by sending him away from your school. Nonviolence does not compel you to keep in your school a student who does not carry out disciplinary rules. *(Harijan, 13 July 1940 (CW 72, p. 226))*

Library

I have some ideas about libraries—about what they should be and what they should do. I will place them before you. First, you must so plan the building of the library that it can be enlarged as the library expands without marring its symmetry. The later additions should not appear as extraneous accretions to the original building. It should provide facilities for arranging occasional lectures, and for students and scholars engaged in research work to come and make use of the books there in an atmosphere of peace. We should aim at making this library the biggest and the best in the world. If we have the will, God will give us the strength to do it. Kakasaheb has suggested that the collection of books with the Vidyapith may be kept here. There is no dearth of art in Gujarat. The famous lattice-work in stone in the mosque at Bhadra has no match in the whole world. Similarly, the needle-work of Ahmedabad is perhaps unrivalled. The delicacy of stone-work of the masons of Ahmedabad has surprised me. I have seen them living in dark and dingy hovels. Artists do not wait for encouragement. If we could find another donor ready to offer fifty thousand rupees, for a museum, we could set up one in this very building. We have to work in such a way that the library may grow and develop from day to day.

It would be better if we could get one or two men who would devote most of their time to it. Don't choose a money-minded businessman, who would merely keep the books safe and in good condition, for the post of librarian. Choose someone who could be depended upon to appreciate the relative worth of different books and select them. In case no one volunteers his services for it free, you should be ready to offer a good salary and appoint a really qualified man. Harijans should be allowed to use the library without any fee, and if books are spoiled or damaged or even stolen, the loss should be borne by the library itself. The Harijans are the poorest of the poor and are entitled to special consideration. In fact, you may extend this concession to all poor people. That will enhance the glory of the institution.

I also repeat the request made by Bhai Rasiklal, namely, the managing body for the library should be carefully chosen from a body of scholars so as to keep the institution alive and growing. Do not think that this body should be composed only of men of practical wisdom, for scholars understand what a library should be like and how it can be made to shine. Carnagie gave large donations to many libraries. The conditions he attached to his donations were accepted by most scholars, except those of Scotland. They frankly told Carnagie that if he insisted on his conditions they would not accept the donation. How could he know, they asked, what books would be useful to the library? The artists do not sell their art. There are in Gujarat large collections of precious books.

But they are in the possession of *banias.* The Jains have fine collections of old books of great historical value, but they are lying useless tied up in silken sheaths. I have wept over the sight of these books which serve no purpose by being in the hands of the *banias* who know nothing except how to make money. I would go as far as to say that in their hands the Jaina religion itself is dying of starvation by being in the stranglehold of money. Is it possible to count dharma against money? In fact, money should be only the means of dharma. I, therefore, ask you to include able scholars in the managing body of the library. Find out how to do this, and see that you do it. *(Extract from speech delivered at foundation-laying ceremony of the Ahmedabad Sangrahalaya, Satyagraha Ashram – Harijanbandhu, 1 October 1933, (True Education, pp. 169–70))*

Textbooks

I have written a book called *Balpothi,* not much worth talking about. If I sit down to read it, I can finish it in five minutes. If I read it a little carefully, I would finish it in ten minutes. I have not read the comments on it which have been received. I know that many of these are not likely to please me much. There is no measure in the praise or censure generally showered on me and, therefore, either has little effect on me. However that be, the idea behind that book is great.

It is that a teacher should impart education only by word of mouth; that he cannot do so with the help of books and textbooks. Who knows what stuff gets into the brains of children in countries where there are heaps of textbooks! The devil takes possession of them, the children's thinking power is reduced to nil. This conclusion of mine is based on my experience of countless children and on discussions with many teachers. I used to move about with wide-open eyes in South Africa. There was a conflagration in the country, and moving even in the midst of that I observed this thing. Let us compare two schools: one in which teachers are supplied with textbooks and another in which they have to teach without the use of a single textbook.

The teachers in both are equally gifted. The one, then, which has no textbooks to use will be able to give more to the pupils than the one which has them. I do not want children to have any text books. The teachers may, if they wish, read them. We may write as much for them as we choose. If you write for children, you will make the teachers mechanical and destroy their originality and initiative. I do not, of course, wish to arrest the progress of teachers. I merely want that you should also know this point of view of mine. The authors of textbooks are experienced writers. Where the people need their books, by all means let them buy them, but please understand what lies behind my attitude.

You may ask me if I have worked as a teacher. My view is based on considerable experience and I have thought a great deal about education. Kindly think about the matter from the point of view indicated by me and go a little slow. The point of what I am saying is that, if you wish to bring out books for lakhs of children, well, Gujarat does not have the money for that and it will lose interest in this business; secondly, we should not burden the children's brains with these books. *(Navajivan 3 August 1924 (CW 24, pp. 488–90))*

Choking Load of Books

Pupils should know to discriminate between what should be received and what rejected. It is the duty of the teacher to teach his pupils discrimination. If we go on taking in indiscriminately we would be no better than machines. We are thinking, knowing beings and we must in this period distinguish truth from untruth, sweet from bitter language, clean from unclean things and so on.

But the student's path today is strewn with more difficulties than the one of distinguishing good from bad things. The *rishis* taught their pupils without books. They only gave them a few *mantras* which the pupils treasured in their memories and translated in practical life. The present day student has to live in the midst of heaps of books, sufficient to choke him. *(Young India, 29 January 1925 (Towards New Education pp. 39-37))*

Textbooks for Teachers

For India a multiplicity of textbooks means deprivation of the vast majority of village children of the means of instruction. Textbooks, therefore, in India must mean, principally and for the lower standards, textbooks for teachers, not pupils. Indeed, I am not sure that it is not better for the children to have much of the preliminary instruction imparted to them vocally. To impose on children of tender age a knowledge of the alphabet and the ability to read before they can gain general knowledge is to deprive them, whilst they are fresh, of the power of assimilating instruction by word of mouth. Should, for instance, a lad of seven wait for learning the Ramayana till he can read it? The results that we arrive at when we think of the few lakhs living in the cities of India are wholly different from those we obtain, we think, in terms of the millions of rural India. *(Young India, 16 September 1926 (CW 31, p. 410))*

Books versus Need-based Learning

There seems to me to be no doubt that in the public schools the books used, especially for children, are for the most part useless when they are not harmful. That many of them are cleverly written cannot be denied. They might even be the best for the people and the environment for which they are written. But they are not written for Indian boys and girls, not for the Indian environment. When they are so written, they are generally undigested imitations hardly answering the wants of the scholars. In this country, wants vary according to the provinces and the classes of children. For instance, want of Harijan children are, in the beginning stages at least, different from those of the others.

I have, therefore, come to the conclusion that books are required more for the teachers than for the taught. And every teacher, if he is to do full justice to his pupils, will have to prepare the daily lesson from the material available to him. This too, he will have to suit to the special requirements of his class.

Real education has to draw out the best from the boys and girls to be educated. This can never be done by packing ill, assorted and unwanted information into the heads of the pupils. It becomes a dead weight crushing all originality in them and turning them into mere automata. If we were not ourselves victims of the system, we would long ago have realized the mischief wrought by the modern method of giving mass education, especially in a case like India's.

Attempts have undoubtedly been made by many institutions to produce their own textbooks with more or less success. But in my opinion they do not answer the vital needs of the country. I lay no claim to originality for the views I have endeavoured to set forth here. They are repeated here for the benefit of the managers and teachers of Harijan schools, who have a tremendous task before them. They dare not be satisfied with mere mechanical work resulting in simply making the children under their charge indifferently and in a parrotlike manner learn the books chosen anyhow. They have undertaken a great trust which they must discharge courageously, intelligently and honestly.

The task is difficult enough but not so difficult as one would imagine, provided the teacher or the manager puts his whole heart into the work. If he becomes a parent to his pupils, he will instinctively know what they need and set about giving it to them. If he has it not to give, he will proceed to qualify himself. And seeing that we have started with the idea that the boys and girls have to have instruction in accordance with their wants, no extraordinary cleverness or possession of external knowledge is required in a teacher of Harijan and, for that matter, any other children.

And when it is remembered that the primary aim of all education is, or should be, the moulding of the character of pupils, a teacher who has a character to keep need not lose heart. *(Harijan, 1 December 1933 (CW 56, pp. 295-6))*

Craze for Changing Textbooks

The craze for ever-changing textbooks is hardly a healthy sign from the educational standpoint. If textbooks are treated as a vehicle for education, the living word of the teacher has very little value. A teacher who teaches from textbooks does not impart originality to his pupils. He himself becomes a slave of textbooks and has no opportunity or occasion to be original. It therefore seems that the less textbooks there are the better it is for the teacher and his pupils. Textbooks seem to have become an article of commerce. Authors and publishers who make writing and publishing a means of making money are interested in a frequent change of textbooks. In many cases teachers and examiners are themselves authors of textbooks.

It is naturally to their interest to have their books sold. The selection board is again naturally composed of such people. And so the vicious circle becomes complete. And it becomes very difficult for parents to find money for new books every year. It is a pathetic sight to see boys and girls going to school loaded with books which they are ill able to carry. The whole system requires to be thoroughly examined. The commercial spirit needs to be entirely eliminated and the question approached solely in the interest of the scholars. It will then probably be found that 75 per cent of the textbooks will have to be consigned to the scrap-heap. If I had my way, I would have books largely as aids to teachers rather than for the scholars. Such textbooks as are found to be absolutely necessary for the scholars should be circulated among them for a number of years so that the cost can be easily borne by middle class families. The first step in this direction is perhaps for the State to own and organize the printing and publishing of textbooks. This will act as an automatic check on their unnecessary multiplication. *(Harijan, 9 September 1939 (CW 70, p. 153))*

Unhealthy Textbooks

There is in Wardha a girls' school. Several girls are preparing there for the Sammelan examination. Both teachers and girls complain that not all the prescribed textbooks are fit to be read. It has been complained that they are too full of erotic matter. There is erotic literature in Hindi. Shri Benarsidas Chaturvedi had drawn my attention to this a few years ago. The literature of the language which we wish to make our national language should be pure, radiant and lofty. Nowadays there is a good deal of obscene literature in Hindi. Editors of periodicals are either not careful or they deliberately encourage obscenity in the writings. In my opinion the Sammelan should not remain indifferent in this matter. Good writers should get encouragement from the Sammelan. People should also get some help from the Sammelan in choosing the right books. The task no doubt is difficult but we cannot run away from difficulties. *(Speech at Hindi Sahitya Sammelan, Indore, 20 April 1935 (CW 60, pp. 449–50))*

Teacher and Textbooks

Nowadays the teacher's task has in fact been reduced to that of a postman or a foreman. It consists only of placing books written by educationists in the hands of pupils and of supervising whether they make use of these or not. In addition to this, what other skill do you expect the teachers to possess?

The science of education has been developed to the extent where the term 'teacher' may be defined as one who can clarify the meaning of difficult passages and prepare abstracts of long chapters. Why should we not now accept this ideal?

I keep on feeling that teachers in the true sense of the word are essential, no matter how good the textbooks are. A good teacher would never content himself with summarizing or explaining the meaning of difficult passages. Time and again, he would go beyond the textbooks and present his subject to the pupil in a vivid manner in the same way as an artist does. The best textbook may be compared to the best photograph. However, just as a painting by an artist although second rate is invariably superior to a photograph, similar is the case with a real teacher. A true teacher introduces the pupil to his subject, creates in him interest for the subject and enables him to understand it independently. In my opinion, one who explains difficult passages and prepares abstracts can never be regarded a good teacher. Our endeavours should be to turn out true teachers who could be infused with a spirit of service. It is not that stray instances of such teachers are not to be found even today. *(Navajivan, 16 June 1928 (CW 36, pp. 352–3) (Translated from Gujarati))*

Language and Spellings

The anarchy prevailing in Gujarati spelling is perhaps unparalleled in any other language. It is not found in Marathi, Bengali, Tamil or Urdu. I have not heard of it in any other Indian language. It is to be found in no European language. What epithet except barbarous can one apply to a people who speak a language with unorganized spelling? Man's language develops as he progresses. A man can be judged in several matters by the language he speaks.

The Government of Bombay took quite some time to come to a decision, but they deserve to be congratulated on having at last arrived at one. I hope all journalists and authors will be guided by the dictionary prepared by the Vidyapith. The Vidyapith should provide the necessary means to facilitate this. Every lover of language must have in his pocket or on his desk a Gujarati dictionary as he would have an English dictionary if he were writing English. Gujarati writers must be as proud of the purity of their language as the English are of theirs.

An Englishman who cannot spell correctly is considered uncivilized. But let us leave aside English. Why should we not devote as much attention to our mother tongue as the students studying in our English schools give or are required to give to English spelling? The Vidyapith should immediately provide facilities for this purpose. The Vidyapith dictionary is of course there. But a simpler and cheaper pocket edition should be prepared. An attempt has been made in the said dictionary to include as many words as possible along with their meanings in brief. It is enough if the pocket edition gives only the spelling and not all words need be included. Only words whose spelling is doubtful should be included. *(Harijanbandhu, 4 February 1940 (Translated from Gujarati) (CW 71, pp. 176-7))*

Music

Nowhere do I find a place given to music. It exercises a powerful influence over us. We do not realize this vividly enough, otherwise we would have done everything possible to teach music to our boys and girls. The Vedic hymns seem to follow musical tunes in their composition. Harmonious music has the power to soothe the anguish of the soul. At times, we find restlessness in a large gathering. This can be arrested and calmed if a national song is sung by all. That hundreds of boys may sing a poem full of courage and the spirit of adventure and bravery and be inspired with the spirit of heroism is no commonplace fact. We have an example of the power of music in the fact that boatmen and other labourers raise, in unison, the cry of Harahar and Allabeli and this helps them in their work. I have seen English friends trying to fight cold by singing songs.

Our boys learn to sing songs from popular plays in all manner of tunes and without regard to time and place, and try their hands, on noisy harmoniums and other instruments, and this does them harm. If, instead, they were to be correctly trained in music, they would not waste their time singing, or attempting to sing, music-hall songs. Just as a trained singer never sings out of tune or at the wrong time, even so one who has learnt classical music will not go in for street music. Music must get a place in our efforts at popular awakening. *(CW 14, p. 30)*

Mass Music

Music means rhythm, order. Its effect is electrical. It immediately soothes. Unfortunately like our *shastras,* music has been the prerogative of the few. It has never become nationalized in the modern sense. If I had any influence with volunteer boy scouts and Seva Samiti organizations, I would make compulsory a proper singing in company of national songs. And to that end I should have great musicians attending every Congress or Conference and teaching mass music. *(Young India, 8 September 1920 (CW 18, p. 241))*

Music and Other Arts

Our conversation having that morning centred round music, Mahatmaji told me in passing how fond he really was of music even though he could not boast of the power of any expert or analytic appreciation. He had said:

> *I am so fond of music that once, while I was in a South African Hospital and ailing from a bruise on my upper lip, I felt greatly soothed as the daughter of a friend of mine sang the song 'Lead, Kindly Light' at my request.*

On my asking him if he knew any of the beautiful songs of Mirabai, he said:

> *Yes, I have heard a good many of them. They are so beautiful. It's because they come from the heart and not from any desire to compose or to please a public.*

I called the same evening at his request. After the music, I saw that it had affected him visibly. For I thought I saw his eyes glisten even in that none-too-bright light of the hospital.

"I feel," said I after a short pause, "that our beautiful music has been sadly neglected in the schools and colleges." Mahatmaji replied:

Yes, it has, I have always said so.

Srijut Mahadeo Desai who was present throughout our conversation corroborated this. "I am glad to hear you say so.

Because I have been all along under the impression that you would be against all arts such as music."

I! Against music! Well, I know, I know.......There are so many superstitions rife about me that it has become now almost impossible for me to overtake those who have set them afloat. As a result, my friends only smile at me when I try to lay any claim to being an artist myself.

"I am glad to hear this; because I have been given to understand that in your philosophy of life, which is one of unqualified asceticism, arts like music can hardly aspire to any place." Mahatmaji emphatically said:

But I maintain that asceticism is the greatest art in life.

"What I however meant by art just now is a somewhat different activity such as music or painting or sculpture for the matter of that. And I had thought that you would be rather opposed to them than otherwise." Mahatmaji said:

> *I, opposed to arts like music! Why, I cannot even conceive of an evolution of the religious life of India without music. I do say I am a lover of music as well as the other arts. Only, my values may be different from the accepted ones, that's all. I am doubtless against much that passes for art in these days. I do not for instance call that art which demands an intimate knowledge of its technique for its appreciation. If you go to the Satyagraha Ashram, you will find the walls bare. And my friends object to this. I admit I don't have paintings on the walls of my Ashram. But that is because I think that the walls are meant for sheltering us, and not because I am opposed to art as such. For have I not gazed and gazed at the wonderful vault of the starry sky – hardly ever tiring of the same? And I do say that I can never conceive of any painting superior to the star-studded sky in its satisfying effect on the mind. It has bewildered me, mystified me – sent me into the most wonderful ecstatic thrills imaginable. Side by side with this wondrous mystery of God's artistic handi-work, does not that of man appear to be the merest tinsel?*

I said: "I agree with you when you say that Nature is a great artist, as also when you inveigh against the regrettable prostitution of art, which unhappily so often passes for art. I differ also from those artists who have acquired the habit of saying that art is even greater than life."

Exactly. Life is and must always be greater than all the arts put together. I go still further. For I say that he is the greatest artist who leads the best life. For what is art without the background and setting of a worthy life? An art is to be valued only when it ennobles life. I object emphatically only when people say that art is everything, that it does not matter even if life has to be held subservient to its (*i.e.*, art's) fulfilment. I have then to say that my values are different, that is all. But fancy people saying that I am opposed to all arts on that account!

An interview with Dilip Kumar Roy, an exponent of Indian music and inmate of the Aurobindo Ashram, Pondicherry. *(The Bombay Chronicle, 5 February 1924 (CW 23, pp. 192–4))*

Music—A Divine Art

Why do you always attach so much importance to music?

It is sad that the study of music is generally neglected in our country today. Without it, the entire educational system seems to me to be incomplete. Music brings sweetness to the individual and to the social life of the people. Even as *pranayama is* necessary for the regulation of breath, so is music for disciplining the voice. Dissemination of the knowledge of music among the people will greatly help in controlling and stopping the music which is a usual feature of public meetings in this country. Music pacified anger and its judicious use is highly helpful in leading a man to the vision of God.

It does not mean shouting and shrieking a tune anyhow like a rigmarole, nor does it mean the singing of stage songs. I have already referred to its ordinary meaning above, but its deeper meaning is that our whole life should be sweet and musical like a song. It goes without saying that life cannot be made like that without the practice of virtues such as truth, honesty, etc. To make life musical means to make it one with God, to merge it in Him. He who has not rid himself of raga and dwesha, *i.e.*, likes and dislikes, who has not tasted of the joy of service, cannot have any understanding of celestial music. A study of music, which does not take account of this deeper aspect of this divine art, has little or no value for me. *(Navjivan, 1 July 1928 (CW 37, pp. 2–3) (Translated from Gujarati))*

Music and Harmony

There is a famous classical saying which has now become a proverb that the man 'that hath no music in himself' is either an ascetic or a beast. We are far from being ascetics, and to the extent that we are devoid of music we are near allied to beasts. To know music is to transfer it to life. The prevalent discord of today is an indication of our sad plight. There can be no Swaraj where there is no harmony, no music. Where there is discord and every one striking his own tune, there is bad government or anarchy. Work for Swaraj fails to appeal to us because we have no music in us. When we have millions of people singing together in harmony or taking God's name in unison, making one music, we shall have taken the first step to Swaraj. If we cannot achieve this simple thing, how can we win Swaraj.

Where there is filth and squalor and misery there can be no music. It implies an atmosphere quite the contrary. If we put a broad interpretation on music, *i.e.*, if we mean by it union, concord, mutual help, it may be said that in no department of life can we dispense with it. Music today has been degraded to mean the vocal effort of a singing girl. We fight shy of sending our sisters and daughters to music schools. There seems to be a superstition that their voice is best when it is devoid of sweetness. That explains why Dr. Hariprasad has had to express satisfaction with an attendance of ten students.

Music, truly speaking, is an ancient and sacred art. The hymns of Samaveda are a mine of music, and no ayat of the Koran can be recited unmusically. David's Psalms transport you to raptures and remind you of the hymns from Samaveda. Let us revive this art and patronize the school of music.

We see Hindu and Musalman musicians sitting cheek by jowl and partaking in musical concerts. When shall we see the same fraternal union in other affairs of our life? We shall then have the name of Rama and Rahman simultaneously on our lips.

I am glad some of you here are patronizing music. If many more send their children to the music class it will be part of their contribution to national uplift.

But to go a step further. If we would see music in millions of our homes, we should all wear Khadi and spin. The music we have had today was sweet indeed but it is a privilege of the favoured few. The music of the spinning wheel can be a free gift to all and is therefore sweeter. It is the hope and solace and mainstay of the millions, and for me therefore truly good music. *(Young India, 15 April 1926 (CW 30, pp. 159–60))*

Music Fills the Soul

A student of the Gujarat Vidyapith asks:

"What has been the influence of music on your life?"

Music has given me peace. I can remember occasions when music instantly tranquillized my mind when I was greatly agitated over something. Music has helped me to overcome anger. I can recall occasions when a hymn sank deep into me though the same thing expressed in prose had failed to touch me. I also found that the meaning of hymns discordantly sung has failed to come home to me and that it burns itself on my mind when they have been properly sung.

When I hear Gita verses melodiously recited I never grow weary of hearing and the more 1 hear the deeper sinks the meaning into my heart. Melodious recitations of the Ramayana which I heard in my childhood left on me an impression which years have not obliterated or weakened.

I distinctly remember how when once the hymn 'The path of the Lord is meant for the brave, not the coward' was sung to me in an extraordinarily sweet tune, it moved me as it had never before. In 1907 while in the Transvaal I was almost fatally assaulted, the pain of the wounds was relieved when at my instance Olive Doke gently sang to me 'Lead kindly light'.

Let no one infer from this that I know music. On the contrary it would be more correct to say that my knowledge of music is very elementary. I cannot critically judge music. All I can claim is that I have a natural ear for good homely music.

I do not mean to suggest either that because the influence of music has been uniformly good on me it must act similarly on others. On the contrary I know that many people employ music to feed their carnal passions. To sum up, therefore, we may say that the influence of music will differ according to temperaments. As Tulsidas has sung:

> *The Lord of Creation created everything in this world as an admixture of good and evil. But a good man selects the good and rejects the evil even as the fabled swan is said to help himself to cream leaving the water in the milk. (Young India, 10 January 1929 (CW 38, p. 90))*

Music in Schools

Pandit Khare of Gandharva Mahavidyalaya, who has dedicated his life to the spread of pure music among boys and girls, reports the great progress being made in Ahmedabad in particular and Gujarat in general, and he deplores the fact that the education authorities do not seem to countenance the introduction of music in the curricula of education. In the Pandit's opinion, based upon wide experience, it should form part of the syllabus of primary education. I heartily endorse the proposition. The modulation of the voice is as necessary as the training of the hand. Physical drill, handicrafts, drawing and music should go hand in hand in order to draw the best out of the boys and girls and create in them a real interest in their tuition. *(Harijan, 11 September 1937 (CW 66, p. 121))*

True Art is Expression of the Soul

How is it that many intelligent and eminent men, who love and admire you, hold that you consciously or unconsciously have ruled out of the scheme of national regeneration all considerations of Art? I am sorry that in this matter I have been generally misunderstood. There are two aspects of things — the outward and the inward. It is purely matter of emphasis with me. The outward has no meaning except in so far as it helps the inward. All true Art is thus the expression of the soul. The outward forms have value only in so far as they are the expression of the inner spirit of man.

Hesitatingly: The great artists themselves have declared, that Art is the translation of the urge and unrest in the soul of the artist into words, colours, shapes, etc.

Yes, Art of that nature has the greatest possible appeal for me. But I know that many call themselves as artists, and are recognized as such, and yet in their works there is absolutely no trace of the soul's upward urge and unrest.

Have you any instance in mind?

Yes, take Oscar Wilde. I can speak of him, as I was in England at the time that he was being much discussed and talked about. I have been told that Oscar Wilde was one of the greatest literary artists of modern times.

Yes, that is just my trouble. Wilde saw the highest Art simply in outward forms and therefore succeeded in beautifying immorality. All true Art must help the soul to realize its inner self. In my own case, I find that I can do entirely without external forms in my soul's realization. I can claim, therefore, that there is truly sufficient Art in my life, though you might not see what you call works of Art about me. My room may have blank walls; and I may even dispense with the roof, so that I may gaze out upon the starry heavens overhead that stretch in an unending expanse of beauty. What conscious Art of man can give me the panoramic scenes that open out before me, when I look up to the sky above with all its shining stars? This, however, does not mean that I refuse to accept the value of productions of Art, generally accepted as such, but only that I personally feel how inadequate these are compared with the eternal symbols of beauty in Nature. These productions of man's Art have their value only so far as they help the soul onward towards self-realization.

But the artists claim to see and to find Truth through outward beauty. Is it possible to see and find Truth in that way?

I would reverse the order. I see and find Beauty in Truth or through Truth. All Truths, not merely true ideas, but truthful faces, truthful pictures, or songs, are highly beautiful. People generally fail to see Beauty in Truth, the ordinary man runs away from it and becomes blind to the beauty in it. Whenever men begin to see Beauty in Truth, then true Art will arise.

But cannot Beauty be separated from Truth, and Truth from Beauty?

I should want to know exactly what is Beauty. If it is what people generally understand by that word, then they are wide apart. Is a woman with fair features necessarily beautiful?

Yes.

Even if she may be of an ugly character?

But her face in that case cannot be beautiful. It will always be the index of the soul within. The true artist with the genius of perception will produce the right expression.

But here you are begging the whole question. You now admit that mere outward form may not make a thing beautiful. To a true artist only that face is beautiful which, quite apart from exterior, shines with the Truth within the soul. There is then, as I have said, no Beauty apart from Truth.

On the other hand, Truth may manifest itself in forms which may not be outwardly beautiful at all. Socrates, we are told, was the most truthful man of his time and yet his features are said to have been the ugliest in Greece. To my mind he was beautiful, because all his life was a striving after Truth, and you may remember that his outward form did not prevent Phidias from appreciating the beauty of Truth in him, though as an artist he was accustomed to see Beauty in outward forms also!

But, Bapuji, the most beautiful things have often been created by men whose own lives were not beautiful.

That only means that Truth and untruth often coexist; good and evil are often found together. In an artist also not seldom the right perception of things and the wrong coexist. Truly beautiful creations come when right perception is at work. If these moments are rare in life they are also rare in Art.

If only truthful or good things can be beautiful, how can things without a moral quality be beautiful?....... Is there truth, Bapuji, in things that are neither moral nor immoral in themselves? For instance, is there truth in a sunset or a crescent moon that shines amid the stars at night?

Indeed these beauties are truthful, inasmuch as they make me think of the Creator at the back of them. How else could these be beautiful, but for the Truth that is in the centre of creation? When I admire the wonder of a sunset or the beauty of the moon my soul expands in worship of the Creator. I try to see Him and His mercies in all these creations. But even the sunsets and sunrises would be mere hindrances, if they did not help me to think of Him. Anything which is a hindrance to the flight of the soul, is a delusion and a snare; even, like the body, which often does hinder you in the path of salvation.

I am grateful to hear your views on Art, and I understand and accept them. Would it not be well for you to set them down for the benefit of the younger generation in order to guide them aright?

That I could never dream of doing, for the simple reason that it would be an impertinence on my part to hold forth on Art. I am not an art student, though these are my fundamental convictions. I do not speak or write about it, because I am conscious of my own limitations. That consciousness is my only strength. Whatever I might have been able to do in my life has proceeded more than anything else out of the realization of my own limitations. My functions are different from the artist's and I should not go out of my way to assume his position. In conversation with Ramachandran, a young student from Shantiniketan. *(Young India, 13 November 1924 and 20 November 1924 (CW 25, pp. 248–50))*

Music and Painting

The art of painting means expression of the emotions of the artist through line and colour. If this definition of painting were to be accepted, would you include painting as an essential part of the scheme of national education which should be universally taught to all? I have never disparaged drawing and painting, though I have certainly deprecated the blots of ink and colour passing under its name. I doubt if painting as defined by the artist could be made universal. There is this difference between music and painting: While painting can be learnt only by a few who have a natural aptitude for it, music must be and can be learnt by all. In painting too, drawing of straight lines and the figures of animate and inanimate objects can be taught to all. It is certainly useful and necessary and I want it to be taught to every child before it is taught the alphabet. *(Navajivan, 1 July 1928 (CW 37, p. 3))*

The Speaking Painting

Though I was happy and proud to see what I saw in the Exhibition this morning, and felt that I had not seen anything of the kind before in Gujarat, let me tell you that I missed what I would call a speaking painting. Why should I need an artist to explain a work of art to me? Why should it not speak out to me itself? I tell you what I mean. I saw in the Vatican art collection a statue of Christ on the Cross which simply captured me and kept me spell-bound. I saw it five years ago, but it is still before me. There was no one there to explain its charm to me. Here in Belur in Mysore I saw in the ancient temple a bracket in stone made of a little statuette which spoke out to me without anyone to help me to understand it. It was just a woman, half-naked, struggling with the folds of her cloths to extricate herself from the shafts of Cupid who is after all lying defeated at her feet in the shape of a scorpion. I could see the agony on the form—the agony of the stings of scorpion. That at any rate was my interpretation of it. *(Harijan. 14 November 1936 (True Education, p. 176))*

Literature in Quest for Truth

I ask writers: "Will you, through your creations, bring me sooner to God?" If their reply is in the affirmative, I will be a slave to their works. If the work of any writer bores me, it is not my dullness that is to blame but his art itself. A gifted writer should so perfect his art that the reader would be simply absorbed in his work. I am sorry that our literature has little of this kind of thing. There is nothing the masses can learn from the literature of today. There is not one idea in this literature by virtue of which it may endure for a week, or a year or a whole age.

Let us, then, see what literature we possess in the holy books we have had with us from ancient times. The satisfaction they give we don't derive from our modern literature. Even a barely passable translation of any of those works is more interesting to read than anything of the latter. There is much indeed, some will say, in contemporary literature. That may be, but it is an exhausting task to search for that "much". Whoever gives us today anything like what Tulsidas and Kabir gave?

Live as you may,

Realize God anyhow, anyway.

We never see these days anything of this kind. Where do we find now what we received in the age of Akha?

I returned to India after twenty years in South Africa and, looking around, I discovered that we lived in a state of fear. A people in such a state cannot express itself fearlessly. If we have to write under the weight of suppression, the springs of poetry in us will not flow nor will truth come floating on the wave. The same is true about newspapers. With the Press Act hanging over him, the editor cannot write uninhibitedly. With the same Act hanging over the writers, not a single line is written in freedom and hence it is that truth is not presented as it ought to be.

This is a period of transition in India. Crores of people feel that great changes are about to take place, that our poverty will give place to glory, that now the Age of Truth will dawn upon us. I hear these hopes expressed wherever I go. Large numbers of people think that India is about to turn a new leaf. If it does, what sort of writing shall we find on that new leaf? The Reforms which will have been granted will only prove to be a collar and we shall continue to be driven like bullocks, as we are driven today. At such a time, I ask the servants of literature nothing less than that they help us to a vision of God and Truth. They must demonstrate that India is not given to sinful ways, that she will not betray one's faith [in her].

No Indian in Madras has served South India so well as did Pope —not the Pope of the *Iliad* fame. I am ever in love with human beings and would, therefore, always want to steal people's hearts. In order that I might steal the hearts of my brothers of the South, I had to learn their language. I cannot just now quote anything from the writings of the Rev. Pope, but this I will tell you that the poems, or rather the poetry, in Tamil, which even the peasant can enjoy as he waters his field, is just superb.

The watering of the field begins even before the sun has risen. *Bajri* and wheat, everything is covered with pearly dew. The liquid drops on the tree leaves shine like pearls. This is what the men, these peasants, as they water the fields sing about. When I lived at Kochrab, I used to watch the peasants and listen to their songs. Found obscene words in their mouth. Why should this be so? I should like to have an answer to this from Shri Narasinharao here and from the Chairman.

I say to the Sahitya Parishad that, unless you help remove the filthy language from the mouths of our peasants, the sin of our degradation will be on your heads. I want to know from the servants of literature what the condition of the majority of our people is and what they will write for this majority. I will say only this to the Sahitya Parishad and repeat it over and over again: rid yourselves of all your shortcomings.

Lewis thought of writing a book and wrote one for his children. They read it to their profit; men, women and children today may also read it and profit by it. I ask for such literature from our men of letters. I want, not Banabhatta's *Kadambari* but Tulsidas's *Ramayana.* I have my doubts whether *Kadambari* will be with us for ever, but Tulsidas's work will certainly endure. Let us at present get just *roti,* ghee and milk from our literature. Later on we shall add almonds, pistachio nuts, etc. and produce something like *Kadambari.*

If the meek people of Gujarat—a people filled with sweetness, whose goodness is without bounds, a people so very simple-minded and having unswerving faith in God—if these people are to go forward, their men of letters should sing and write for labourers and peasants in the fields.

It is my heartfelt prayer that our people may learn to write the truth, speak the truth and live the truth. *(Speech at Gujarat Sahitya Parishad, Ahmedabad. Navajivan, 4 April 1920 (CW 17, pp. 301–03) (Translated from Gujarati))*

Literature for the Deprived

I want art and literature that can speak to the millions. I have given you an outline of the picture; you will fill in the details. I have had my say. My heart is weeping at the present moment, but time has made it hard enough not to break even when there are occasion for it. As I think of Segaon and its skeletons, (at this stage he did, however, break down! After a little pause he continued) as I think of Segaon and its folk, I can't help saying that our literature is a miserable affair. Principal Anandshankar Dhruva sent me a list of a hundred books, but none of them would do for them. What am I to place before them? And their women! Is there any relation, I wonder, between them and the Ahmedabad ladies I see in front of me?

The Segaon women know no literature. They cannot even repeat the *ramadhun* with me. They simply know how to drudge and slave away. Reckless of sun or rain, of snakes or scorpions, they fetch water, they cut grass and hew wood, and look upon me as their benefactor if I give them work and a few coppers. What am I to take to these dumb sisters? Those dumb millions do not live in Ahmedabad but in the Indian villages. I know what to take to them. But I cannot tell you. I am no speaker, neither is the pen my profession. I have written what I have, because I could not help it, and at one time I was dumb, so much so that my friends used to call me a dunce, until I went to the courts where too it was with difficulty that I opened my lips. It is not my business to speak or to write. My business is to live amongst them and show them how to live. The key to Swaraj is not in the cities but in the villages, and so I have settled in a village—a village too, not of my seeking, but which came to me." *(Harijan, 14 November 1936 (True Education, p. 177))*

Wrong Apotheosis of Women

He next dwelt on a topic on which he had spoken in the Subjects Committee, but could not have any resolution thereon as he did not find the proper atmosphere. The occasion was a letter addressed to him by the ladies in charge of a women's movement called *Jyoti Sangh.* The letter enclosed copy of a resolution they had passed condemning the present-day tendencies in literature regarding the presentation of women. There was, Gandhiji felt, considerable force in the complaint, and he said: "The gravest of their charge is that the present-day writers give an entirely false picture of women. They are exasperated at the sickly sentimentality with which you delineate them, at the vulgar way in which you dwell on their physical form. Does all their beauty and their strength lie in their physical form, in their capacity to please the lustful eye of men? Why, the writers of the letter justly ask, should we be eternally represented as meek submissive women for whom all the menial jobs of the household are reserved, and whose only deities are their husbands?

Why are they not delineated as they really are? We are, they say, neither etherial damsels, nor dolls, nor bundles of passions and nerves. We are as much human beings as men are, and we are filled with the same urge for freedom. I claim to know them and their minds sufficiently well. There was a time in South Africa when I was surrounded by numerous women, all their menfolk having gone to jails. There were some sixty inmates and I had become the brother and father of all the girls and women. Let me tell you that they grew in strength and spirit under me, so much so that they ultimately marched to jails themselves.

"I am told that our literature is full of even an exaggerated apotheosis of women. Let me say that it is an altogether wrong apotheosis. Let me place one simple test before you. In what light do you think of them when you proceed to write about them? I suggest that before you put your pens to paper, think of women as your own mother, and I assure you the chastest literature will flow from your pens even like the beautiful rain from heaven which waters the thirsty earth below. Remember that a woman was your mother before a woman became your wife.

Far from quenching their spiritual thirst some writers stimulate their passions, so much so that poor ignorant women waste their time wondering how they might answer to the description our fiction gives of them. Are detailed descriptions of their physical form an essential part of literature, I wonder? Do you find anything of the kind in the Upanishads, the Quran or the Bible? And yet do you know that the English language would be empty without the Bible? Three parts Bible and one part Shakespeare is the description of it. Arabic would be forgotten without the Quran. And think of Hindi without Tulsidas! Do you find in it anything like what you find in present day literature about women? *(Harijan, 21 November 1936 (True Education, pp. 179–180))*

Folk Literature

We must not only seek to know the picturesque language of the village folk, but also to spread a knowledge of modern useful literature among the villagers. It is a shame that Chaitanya's lyrics are a sealed book to people outside Bengal and Orissa. Few of us here may know the name of Tiruvalluvar. People in the North are innocent even of the great saint's name. Few saints have given us treasures of knowledge contained in pithy epigrams as he has done.

In this context, I can at this moment recall the name only of Tukaram.

But for that purpose not only the existing literary treasures had to be made available in a language which could be easily learnt by the masses in all the provinces, but even new literature had to be created—new literature of a healthy and health-giving type. *Harijan,* 2 May 1936 (*CW* 62, p. 346)

Global Culture versus Mother Tongue

I do not want my house to be walled in on all sides and my windows to be stuffed. I want the cultures of all lands to be blown about my house as freely as possible. But I refuse to be blown off my feet by any. I would have our young men and women with literary tastes to learn as much of English and other world languages as they like, and then expect them to give the benefits of their learning to India and to the world like a Bose, a Roy or the Poet himself. But I would not have a single Indian to forget, neglect or be ashamed of his mother tongue, or to feel that he or she cannot think or express the best thoughts in his or her own vernacular. Mine is not a religion of the prison-house. *(Young India, 1 June 1921)*

Cultural Diversity

Nothing can be farther from my thought than that we should become exclusive or erect barriers. But I do respectfully contend that an appreciation of other cultures can fitly follow, never precede, an appreciation and assimilation of our own. It is my firm opinion that no culture has treasures so rich as ours has. We have not known it, we have been made even to deprecate its study and depreciate its value. We have almost ceased to live it. An academic grasp without practice behind it is like an embalmed corpse, perhaps lovely to look at, but nothing to inspire or ennoble.

My religion forbids me to belittle or disregard other cultures, as it insists under pain of civil suicide upon imbibing and living my own. It stands for synthesis of the different cultures that have come to stay in India, that have influenced Indian life, and that, in their turn, have themselves been influenced by the spirit of the soil. This synthesis will naturally be of the Swadeshi type, where each culture is assured its legitimate place....

It [Indian civilization] is a mingling of the cultures represented by the different faiths and influenced by the geographic and other environments in which the cultures have met. Thus Islamic culture is not the same in Arabia, Turkey, Egypt and India, but it is itself influenced by the conditions of respective countries. Indian culture is, therefore, Indian. It is neither Hindu, Islamic nor any other, wholly. It is a fusion of all and essentially Eastern. And everyone who calls himself or herself an Indian is bound to treasure that culture, be its trustee and resist any attack upon it.

The Indian culture of our times is in the making. Many of us are striving to produce a blend of all the cultures which seem today to be in clash with one another. No culture can live if it attempts to be exclusive.

There is no such thing as pure Aryan culture in existence today in India. Whether the Aryans were indigenous to India or were unwelcome intruders does not interest me much. What does interest me is the fact that my remote ancestors blended with one another with the utmost freedom and we of the present generation are a result of that blend. Whether we are doing any good to the country of our birth and the tiny globe which sustains us or whether we are a burden, the future alone will show.

Either people of different faiths having lived together in friendship have produced a beautiful blend of cultures, which we shall strive to perpetuate and increasingly strengthen the shape

[of], or we shall cast about for the day when there was only one religion represented in Hindustan and retrace our steps to that exclusive culture.

It is just possible that we might not be able to find any such historical date and if we do and we retrace our steps, we shall throw our culture back to that ugly period and deservedly earn the execration of the universe.

Western versus Eastern Culture

Of myself, whilst I have freely acknowledged my debt to Western culture, I can say that whatever service I have been able to render to the nation has been due *entirely* to the retention by me of Eastern culture to the extent it has been possible. I should have been thoroughly useless to the masses as an anglicized, denationalized being, knowing little of, caring less for and perhaps even despising their ways, habits, thoughts and aspirations.

European civilization is no doubt suited for the Europeans, but it will mean ruin for India if we endeavour to copy it. This is not to say that we may not adopt and assimilate whatever may be good and capable of assimilation by us, as it does not also mean that even the European will not have to part with whatever evil might have crept into it.

The incessant search for material comforts and their multiplication is such an evil; and I make bold to say that the Europeans themselves will have to remodel their outlook if they are not to perish under the weight of the comforts to which they are becoming slaves. It may be that my reading is wrong, but I know that for India to run after the Golden Fleece is to court certain death.

Let us engrave on our hearts the motto of a Western philosopher, 'Plain living and high thinking'.

Today it is certain that the millions cannot have high living and we the few who profess to do the thinking for the masses run the risk, in a vain search after higher living, of missing high thinking. *(The Mind of Mahatma Gandhi, pp. 430–32.)*

5

Meaning of Gandhian Education

True Value of Education

The real difficulty is that people have no idea of what education truly is. We assess the value of education in the same manner as we assess the value of land or of shares in the stock-exchange market. We want to provide only such education as would enable the student to earn more. We hardly give any thought to the improvement of the character of the educated. The girls, we say, do not have to earn; so why should they be educated? As long as such ideas persist there is no hope of our ever knowing the true value of education.

Not Mere Literacy

In Western countries education is so highly valued that senior teachers are treated with much respect. There are at present in England, schools that have been running for hundreds of years and have turned out many renowned men. One of these famous schools is Eton. A few months ago the Old Boys of Eton presented an address to the Head Master, Dr. Weir, who is well known throughout the British Empire. Writing about the occasion, *The Pall Mall Gazette*, a well-known journal in England, has explained the nature of real education. Its comments deserve the attention of us all. The writer in *The Pall Mall Gazette* says:

> *We hold that real education does not consist merely in acquainting oneself with ancient or modern books. It consists in the habits which one knowingly or unknowingly imbibes from the atmosphere, one's surroundings and the company one keeps and above all in work. It is all very well to acquire a stock of knowledge from good books or from other sources. But the more important thing is to learn humanity. The primary function of teachers is, therefore, not to teach the alphabet, but to inculcate humanity. Aristotle said that virtue is not learnt by reading big volumes. It is by doing good deeds that we learn virtue. Another great writer also says that it is well for one to know what is good, but one will be considered a happy person only if one acts upon that knowledge.*

Judged by these standards, English schools will not be found wanting. If we think of English schools as places for turning out human beings, we shall see that they give us statesmen and administrators. Those educated in German schools may have greater knowledge, but if they become also men of action like the pupils of Eton, it is not by virtue of their training in the schools. Despite the defects that may exist in English schools, it is these that produce true men. They are men who are ever ready to meet an enemy threatening at the gates of England. We can readily realize how a country that invests education with such a noble purpose becomes prosperous. India's star will shine bright when Indian children receive such education. Parents, teachers and pupils ought to ponder over the passage quoted above. It would not do merely to know it, it is necessary to act upon it. That is to say, parents should provide for excellent education, teachers should discharge their responsibility and pupils should recognize that mere literacy is not education.

Education as Training

Now I have read a great deal in the prison. I have been reading Emerson, Ruskin and Mazzini. I have also been reading the *Upanishads*. All confirm the view that education does not mean a knowledge of letters but it means character building, it means a knowledge of duty. Our own word literally means 'training'. If this be the true view and it is to my mind the only true view, you are receiving the best education—training—possible.

Education as Service

True education lies in serving others, oblige them without the least feeling of one-uppishness. The more mature you grow, the more you will realise this. A great deal of religious obligations on us are fulfilled when we nurse the sick. I am not worried about your bookish learning so long as you perform your duties and observe solemn ethical conduct. For me carrying out the fundamentals of ethics is *duty*. I shall support you if you want to study further out of your love for it or for excellence. But I won't scold you if you do not do it. Try your best to carry out the decisions you have made. Write to me what you do at the press, at what time do you get up and about your work at the farm.

Service before Self

I was extremely glad to read your letter of the 21st (ultimo) about Mr. West. I read the letter twice. I felt proud of you and thanked God that I had such a son. I wish you to remain such for ever. To do good to others and serve them without any sense of egoism—this is real education. You will realize this more and more as you grow up. What better way of life can there be than serving the sick? Most of religion is covered by it.

Moral Path

The true occupation of man is to build his character. It is not quite necessary to learn something special for earning [one's livelihood]. He who does not leave the path of morality never starves, and is not afraid if such a contingency arises.

Living a Good Life

The service you are rendering to Mr. West and others is the best study for you. He who does his duty is all the while studying. You say that you had to leave your studies; but it is not so. You are certainly studying when you are serving. It would be correct to say that you had to give up reading books. There is no harm in thus leaving studies. One can get academic education later on. One cannot say that one will get an opportunity of serving others later on...' Let this be inscribed in your heart that, since your mind is pure, you will not fall ill while serving others. And even if you fall ill, I will not worry. You and I, all of us, will achieve perfection only by being moulded in this manner. Learning to live a good life is in itself education. All else is useless. *(Letter to Manilal Gandhi, 12 October 1909 (CW 9, p. 475))*

Laying Strong Foundation

What is the meaning of education? It simply means a knowledge of letters. It is merely an instrument, and an instrument may be well used or abused. The same instrument that may be used to cure a patient may be used to take his life, and so may a knowledge of letters. We daily observe that many men abuse it and very few make good use of it; and if this is a correct statement, we have proved that more harm has been done by it than good.

The ordinary meaning of education is a knowledge of letters. To teach boys reading, writing and arithmetic is called primary education. A peasant earns his bread honestly. He has ordinary knowledge of the world. He knows fairly well how he should behave towards his parents, his wife, his children and his fellow villagers. He understands and observes the rules of morality. But he cannot write his own name. What do you propose to do by giving him a knowledge of letters? Will you add an inch to his happiness? Do you wish to make him discontented with his cottage or his lot? And even if you want to do that, he will not need such an education. Carried away by the flood of Western thought we came to the conclusion, without weighing pros and cons, that we should give this kind of education to the people.

Now let us take higher education. I have learned Geography, Astronomy, Algebra, Geometry, etc. What of that? In what way have I benefited myself or those around me? Why have I learned these things? Professor Huxley has thus defined education:

> *That man, I think, has had a liberal education who has been so trained in youth that his body is the ready servant of his will and does with ease and pleasure all the work that as a mechanism it is capable of; whose intellect is a clear, cold, logic engine with all its parts of equal strength and in smooth working order;... whose mind is stored with a knowledge of the fundamental*

> *truths of nature;... whose passions are trained to come to heel by a vigorous will, the servant of a tender conscience;... who has learnt to hate all vileness and to respect others as himself. Such a one and no other, I conceive, has had a liberal education, for he is in harmony with nature. He will make the best of her and she of him.*

If this is true education, I must emphatically say that the sciences I have enumerated above I have never been able to use for controlling my senses. Therefore, whether you take elementary education or higher education, it is not required for the main thing. It does not make men of us. It does not enable us to do our duty.

Reader: If that is so, I shall have to ask you another question: What enables you to tell all these things to me? If you had not received higher education, how would you have been able to explain to me the things that you have?

Editor: You have spoken well. But my answer is simple: I do not, for one moment, believe that my life would have been wasted, had I not received higher or lower education. Nor do I consider that I necessarily serve because I speak. But I do desire to serve and in endeavouring to fulfil that desire, I make use of the education I have received. And, if I am making good use of it, even then it is not for the millions, but I can use it only for such as you, and this supports my contention. Both you and I have come under the bane of what is mainly false education. I claim to have become free from its ill effect, and I am trying to give you the benefit of my experience and in doing so, I am demonstrating the rottenness of this education.

Moreover, I have not run down a knowledge of letters in all circumstances. All I have now shown is that we must not make of it a fetish. It is not our *Kamadhuk*. In its place it can be of use and it has its place when we have brought our senses under subjection and put our ethics on a firm foundation. And then, if we feel inclined to receive that education, we may make good use of it. As an ornament it is likely to sit well on us. It now follows that it is not necessary to make this education compulsory. Our ancient school system is enough. Character-building has the first place in it and that is primary education. A building erected on that foundation will last. *(Hind Swaraj, Chapter XVIII, 21 November 1909 (CW 10, pp. 54–55))*

The Three R's

But although much good and useful work can be done without a knowledge of the three R's, it is my firm belief that we cannot always do without such knowledge. It develops and sharpens one's intellect, and it increases our capacity of doing good. I have never placed an unnecessarily high value on the knowledge of the three R's. I am only attempting to assign its proper place to it.

Again, the true knowledge of self is unattainable by the millions who lack such education. Many a book is full of innocent pleasure, and this will be denied to us without education. It is no exaggeration to say that a human being without education is not far removed from an animal. Education, therefore, is necessary for women as it is for men. *(Speech at Bhagini Samaj, Bombay, 20 February 1918 (CW 14, p. 206))*

Education as Liberation

"That is true education which leads to freedom." That alone is true education which enables us to preserve our dharma. This is the motto accepted by our university. The idea has appealed to me very much: "That is true education which leads to freedom." That which liberates is education. Liberation is of two kinds. One form of liberation consists in securing the freedom of the country from foreign rule. Such freedom may prove short-lived. The other kind of liberation is for all time. In order to attain *moksha,* which we describe as our *paramadharma,* we should have freedom in the worldly sense as well. He who is ridden with many fears cannot attain the ultimate *moksha.* If one would attain this, would achieve the highest end of human effort, one has no choice but to attain that *moksha* which is nearest to one. That education which delays our freedom is to be shunned, it is Satanic, it is sinful. Whatever the quality of the education given in Government schools and colleges, it is to be shunned because the Government which imparts it is Satanic and deserves to be shunned. *(Speech to students, Ahmedabad, 18 November 1926 (CW 18, p. 471))*

Education as Assimilation

But I must advise you, students, to read these prize-books carefully, to reflect over their real import and, keeping in mind all the profound truths set out in them, follow the path enjoined by religion. Whether you are a girl or a boy, you will grow up one day and have to carry a heavy burden of worldly duties; give some thought, therefore, to the future. Truth is revealed not only in our scriptures but in the scriptures of other religions as well.

It is the duty of students to assimilate whatever they have learnt. They should have religious and moral instruction, as much of it as they can usefully apply. They need education in such measure that it would not become too much of a useless burden on them. I should like to address a few words exclusively to students. Men and women students, you will benefit from what you have learnt only to the extent that you have assimilated it. That should be the object of this institution too. You should ponder over the element of truth in whatever books of religion you read. If you cling to truth, success is yours. I would advise you from my experience, to profit well from your education. That will be to your advantage and to your country's as well. *(Speech to students in Bombay, 14 February 1915 (CW 13, p. 23))*

Overcoming Fear

Speaking about the timidity induced by their education, Gandhiji said: We may feel in our heart any measure of devotion for Tilak Maharaj, but where is the student who will express it freely?

For us, fear has become synonymous with life. What is the use of that education which does not help us to overcome fear, but which, on the contrary, strengthens it? What kind of an education is it which does not teach us to follow truth and to cultivate devotion for the country? *(Speech at students' meeting, Agra, 23 November 1920 (CW 19, p. 16))*

Culture of the Heart

There is one thing which, as I am speaking to you occurs to me, which comes to me from my early studies of the Bible. It seized me immediately. I read the passage:

But seek ye first the Kingdom of God, and his righteousness; and all these things shall be added unto you.

I tell you that if you will understand, appreciate and act up to the spirit of this passage, you won't even need to know what place Jesus or any other teacher occupies in your heart. If you will do the proper scavenger's work, clean and purify your hearts and get them ready, you will find that all these mighty teachers will take their places without invitation from us. That, to my mind, is the basis of all sound education. Culture of the mind must be subservient to the culture of the heart. May God help you to become pure! *(Speech at Central College, Jaffna, The Hindu, 2 December 1927 (CW 35, p. 343))*

Learning and Courage

Let them (students) realize that learning without courage is like a waxen statue beautiful to look at but bound to melt at the least touch of a hot substance. (*Young India*, 12 July 1928, p. 236).

Character vs Knowledge

In brief, formation of character should have priority over knowledge of the alphabet. If this order is reversed, the attempt would be like putting the cart before the horse and making it push the cart with its nose, and would meet with the same success as the latter course. *(9 January 1924 (CW 37, p. 248))*

Education as Contemplation

Education, character and religion should be regarded as convertible terms. There is no true education which does not tend to produce character, and there is no true religion which does not determine character. Education should contemplate the whole life. Mere memorizing and book-learning is not education. I have no faith in the so-called systems of education which produce men of learning without the backbone of character. *(Interview with W.W. Hall, October 1928 (CW 37, p. 320))*

Education of the Whole Child

Education does not mean a knowledge of the alphabet. This type of knowledge is only a means to education. Education implies a child's learning how to put his mind and all his senses to good use. That is to say, he really learns how to use his hands, feet and other organs of action and his nose, ear and other organs of sense. A child who has acquired the knowledge that he should not use his hands for stealing or for killing flies nor for beating up his companions or younger brothers and sisters has already begun his education. He has started it, we can say, when he understands the necessity of keeping his body, his teeth, tongue, ears, head, nails, etc., clean and keeps them clean. That child has made good progress in education who does not indulge in mischief while eating and drinking, eats and drinks alone or in society in a proper manner, sits properly and chooses pure foodstuffs knowing the difference between pure and impure foodstuffs, does not eat like a glutton, does not clamour for whatever he sees and remains calm even if he does not get what he wants.

Even that child has advanced on the road to education whose pronunciation is correct, who can recount to us the history and geography of the country surrounding him without knowing those terms and who understands what his country means. That child has made very good progress in his education who can understand the difference between truth and untruth, worth and worthlessness and chooses the good and the true, while rejecting the bad and the untrue. *(Navajivan, 2 June 1929 (CW 41, p. 6))*

Education as Self-discipline

All your scholarship, all your study of Shakespeare and Wordsworth would be vain if at the same time you do not build your character, and attain mastery over your thoughts and actions. When you have attained self-mastery and learnt to control your passions you will not utter notes of despair. You cannot give your hearts and profess poverty of action. To give one's heart is to give all. You must, to start with, have hearts to give. And this you can do if you will cultivate them. *(Speech to students, Agra, 19 September 1929 (CW 41, p. 391))*

Right Learning

I have been all this time looking at the motto in front of me: "Learning owes its worth to dharma." What the motto says is true.

I have discovered in the course of my travels in India that, without dharma, learning is barren. This raises the question: "What is right learning?" I have given my reply often enough. We shall settle afterwards the issue of what manner of learning to provide. For the present, we may follow one definite method and include religious instruction in it. Religion is not a matter for reflection but of conduct. It is not a subject for talking about, be it noted. Teachers can create the thing only by their conduct. Gurjarat itself should produce such teachers; it is shameful to go looking for them outside. *(Speech at foundation laying of Vanita Vishram, Ahmedabad, 13 July 1919; (CW 15, p. 410) (Translated from Gujarati))*

Becoming Strong

In the circumstances in which you pursue your studies, you can only learn to fear man. I would say, on the other hand, that he alone is a real M.A. who has given up the fear of man and has learnt to fear God. Any education you receive will have justified itself only when you have become so strong that you will not beg of anyone for your living. It will have justified itself when the feeling has grown in you that, so long as you are strong of limb, you need not humble yourselves before anyone for a livelihood. *(Speech at students' meeting, Banaras; Navajivan, 5 December 1920 (CW 19, p. 27))*

Literary Training

Literary training by itself adds not an inch to one's moral height and that character-building is independent of literary training. *(Young India, 1 June 1921, p. 172)*

Development of Body, Mind and Spirit

The English word 'education' etymologically means 'drawing out'. That means an endeavour to develop our latent talents. The same is the meaning of *kilavani*, the Gujarati word for education. When we say that we develop a certain thing, it does not mean that we change its kind or quality, but that we bring out the qualities latent in it. Hence 'education' can also mean 'unfoldment'. In this sense, we cannot look upon knowledge of the alphabet as education. This is true even if that knowledge gains us the M.A.

degree or enables us to adorn the place of a Shastri in some *pathshala* with the requisite knowledge of Sanskrit. It may well be that the highest literary knowledge is a fine instrument for education or unfoldment, but it certainly does not itself constitute education.

True education is something different. Man is made of three constituents, the body, mind and spirit. Of them, spirit is the one permanent element in man. The body and the mind function on account of it. Hence we can call that education which reveals the qualities of spirit. That is why the seal of the Vidyapith carries the dictum 'Education is that which leads to *moksha*'.

Education can also be understood in another sense; that is, whatever leads to a full or maximum development of all the three, the body, mind and spirit, may also be called education. The knowledge that is being imparted today may possibly develop the mind a little, but certainly it does not develop the body and spirit. I have a doubt about the development of the mind too, because it does not mean that the mind has developed if we have filled it with a lot of information. We cannot therefore say that we have educated our mind. A well-educated mind serves man in the desired manner. Our literate mind of today pulls us hither and thither. That is what a wild horse does. Only when a wild horse is broken in can we call it a trained horse. How many 'educated' young men of today are so trained?

Now let us examine our body. Are we supposed to cultivate the body by playing tennis, football or cricket for an hour every day? It does, certainly, build up the body. Like a wild horse, however, the body will be strong but not trained. A trained body is healthy, vigorous and sinewy. The hands and feet can do any desired work. A pickaxe, a shovel, a hammer, etc. are like ornaments to a trained hand and it can wield them. That hand can ply the spinning-wheel well as also the ring and the comb while the feet work a loom.

A well trained body does not get tired in trudging 30 miles. It can scale mountains without getting breathless. Does the student acquire such physical culture? We can assert that modern curricula do not impart physical education in this sense.

The less said about the spirit the better. Only a seer or a seeker can enlighten the soul. Who will awaken that dormant spiritual energy in us all? Teachers can be had through an advertisement. Is there a column for spiritual quest in the testimonials which they have to produce? Even if there is one, what is its value? How can we get through advertisements teachers who are seekers after self-realisation? And education without such enlightenment is like a wall without a foundation or, to employ an English saying, like a whited sepulchre. Inside it there is only a corpse eaten up or being eaten by insects. *(Navajivan Education Supplement, 28 February 1926 (CW 30, pp. 58-59))*

Science and Responsibility

At the time when emphasis in education is put more upon literary knowledge than upon character building, the following from the article of Principal Jacks in the *Sunday School Chronicle* will be read with profit:

> *Our life presents itself as an endless movement, in which the march of science never quite overtakes the final problem of its own application. The point where responsibility rests upon us all is always just ahead of the last point reached by advancing science. The more the pursuer quickened his pace the more the fugitive quickens his. This inability of science to overtake responsibility is what I mean by its limitations. Applied science will tell you how to make a gun, but it will not tell you when to shoot nor whom to shoot at. You say that moral science will look after that. I answer that moral science in revealing the right use of my gun, inevitably reveals the wrong use also, and since the wrong will often serve my selfish purpose better than the right, my neighbours run a new risk of being shot at and plundered. A bad man armed with moral science is another name for the devil. If Mephistopheles had been examined in moral science in the University of London, he would have carried off all the prizes. At that point moral science and natural science are both in the same boat. How shall we name this fugitive thing which science never catches? I have called it life, others call it spirit or soul or sense, or perhaps the will. I do not think it matters greatly what we call it, so long as we*

recognize that it exists and that it carries in its arms the fortunes of mankind. Let education look to that. This is the point where all the enterprise of education and all the activities of religion come to their focus – the point of responsibility. If we do it at all other points and leave the point of responsibility uncared for, we shall inevitably come to grief. (Young India, 30 September 1926)

Against Atheism

My association with the students of our country dates back to 10 years, since my return to India. I know the hardships and the difficulties of the students. I have been seeing them every day. I also know their weak points. It has been my privilege to have a corner in their hearts.

They have not hesitated to open their hearts to me, to tell me even what they had concealed from their parents. I do not know how I could bring them peace, or what message I could give them. I share in their sorrows, and I have been striving to alleviate their hardships. But in this world, we have to look only to God for help. None other could render any effectual help.

There is no sin equal to that of disbelieving in Him, in denying Him. Amongst the students of today the spirit of atheism is gaining ground. I am deeply grieved that things should be so. Whenever I see Hindu students, I ask them to think of God, to pray, to repeat Ramanama. They ask me where is God, where is Rama and such other questions. When I see Musalman youths and ask them to read the Koran, and to live the life enjoined therein, they also ask me similar questions.

The education which leads to the negation of God cannot make for the service of the country nor of humanity. In your address, you have referred to my service to my country. Whatever I have been doing is done with a sense of my duty to God. And this I consider to be the right thing. God is not seated in the skies, in the heavens, or elsewhere. He is enshrined in the heart of everyone – be he a Hindu, Mohammedan, Christian or Jew, man or woman. *(Speech to students, Mysore – The Hindu, 21 July 1927 (CW 34, pp. 203–04))*

Education and Culture

"Culture" means refinement of feelings and "education" means knowledge of literature. Education is a means and culture is the end. The latter is possible even without education. For instance, if a child is brought up in a truly cultured family, it will unconsciously imbibe culture from its environment. In our country at any rate, present-day education and culture have no connection with each other. If the educated still retain some culture, that is in spite of their education. This fact shows that the roots of our culture are deep. *(Letter to Premabehn Kantak – 5 January 1931 (CW 45, pp. 63–64))*

Strengthening of Character

In my wanderings among the students I made the discovery at an early stage of the movement that in order to conduct a movement of this kind character must be the foundation. We also found that real education consists not in packing the brain with so many facts and figures, not in passing examinations by reading numerous books but in developing character. I do not know to what extent you students of France lay stress upon character rather than upon intellectual studies, but I can say this that if you explore the possibilities of nonviolence you will find that without character it will prove a profitless study. *(Speech at meeting of students, Marseilles – Young India, 1 October 1931 (CW 47, p. 422))*

Knowledge of the Self

True education is that which helps us to know the *atman*, our true self, God and Truth. To acquire this knowledge, some persons may feel the need for a study of literature, some for a study of physical sciences and some others for art. But every branch of knowledge should have as its goal knowledge of the self. That is so in the Ashram. We carry on numerous activities with that aim in view. All of them are, in my sense of the term, true education. Those activities can also be carried on without any reference to the goal of knowledge of the self. When they are so carried on, they may serve as a means of livelihood or of something else, but they are not education. In an activity carried on as education, a proper understanding of its meaning, devotion to duty and the spirit of service are necessary. *(10 July 1932 (CW 50, p. 182))*

Ideal Education

When it is remembered that the primary aim of all education is, or should be, the moulding of the character of pupils, a teacher who has a character to keep need not lose heart. *(Harijan, 1 December 1933, p. 3 (CW 56, p. 296))*

Real Education

Real education has to draw out the best from the boys and girls to be educated. This can never be done by packing ill-assorted and unwanted information into the heads of the pupils. It becomes a dead weight crushing all originality in them and turning them into mere automata. *(Harijan, 1 December 1933 (CW 56, p. 295))*

Book of Humanity

Real education consists in drawing the best out of yourself. What better book can there be than the book of humanity? *(Harijan, 30 March 1934, p. 55)*

Education of the Hand

Literary education should follow the education of the hand—the one gift that visibly distinguishes man from beast. It is a superstition to think that the fullest development of man is impossible without a knowledge of the art of reading and writing. That knowledge undoubtedly adds grace to life, but it is in no way indispensable for man's moral, physical, or material growth. *(Harijan, 8 March 1935, p. 28)*

Fighting Social Evils

All this means education of a character that will revolutionize the mentality of the youth of the nation. Unfortunately the system of education has no connection with our surroundings which therefore remain practically untouched by the education received by a microscopic minority of the boys and girls of the nation. Whilst, therefore, whatever can be done to abate the evil must be done, it is clear to me that this evil and many others which can be named can only be tackled if there is education which responds to the rapidly changing conditions of the country. How is it that so many boys and girls who have even passed through colleges are found unable or unwilling to resist the manifestly evil custom which affects their future so intimately as marriage does? Why should educated girls be found to commit suicide because they are not suited? Of what value is their education if it does not enable them to dare to defy a custom which is wholly indefensible and repugnant to one's moral sense? The answer is clear. There is something radically wrong in the system of education that fails to arm girls and boys to fight against social or other evils. That education alone is of value which draws out the faculties of a student so as to enable him or her to solve correctly the problems of life in every department. *(Harijan, 23 May 1936 (CW 62, p. 436))*

Making the Whole Man

Man is neither mere intellect, nor the gross animal body, nor the heart or soul alone. A proper and harmonious combination of all the three is required for the making of the whole man and constitutes the true economics of education.... I hold that true education of the intellect can only come through a proper exercise and training of the bodily organs, *e.g.*, hands, feet, eyes, ears, nose, etc. In other words an intelligent use of the bodily organs in a child provide the best and quickest way of developing his intellect. But unless the development of the mind and body goes hand in hand with a corresponding awakening of the soul, the former alone would prove to be poor lopsided affair. By spiritual training I mean education of the heart. A proper and all-round development of the mind, therefore, can take place only when it proceeds *pari passu* with the education of the physical and spiritual faculties of the child. They constitute an indivisible whole. According to this theory, therefore, it would be a gross fallacy to suppose that they can be developed piecemeal or independently of one another. *(Harijan, 8 May 1937, p. 104)*

Self-supporting Schools

By education I mean an all-round drawing out of the best in child and man—body, mind and spirit. Literacy is not the end of education nor even the beginning. It is only one of the means whereby man and woman can be educated. Literacy in itself is no education. I would therefore begin the child's education by teaching it a useful handicraft and enabling it to produce from the moment it begins its training. Thus every school can be made self-supporting, the condition being that the State takes over the manufactures of these schools. *(Harijan, 31 July 1937 (CW 65, p. 450))*

Training in Crafts

Do not think that I say this because I wish to run down book-learning. I fully understand its value. You will not easily come across many men who put such knowledge to better use than I do. My purpose in saying this is to put training in crafts on the same footing as education in letters. Those who thoroughly understand this point will never be eager for a literal education at the cost of training in crafts. Their book-learning will shine better and also prove of greater benefit to the people. *(Letter to Ashram boys and girls, 17 December 1932 (CW 52, p. 226))*

Nayee Taleem

It is necessary to understand the newness of *Nayee Taleem*. The new scheme of basic education will retain whatever was good in the old system. However, it will have newness in abundance. If there is something genuinely new in it, it should result in hope taking up place of despondency, food of poverty, work of unemployment, unity of dissensions and in our boys and girls learning along with reading and writing some craft, for only through the latter will they gain the knowledge of the alphabet. *(Utmanzai, 14 October 1938 (CW 67, p. 438))*

Making the Right Choice

Our education has got to be revolutionized. The brain must be educated through the hand. If I were a poet, I could write poetry on the possibilities of the five fingers. Why should you think that the mind is everything and the hands and feet nothing? Those who do not train their hands, who go through the ordinary rut of education, lack 'music' in their life. All their faculties are not trained. Mere book knowledge does not interest the child so as to hold his attention fully. The brain gets weary of mere words, and the child's mind begins to wander. The hand does the things it ought not to do, the eye sees the things it ought not to see, the ear hears the things it ought not to hear, and they do not do, see, or hear, respectively, what they ought to. They are not taught to make the right choice and so their education often proves their ruin. An education which does not teach us to discriminate between good and bad, to assimilate the one and eschew the other is a misnomer. *(Discussion with Teacher Trainees – Harijan, 18 February 1939 (CW 68, pp. 372–73))*

Freedom from Servitude

The ancient aphorism, "Education is that which liberates", is as true today as it was before. Education here does not mean mere spiritual knowledge, nor does liberation signify only spiritual liberation after death. Knowledge includes all training that is useful for the service of mankind and liberation means freedom from all manner of servitude even in the present life. Servitude is of two kinds: slavery to domination from outside and to one's own artificial needs. The knowledge acquired in the pursuit of this ideal alone constitutes true study. *(Harijan, 10 March 1946, p.38 (CW 83, p. 208))*

Culture as the Foundation

I attach far more importance to the cultural aspect of education than to the literary. Culture is the foundation, the primary thing which the girls ought to get from here. It should show in the smallest detail of your conduct and personal behaviour, how you sit, how you walk, how you dress, etc., so that anybody might be able to see at a glance that you are the products of this institution. Inner culture must be reflected in your speech, the way in which you treat visitors and guests, and behave towards one another and your teachers and elders. *(Speech at Kasturba Balika Ashram, 20 April 1946 (CW 84, p. 36))*

Education for a New World

Education must be of a new type for the sake of the creation of a new world. *(Harijan, 19 January 1947, p. 494)*

6

Gandhi on Education at Various Stages

Infant Education

We should try to draw all the children towards us. We should admit that it is our fault if some do not come to us. They should all want to come to us.

We should treat those children who come to us as our own children. If their body and mind become sound and they acquire normal discipline, we should be satisfied that our purpose has been served.

I have taught many boys. I never allowed them to indulge in mischief. If they were under my care, I would educate them in such a way that they would learn from their very childhood that the desire to destroy was a very bad thing. Whatever they do, they should create something, produce something. There is an art in making anything and whatever they make should be artistic.

I do not believe that children are either good or bad from their very birth. Some tendency is there, but we have to mould them. This means that an infant starts learning right from the time of conception. At that time I would teach the mother. That would be a part of adult education. The training of the infant begins from that stage. We have to train the future generation on these lines. Till the child is separated from the mother, I would teach the mother. The infant is ever moving its hands and feet and is able to do something. If we are able to take under our care children of two or two and a half years of age and if they learn to move their hands and feet according to our method, I cannot set any limits to their progress.

If the child is put under our care, he will not destroy anything. He will feel hurt in doing so.

Whatever education we give to the children, it should be constructive and creative but never destructive.

When the child starts speaking, he starts learning a language. First you should teach him to distinguish different colours. Begin teaching him the letters of the alphabet only with the help of the pictures. Don't you have charts showing 1-2, A-B and so on? Reading, writing and arithmetic will come in due course of time and the child will not be overstrained. His education should be a form of play.

Whatever thing he makes should be useful. In this way his mind and hands and feet develop in coordination.

There are no distinctions between work and play in basic education. For a child everything is play. I would go so far as to say that thus his whole life becomes a kind of game. I have been doing this for many years now. I never feel that it is time for play and I should go and play. For me even writing is a game. Under basic education of my conception children will learn while playing. *(Speech to teachers, Sevagram, 17 February 1946 (Translated from Hindi))*

Early Childhood Education

Educating children should be normally the easiest of things; but somehow it has become, or been made, the most difficult. Experience shows that the children are always learning one thing or another whether we notice it or not and whether what they learn is good or bad. This may seem strange to some readers. But if we would consider carefully—who is a child; what is education and who is best qualified to teach the children?—the observation made above would not seem strange and might even appear quite correct.

By children we mean young boys and girls not more than 10 years of age. Then, education does not mean simply the knowledge of letters—the capacity to read and write. The knowledge of letters is only one of the means to education. Really speaking, education consists in learning to use in the right way all one's sense-organs, including the mind.

In other words, the child should know how to use his organs of action such as hands and feet, etc. as also his organs of knowledge such as the nose, the eyes, etc. A boy who knows that he should not use his hands in stealing things or killing flies or beating the younger brothers, sisters and playmates has already made a good beginning on his way to education.

The same may be said of the boy who understands the need for keeping his teeth, tongue, ears, eyes, nails, etc. clean and does so. A boy who does not indulge in pranks while eating or drinking, who has learnt to eat and drink in the right manner whether alone or in company, who knows the distinction between wholesome and unwholesome food and chooses the former, who does not overeat, who does not ask for every new thing that he sees and who, when he asks for it and does not get it, remains quiet, may be said to have progressed quite a great deal in his education.

Whose pronunciation is good, who can tell the history and geography of his region—even though he may not know these terms,—who knows what is meant by the motherland, he has traversed a fairly good distance on the road to education. Similarly with him who has learnt to distinguish between truth and untruth, between good and evil and who invariably chooses what is true and good, there is no need to further elaborate the point. The readers can fill in the picture themselves.

Only I should make one thing clear: there is no need of the knowledge of reading and writing in order to learn the things I have spoken of above. To make the boys to learn the alphabet is to put an undue burden on their young minds and to misuse their eyes and hands. A rightly educated boy gets to learn reading and writing almost without any effort and, what is more, gladly at the proper time. At the present time, however, this thing becomes a heavy burden upon him.

Much of the valuable time which could be put to better use goes to waste and in the end, instead of producing shapely letters or acquiring a finely articulated pronunciation, all that they succeed in doing is to produce misshapen letters and cultivate a bad handwriting. As for reading, they read much which had better been left unread and read it indifferently without any sense of pronunciation. To call it education is to abuse that august term. The boy must first get elementary knowledge before learning to read and write. If this is done our poor country would be saved from much unnecessary expense incurred on various readers and children's books and many other evils. If children's readers are at all thought necessary they should be written for use by the teachers and not for boys of my conception. But for our drifting with the current vogue this thing should be as clear to us as daylight.

The boys can get the education I have spoken of only at home and that too only through the mother. In a way, all boys do get some sort of an education from the mother. But seeing that the home has disintegrated, so to say, and seeing that most parents are not equal to the task, the boys should be placed in surroundings where they will get the same atmosphere as they do at home. Since of all persons the mother is the most competent to undertake the duty of educating the children, this particular task should be entrusted only to women. As a rule men are far behind women in respect of love and patience. If this is true the question of the education of children cannot be solved unless efforts are made simultaneously to solve the women's education. And I have no hesitation in saying that as long as we do not have real mother-teachers who can successfully impart true education to our children they will remain uneducated even though they may be going to schools.

Let me now set forth in brief an outline of the children's education. Suppose that a mother-teacher is entrusted with five children. These children have no training in manners. They do not speak distinctly. They do not know how to walk or even to sit in the right manner. The nose, eyes, ears, and nails are dirty. Asked to sit, they stretch out their legs and when they speak, they mumble. They have no knowledge of directions. The clothes are untidy and the pockets are filled with dirty titbits which they are always taking out and putting in their mouths. The border of the cap on the head has turned black and sticky and it gives out a foul odour. Now the teacher in question can train them only if she has the heart of a mother. The first lesson she has to give them would be that of cleanliness. She will drench them with her love and amuse them in various ways as only mothers know how to do and as did Kaushalya her Rama and thus she will bind them to herself with the ties of love and so will be in a position to secure from them willing compliance to all that she wants. She will know no rest until these boys have learnt to keep neat and tidy, until their teeth, ears, hands and feet are clean, until they learn to take care of their clothes and have improved their pronunciation. Having accomplished this she will first teach them *Ramanama*—the name of Lord God. He has many names and it does not matter by which name He is called.

The next in order after *dharma* is *artha, i.e.,* the temporal knowledge. So she will now set out to teach them arithmetic. She will get them to learn the multiplication tables and teach them addition and subtraction—as much of it as can be managed orally. The boys must know the place where they live. So she will tell them of the rivers and rivulets, hills, buildings of interest, etc. and in the process give them the knowledge of directions. She will improve her own knowledge for the sake of the children. History and geography are not to be treated as separate subjects in this method. Both will be taught by way of stories. She will not however be content with this. A Hindu mother will recite Sanskrit verses to her children from their infancy, so that they get used to the pronunciation of Sanskrit words. She will get them to learn Sanskrit verses in praise of God. A patriotic mother will of course teach them Hindi too.

She will therefore converse with them in Hindi. She will read out to them selected passages from Hindi books and thus make them bilingual. She will not teach them the alphabet yet, but she will certainly give them the brush. She will get them to trace the geometrical figures—to draw straight lines and circles. A boy who cannot draw a flower or a water-jug or a triangle cannot be said to be educated. Again, she will not but introduce them to good music. She will not tolerate the children being unable to sing in unison the national song or hymns, etc. She will teach them to sing to the accompaniment of time. If possible, she will give them *ektara,* or *jhanjh.* To make them physically fit she will get them to do physical exercises, to practise running and jumping. Then, the boys should also be taught the love of service and various skills. She will therefore teach them spinning with all the ancillary processes beginning from the picking of cotton pods. And these boys will willingly spin for at least half an hour every day.

Most of the textbooks which we have today are useless for this purpose. The mother-teacher therefore will find out or produce new ones and her love for the children will help her in this task. Every village has its own history and geography; naturally it will have its own history-book and geography-book. The arithmetical exercises too will be new. The mother-teacher will prepare the lessons she wants to teach the children herself everyday. She will produce new sums and will always have many new things to say to the boys—which she will note down in her notebook when she prepares the lesson. Her lesson in the class will thus be not a mechanical performance but something lively and creative.

The syllabus will vary according to the progress of the children. It should therefore be drawn up after every three months. The children constituting the class come from different homes—each has his own different background of nurture. We cannot therefore have the same syllabus for all of them. At times it may be necessary even to induce them to unlearn what they have learnt. For example, if a six or seven year old child has learnt to trace letters in a slovenly way or has picked up the habit of reading without trying to understand what he reads, the mother-teacher will see that he unlearns all that. She must cast out the illusion that the child can acquire knowledge only through reading. It is easy enough to understand that even one who never had any training in reading can be wise.

I have not used the word teacher in this article; I have throughout used the word 'mother-teacher' in its place. Because the teacher must really be a mother to the children she teaches. One who cannot take the place of a mother cannot be a teacher.

The child should never feel that he is being taught. Let her simply keep her eye upon him and guide him. A child who spends six hours in the school will possibly be wasting his time while the former will be learning something or the other all the time in terms of real education.

It is likely that we may not get good women-teachers in the existing conditions. That being so we may make use of men for the purpose. In that case these men-teachers will have to fill the place of the mother. But eventually it is the mother who will have to undertake the task. But if I am right any mother who has love for children can easily prepare herself for it. And she can also prepare the children at the same time that she is preparing herself. *(Navajivan, 2 June 1929 (CW 41, pp. 5–9))*

Montessori Education

I have no difficulty in agreeing with the scientific views of Madame Montessori. However, if they are propagated in their Western garb in Indian villages they are more likely to prove useless and might even prove harmful, because in that garb they will be too expensive for Indian villages and ill-adapted to the village atmosphere. It is possible the cities may not feel the expense so much and women influenced by Western ways may be receptive to the ideas presented in Western garb; but even so it will be of no use because India lives not in cities but in its seven lakh villages. Besides, scientific education with Western trappings might prove poisonous to the city dwellers because here education begins the moment the child is conceived and ends no one knows when. These days the cities are created by the foreigners to serve their ends and so they do not represent the villages. They do not protect the interests of the villagers but are becoming their exploiters. *(Letter to Saraladevi Sarabhai, 12 April 1945 (CW 71, pp. 370–71))*

Nursery Education

I saw the work done by teachers trained under Madame Montessori, and carefully observed the working of the Nursery School. Of course the things were foreign and the poor teacher had not digested what she had been taught. What to speak of the children? They could not even observe normal discipline. I am not criticising anyone. I have given the gist of my experience just for your information. Imbibe whatever you find useful and discard the rest. The conclusion I have drawn from this experience is that we shall be able to propagate scientific knowledge of child education only when our teachers are competent. They should have the will to become one with children. I am afraid I am not saying anything new in this. These things are certainly not beyond your range of experience but since I have come to know you and also love you I hope you will not find fault with me for saying the things you already know. *(Letter to Tarabehn Modak, 16 October 1945 (CW 81, p. 364))*

Primary Education

After a great deal of reflection and experimentation I have come to the conclusion that primary education should be given for at least a year without books and even after that the use of books should be restricted to the minimum.

If books are introduced from the very start and the children made to master the alphabet, the development of their various abilities are arrested and their intelligence stunted, although this is the time when it should grow rapidly. A child begins to learn immediately after its birth, but mostly through the eyes and ears or through the senses. And, as soon as he has learnt to speak, *i.e.,* to imitate the sound of words, he begins rapidly to acquire the use of language. Naturally he picks up the same language as that of his parents. If the parents have taste and refinement, he also develops those qualities. He pronounces the words correctly and copies their good manners and conduct. This is his real education. And if our culture and traditions had not fallen apart, children would still be receiving the best kind of education in their homes.

But looking at the deplorable conditions in which we are living at present this cannot be and there is no alternative save to send our boys to schools. But if the child has to go to a school, we must see that it looks like a home to him and the teachers like parents, and the education provided should be such as would be provided in a cultured home. This means that all preliminary teaching should be oral. A child educated in this way would learn in a year ten times more than the boy taught in the other way, *i.e.*, through the alphabet. Oral teaching would enable the children to know the usual rudiments of history and geography much in the same way as they get to know stories, quite easily, in the very first year. They would commit to memory a fairly good number of poems; and they would learn the counting of numbers almost automatically without any effort. And because they would not be subjected to the burden of recognizing and learning the alphabet, the growth of their minds would not be stopped and their eyes would not be misused.

They would use their hands not in tracing different letters—a practice which spoils their handwriting for good—but in drawing the figures of geometry and simple pictures. This would be good preliminary training for the hand, as it would develop both coordination and skill.

And if we want to provide education to the crores of children of Gujarat and of India, this is the only way in which primary education should be imparted to them.

Under the conditions existing in the country it is impossible to give books to children. I admit that if it is necessary to give books to children in the primary stage also, then attempts must be made to do so whatever the expenditure, but if they are considered unnecessary and even harmful then this plea for stopping the use of books in the initial years. The idea should be given a fair trial. A thing which is unnecessary from the moral point of view is always found to be impermissible also from the practical point of view. In an ideal civilization morality and what is called practical policy are not two contradictory things.

Lastly, it is clear that the present group of teachers cannot be expected to give effect to the scheme of education presented here. They may manage to teach the boys the alphabet and also simple arithmetic. But they themselves are ignorant of the type of knowledge which, according to the scheme I have sketched, should be made available to the boys in the very first year of the school. Since they themselves do not speak correctly, how can they then help the boys to form the habit of correct speech?

We will consider this difficulty in the next article. *(Navajivan, 13 May 1928 (Problem of Education, pp. 147–49))*

Secondary Education

A system of education has to be so conceived as to be an instrument of protection of the freedom of a nation.

Hence, we must make our own experiments in education. It may well be that in the course of these experiments we get to know the experiences which Europe has had; but we should never give credence to the idea that everything European is good, or that what is good for Europe under the conditions obtaining there will also be good for us here in India. Granting that this line of reasoning is correct, one of the conclusions it leads us to is that we should evaluate what goes on in the Government schools critically. Knowing as we do that Government education is detrimental to Swaraj and destructive of our civilization, we are likely to get at the right solution for us if we do just the opposite of what is done in the Government schools. Let us now study examples:

There, the medium of education is English. We should know from this that it should never be permitted in national education.

There, they have big expensive buildings. We should know that this is undesirable. The buildings of our school should be simple – as befit the poor.

There, they concentrate on mere literacy and the study of language and literature and neglect the indigenous crafts. Evidently this is not right.

There they leave out the teaching of religion – I mean the basic principles common to all religions and not any particular creed. We know that this has the effect of nullifying the good that the rest of the education might ordinarily do to students. History, as taught in Government schools, if not wholly untrue, is presented essentially from the point of view of the British Government. German, French and American historians would treat and interpret the same material in a different way. Even recent events, as for example, the Punjab Massacre is presented by Government writers in one way and by nationalist writers in quite another light.

Economics, as taught in Government schools, approves of the policies of the Government, while we look at them from a totally different point of view.

While in Government primary schools, the teachers are appointed without any consideration of their character, in our schools they must be men of the highest character. The former have only the minimum qualifications for the work they are expected to do and are paid the lowest salaries. The latter, on the other hand, should be highly qualified men and though they will also be paid low salaries, the reason would be their selflessness and not their helplessness.

This, I think, should give you some idea of the type of education which should be given in our city schools.

Our students should be men who will work for the stabilisation and revitalisation of our rural civilization. They would study the needs of the villagers, try to remove the defects they may discover in them and train their children to become good farmers and good villagers and not to be lured by the dazzle of the cities. Thus, as long as we do not set about to make a radical change in the form and content of the education now going on in the cities, we cannot fulfil one of the important aims of the Vidyapith. Take only one example: We are running three institutions in Ahmedabad—the Mahavidyalaya or the college, the New Gujarati Pathashala, and the Vinaya Mandir or the secondary school. We have the right to run these institutions only if we mean to try to make good villagers of the students studying in them. They should have a thorough knowledge of village life and develop a love for it. Eventually, those of them who pass out of the Mahavidyalaya or the Vinaya Mandir, after having completed their studies, should spread out in the villages and immerse themselves in the service of the people there.

As to how this could be done, we shall consider it in the next article. *(Navajivan, 20 May 1928 (CW 36, pp. 327–29))*

Rural Education

The problem of primary education, *i.e.*, of rural education, can be tackled and solved only if the teachers appreciate and accept the point of view presented by me, and we agree to overhaul and change the curriculum in the Vinaya Mandir and Mahavidyalaya. Today, we hesitate to make any changes out of fear for what people might say, or because the number of students might go down and the institution may suffer in the estimate of the people. But if we could make bold and introduce the necessary changes there would pass out from these schools a group of workers pledged to the service of the villages who would atone in some degree at least for the sin of the cities.

The students passing out of these schools should be first class carders, spinners and weavers. They should be experts in the cultivation of cotton. They should know enough carpentry for the purposes of the village, that is, they should be able to manufacture good Charkhas and should be able if not to manufacture at least to repair the carts and ploughs, etc. Then they should know enough sewing for village-life. Their handwriting must be good, and they should be able to write good simple prose, as also to work out simple arithmetical problems.

They should be intimately conversant with old religious books like the *Ramayana* and *Mahabharata,* and have the ability to interpret them in terms of today. They should know village games and the rules of health. They should be able to recognize simple diseases and cure them through simple home remedies. They should know the art of cleaning the village-wells, tanks and dust-heaps. I could recount many other things. But the point is that our schools should provide such training to the boys as would enable them to serve the villages in every way. And the expenditure incurred on this training should be regarded as having been incurred on education. Such training alone would qualify us to enter and reform village-life.

I am aware that some of you fear that as soon as we introduce these changes and clarify our aim as above our schools would be empty. But even if this fear proves true I would be ready to face it for the sake of truth. But as long as it is the object of the Vidyapith to work out a suitable system of education for the villages, it will be a betrayal of our trust not to do so.

But it is my experience and conviction that if we stick to our aims with undivided loyalty, the people will come to recognize their importance in the end and cooperate with us in their propagation. If we try to discover the reasons of this real or supposed failure we will find that the workers were either not loyal to their aims or only half-hearted in carrying them out. A man who wavers in his faith, as says the *Gita,* is doomed to failure.

It is my firm belief that if there were in our schools teachers who have faith and the spirit of sacrifice, they would be filled with students. People do recognize and appreciate fundamental values. It may seem that this takes an unusually long time to come about in many cases. But this is merely an illusion. The fact is that the right path is also always the shortest.

How does it profit anyone if a school which encourages the desire for sensual pleasures and panders to the weaknesses of people attracts large numbers? Mere numbers do not prove the usefulness of an institution or its success in its chosen task. I am aware that the acceptance of my scheme may lead to but one result, *i.e.,* the students who have come here in the hope of getting the same sort of education as they do in Government school or of acquiring the equipment for a comfortable city-life, will leave our schools. But that would be good. It will save both us and them from an undesirable situation and enable both to serve each other in a disinterested way.

I think I have said enough to have explained my viewpoint in regard to the problem of primary education which was the purpose in writing the present series. I have to add only a little more and then I will close it. And then I hope to discuss a few questions put to me on the subject. If the idea of not introducing the teaching of the alphabet in the first year of primary education is correct, some of its good result should also be visible in our Vinaya Mandirs or secondary schools and the Mahavidyalaya.

There is a great increase in the number of books being brought out today. Books are being published daily. Whoever has or thinks he has a certain command of the language or believes to have studied or reflected a little over a certain thing, becomes impatient to express his ideas in writing and have them printed, and actually thinks that he thereby serves the country. The result is that there is a great strain on the minds of the students and the pockets of the parents! The intellectual growth of the students is paralyzed. The minds become storehouses of strange and unrelated facts and there is no room left in them for original ideas. And those facts too do not fall each into its right place as in a well-arranged plan but lie scattered as the things in the house of a lazy man. Neither can they make any worthwhile use of them nor do they yield any good to the people.

Therefore, if I could have my way, I would not put the large number of books that are being published today into the hands of the people. Even the students who know reading and writing receive most of what they get to learn from the teacher's mouth. So I would advise the students to read only a few selected books. But they should think over what they read and put into practice what appears worthwhile. If they do so, it will make their lives beautiful and pure as also full of strength and energy. They will have learnt to think and discriminate—the hallmark of real education. This is the education which will suit and profit our poor people. It will do good to both the students and the people. The solution of the difficult problem which faces Vidyapith depends upon the capacity of its present teachers to sincerely reflect upon and accept the aims of the Vidyapith and to try to implement them in practice. *(Navajivan, 3 July 1928 (CW 36, pp. 343-45))*

Teacher-Taught Relationship

I believe in *guru-bhakti.* But every teacher cannot be a *guru.* The *guru-shishya*—the teacher-disciple—relation in this sense is something spiritual and springs up spontaneously. In any case it is not an artificial thing or a product of pressure from without. Such teachers still exist in India. (It should not be necessary to sound the warning that I am not speaking here of spiritual teachers who have the power to lead the aspirants to liberation.) Such teachers have no use for flattery. Respect for them must be natural and so is the love of the teacher for his pupil. That being so, the teacher is ever ready to give, and the pupil equally ready to receive. *(Navajivan, 3 July 1928)*

Some Related Questions

Having written the previous three articles about primary education, it is now somewhat easy to answer the following questions:

You once wrote that if the burden of English were lightened it will save a few precious years in the life of the students which are now wasted. What is your estimate of this wastage in terms of years and of the loss it means to society?

Let me first explain what I mean by lightening the burden of English. I do not mean that the students should stop learning English altogether. We may learn it and use it but only as a Frenchman knows and uses English; that is, we should learn and know it as one does a foreign language. If we try to limit our learning of English to this extend, we would not be required to think in English and speak it correctly with the right pronunciation and to write it with the mastery of an Englishman. I am inclined to think that every student wastes at least five years of his life in this useless endeavour. Not only that, this forced labour over a thing for which he feels no genuine attraction cripples his power of original thinking. His body weakens and he becomes almost a blotting-paper—a blind imitator of superfluities. How much more a man can acquire if he spends five years in acquiring knowledge through his mother tongue? How much time and energy would he save? He will easily get to know the best thought through his own language and yet be saved from the great trouble in mastering the difficult pronunciation of a foreign language.

Child education at one end and college education at the other are both very expensive. Are both these to be included in national education? Have you a scheme to provide both and an equally high type of education at a cheaper cost?

I have tried to show in the three previous articles how the education of the children can be made cheaper, even, almost self-supporting. If we could bring the same approach to bear on college education, it too could be made cheaper, and the students well enabled to acquire such knowledge which will strengthen the nation. If by the expression—'an equally high type of education' the correspondent means an education resembling that to be found in Government institution, the question does not arise, because I do not consider Government type of education to be desirable at all. The education offered in national colleges or national schools is different from the former and often original in many ways. Therefore, it is good in its own way.

Do you think that teachers have the right to impart religious instruction to the boys in their charge in whatever way they like?

Teachers have to conform to the policy or policies laid down by the organisation to which they belong; they cannot, therefore, claim the right to give religious education in the way they would like to do it. As in other subject so also in the matter of religious instruction the teacher must carry out the policy decided upon by those in charge of the organisation. Of course, the teacher should be free to choose his method of teaching, but what he teaches will have to be in conformity with the ideals accepted by the organisation in the matter of religion. It is true that while one may teach other subjects by reading a few selected books on those subjects, this is not possible in the case of religious education. In fact, it cannot be imparted through books at all. While instruction in other subjects is mostly through the intellect, in religious education it has to be from the heart to the heart. Therefore, a teacher should not undertake to teach religion unless he is himself deeply religious.

It is also necessary to exercise a certain discrimination. For example, nothing that is likely to promote violence should be taught in a school which accepts nonviolence as the highest form of religion. Similarly, there should be no room for any propaganda against any of the other religions in a school which has adopted for itself the ideal of love, charity and tolerance in regard to all religions. In short, if a school accepts the need for providing religious education, it must also clearly define the content of such education, and not leave it to the whims of the teachers concerned as this would result in chaos.

If it is considered necessary for every student to know at least three to four languages don't you think it is equally necessary to introduce students to the basic tenets, rites, dogmas and superstitions of all the existing religions?

If we want to create a feeling of respect and love among the students towards every religion—which is religion in the true sense of the word and not an irreligion, we must surely provide them a knowledge of its main tenets. I do not think it is necessary to know the superstitions which have crept in into different religions and the special rites pertaining to each of them. In a country like India everyone who keeps his eyes and ears open can easily see for himself what these rites and superstitions are. If we would become seekers of good—wherever we find it, as we must, we should not want to know the rites and superstitions of every religion. They are quite unnecessary. It should be enough to know the rites and superstitions of our own religion and to impress upon the boys the need to reform them wherever necessary. That would itself take up enough of their time.

Since you believe in the *varna, i.e.,* the four-fold division of society, do you accept, or not accept, that education provided to students should differ according to the *varna*?

I do not think that education should differ according to *varna*. There is much that is common between the different *varnas* and the education provided to them should be the same. The chief aim of education is to make of the students decent men and women. And he who would become a decent man would easily learn the laws of conduct governing human society—the laws which add to the glory of men. My conception of *varna* is that since the *varna* division rests on the difference in vocations, and every *varna* has to earn its livelihood through its appointed vocation, it would be found that men belonging to a particular *varna* generally inherit the characteristics of their class. I do not mean that a particular *varna* does not or cannot have the characteristics of the other three *varnas*. A Brahman would not earn his bread by working for others on hire-purchase basis, but if he does not know the art of service or is ashamed of it, he is not a *Brahman* at all. In the same way, though a *Shudra* may not teach the *Vedas*, etc. and has to live on alms voluntarily given, he would surely have been given a sufficient grounding in the *Vedas*, etc. in a well-organized society. Is it true that training in useful crafts automatically includes all other education and that intellectual education is no more than a superficial decoration? If it is true, why do you approve and support the education given by the Mahavidyalaya?

This view is as true as it is false. Where people have idolized intellectual education I say that training in crafts includes all other education, for there is no insurmountable barrier between what is called intellectual education and the crafts. They are not like two watertight compartments without any relation with each other. On the contrary, training in arts and crafts offers full scope for the development of the intellect. And I venture to claim that without it the development of intellect is impossible. If a mason knows just enough to earn his bread, he cannot be said to have had any education. The education of a mason should therefore include: the place of this craft in social life, the science of bricklaying, the need of housing, the requisites of a good house, and the close relation between civilization and houses for human habitation. To think that intellectual education means no more than a knowledge of certain facts is a gross misapprehension. Development of intellect is fully possible without any such knowledge. A teacher who turns the mind of students into a cupboard for storing all manner of facts has himself not learnt even the first lesson in teaching.

The reader must, by now, have gathered from the above why I have called the view stated by the correspondent both true and false. It is false if my view about the training in crafts and intellectual training is accepted. But it is true if the question has been framed keeping in view the misunderstanding which springs from regarding intellectual education and training in useful crafts as two different things. It should be easy to see now why, and on what conditions, I approve and support the Mahvidyalaya and the education provided by it. In the institution of my conception the mason, the carpenter and the weaver will be intelligent social workers and not mere bread-earners who know only as much of their job as may be sufficient for the purpose. I hope for Kabir, Bhoja Bhagat, Akha and Guru Govind springing up respectively from the weavers, cobblers, goldsmiths and peasants studying at the Mahavidyalaya. Who would say that Kabir, Bhoja Bhagat, Akha and Guru Govind were not men with an intellectual education?

If training in crafts be the essence of education why shouldn't you entrust the Vidyapith to a committee composed of carpenters, blacksmiths and weavers? Let them then engage the services of teachers having to do with intellectual education if they so choose.

I think the answer to this question is already covered before. If I had weavers like Kabir I would certainly place the direction of the Vidyapith in their charge, and I am sure 'the teachers having to do with intellectual education' would consider it an honour to work as servants under them. That we did not consider arts and crafts fit to be included in the content of education is the reason why our craftsmen are relegated today to an inferior status in society and we cannot get any help from them in our endeavour to serve society.

It is mentioned in the statement of the aims and objects of Vidyapith that the progress of the country depends on the villages and not on the cities. If it is so, why do you spoil our city boys? Give village education to the village boys, if you must. But the city boys desire to live a city life. Why not arrange to give them an education which would suit them? And don't you get all the money for the Vidyapith from the cities? Of course, we will have nothing to say if you would transfer the Vidyapith to some ideal village and collect the necessary money, grain and cotton locally from the village itself.

Fortunately, this question does not arise in the mind of many city people or city students. How can the city people who have expressed their readiness to atone for the wrong done to the villages ask for the village education to be given to the village boys at their own expense? The Vidyapith has come into existence as a result of the city people's attention being drawn to the villages.

It is the city people who decided to start the Vidyapith after they had their eyes opened. How could the villagers be called upon to pay its bill if it aims specially at the uplift of the villages? It is up to the city people to provide the wherewithal for the education even in the villages for the time being at least. The villagers can bring against us the same charge as we do against the Government. They may well say: "You city people have exploited us and are still exploiting us. Please stop it now. We will forget the past. Some of us realized the reality of the situation and woke up to our duty. We saw the wrong we have done to the villagers and resolved to make amends for it. The first part of this process was to non-co-operate with the Government under whose protection and with whose help we could and still can drain out the sap of life from them.

The next was that as we learnt the deeper implications of noncooperation, we also learnt to reject the illegitimate gains of that cooperation. If, after launching out on noncooperation, we had simply sat quietly, it could justly be said against us that we had not grasped the meaning of noncooperation. Supposing somebody started plundering our house, then it would not be enough not to help him. We must also step in to stop him from his nefarious business as also desist from sharing the spoils. Then only can it be called true noncooperation with the plunderer. This noncooperation can either be violent or nonviolent, riotous or peaceful, based on brute-force or on soul-force. We have chosen to practise nonviolent and peaceful noncooperation based on soul-force.

And we have come to realize in the process that as an expiation for the exploitation of the wealth of the villages which many city people indulge in, we should render some service at least to the villagers. The Vidyapith had its birth as a result of this realisation on our part. And as some of us are wakeful and persistent in our efforts to know the truth, we are realizing the secret of noncooperation more clearly every day, and to that extent trying to give a truer shape to the Vidyapith. This is sufficient reason why a major portion of the money donated by the city people should be spent on bringing education to the villagers. And the education for time being should be carried to them only through the students from the cities trained by the Vidyapith?

I am of the opinion that any other use of the money received by the Vidyapith will be a betrayal of the assurance given to the people. The donors have given the money in the belief that it will be used in providing education which will be of a different kind from the present one and conform to my conception of it.

The Vidyapith has consistently followed a policy of the removal of untouchability for the past eight years. How many *vinitas* and *snatakas* from among the untouchables has it turned out during this period?

The question appears strange, and suggests ignorance to me. The removal of untouchability does not and should not mean that we are to make the so-called "untouchable" boys *vinitas* and *snatakas*. It is quite possible that in the course of time some of them may become *vinitas* and *snatakas*. And that would be welcome. It is also right that the Vidyapith should be ready to help such boys. But to turn out *snatakas* from among the untouchables is in no way a part of the campaign for the removal of untouchability. The Vidyapith has demonstrated its love for the cause of the removal of untouchability by refusing thousands, if not lakhs, of rupees offered to it, by staking its very existence and by foregoing the valuable help of quite a few who were otherwise very able men in organizing its work.

We see quite clearly that in the absence of *Brahmacharya* the nation has become both physically and mentally weak and its capacity for adventure, enterprise and perseverance has gone down. How is it then that you have not included *Brahmacharya* in the last article of the constitution dealing with its aims and objects?

It is a good question. It cannot be proved that the physical and mental weakness afflicting the nation and the slackening of its capacity for adventure and enterprise are all due directly to the absence of *Brahmacharya*. Nor can it be proved that *Brahmacharya* will always result in physical strength. It is not therefore proper to connect *Brahmacharya* with physical strength or weakness—which is after all an ephemeral good—and thus to detract from the importance of that celestial virtue. The people of the West are not *brahmacharis*, but they are not physically or mentally weak. Their capacity for sustained work and enterprise are excellent and exemplary.

It may be said that the Gurkhas, Pathans, Sikhs, Dogras, and the English among the soldiers are not *brahmacharis*, but they have strongly built bodies. They will easily beat the student of our *vyayamshala* in a physical contest. It can thus be proved that it is not quite correct to maintain that physical strength, even a kind of mental energy, capacity for persistent effort and enterprise are impossible to achieve except through *Brahmacharya*. The *Brahmacharya* of my conception—the *Brahmacharya* which leads one to the realisation of *Brahma* is beyond physical and mental fitness. It is itself both the end and the means. I will, therefore, be willing to sacrifice the body to be able to observe it and achieve it. He who is attached to the body can hardly observe unbroken *Brahmacharya.* Examples of its observance by Bhishma and others are likely to misdirect us in this case. Literal acceptance of things mentioned in the *Mahabharata* and *Ramayana* will lead us astray. What is required is to grasp their inner meaning which we should then put into practice. If we do that in the spirit of true inquiry and experimentation we would surely march forward.

The body is not a thing to be carelessly thrown away. It has to be preserved. The body, if it is at times the abode of Ravana, is also the Ayodhya of Rama. If it is *Kurukshetra* – the field of action, it is also *dharmakshetra* – the field of duty. Hence, it cannot be ignored. It has to be kept fit and strong. Physical exercise is therefore necessary. But this is as far as we can go to praise physical exercise and this should be enough to popularize it among the students. We cannot insist on an unbreakable relation between physical exercise and *Brahmacharya.* It will not only be an exaggeration; there is in it the further danger of a person abandoning *Brahmacharya* when he finds himself lagging behind in physical strength in the erroneous belief that the reason for his failure lies in his practice of *Brahmacharya.*

Brahmacharya does not need the support of physical strength. Its importance and need lie elsewhere. The West may have physical strength and mental energy, but they do not have soul-force. How can we entertain any feeling of envy for their physical strength and mental energy when we see that they succumb to inferior passions at every moment, cannot put up with the least opposition to their will, and spend all their energy, industry and enterprise in plundering and destroying other races? How can we think of copying them? Their strength and energy, shows lack of *Brahmacharya;* this is why it has proved disastrous to the real progress of the world, and that is why I have called it satanic. I am not condemning the West, nor belittling it.

There are many in the West who are votaries of truth and other moral principles. There are also many *brahmacharis* there. They understand these undesirable features of Western life I am referring to here. And so we can, in spite of our love and respect for the West, speak of all the sad results its furious endeavours have led to. If the civilization of the West had been raised on the secure foundations of the *Brahmacharya* ideal, the world today would have been a different place. It would not then be the sorry mess it is, but a happy and beautiful habitation of noble men and women. Knowing thus the evil consequences of the non-observance of *Brahmacharya,* we should put forward the ideal of *Brahmacharya* before the people.

Full development of the soul is impossible without it. A man may behave like an unbridled wild horse without *Brahmacharya,* but he cannot achieve refinement and purity which is the mark of culture. There can be no *sattwik, i.e.,* pure and enlightened endeavour and enterprise without *Brahmacharya.* One may seem to have a strong and energetic mind even without *Brahmacharya,* but then it will be a prey to a thousand passions and lures. Similarly, one may have a well-built and strong body even without *Brahmacharya,* but it will not be a truly healthy body. It is not necessary for health to strengthen the muscles and put on fat. A body which, though lean and thin like a chip of wood, can bear cold and sun and rain and yet remain healthy—such a healthy body is impossible to have without *Brahmacharya.* This is not a belief which I have come to hold today; it is an old belief and is moreover based on experience. I can give you numerous examples from my life and from the life of my friends and co-workers as to how every single impure thought wastes man's energy and destroys his soul. I will say, therefore, that those who seek self-realization should preserve their *Brahmacharya* even though the body may decline.

The reason for the weakness of the body and the mind to be found in our students lies elsewhere. The reasons are: child-marriage, the burden of the family, the lack of good food due to poverty, etc. Let not the readers make the mistake of regarding child-marriage as just non-*Brahmacharya.* Great and persistent efforts are necessary in order to eradicate these evil habits. The harmful customs prevailing in society have to be reformed, and the burden of the present artificial type of education should be lightened. This is however a different subject; I will therefore not dwell on it here. I will merely state that our students cannot have a strong and healthy body merely by taking physical exercise.

Efforts will have to be made in all directions; only then may we hope to achieve the results we desire.

Ever since you made your entry into the public life of this country, there has been a tendency to approach you and get your view of a problem whenever a person or persons have been in doubt and have thus failed to reach a clear-cut conclusion. People are eager to know from you whether a certain thing on a certain occasion is right or not. I am only describing the situation as it really is. It shows that all your activity is basically of a religious nature. Would it be right that when you are no more, these decisions be delivered by a body of persons by a majority vote if necessary? If not, is it not necessary to create what may prove to be continuous line of knowledgeable men, versed in the precepts of *dharma*?

I do not deem it worthy that people should approach me and ask me to pronounce judgment on disputable points. It is true that all my activities, whatever their outer form, are fundamentally religious. But the fact that I am asked to pronounce judgments on every disputed matter shows that people have either not understood the principles which I follow in shaping my conduct, or they have doubts about them. And because I am known as the Mahatma or respected as a good man, our people are credulous and not given to thinking for themselves, they continue to put all forms of questions to me.

This may gratify my sense of pride or even help me up to a point in doing my work, but it does not appear to me if it helps in any appreciable way either the people or questioners. Indeed, I have often felt how nice it would be if I stopped making any pronouncements and did whatever suggested itself to me silently. But in that case I must first stop this weekly that I am now conducting, as also severely cut down much of my present correspondence. That, however, would need a courage which I do not feel within myself. But, there is the great friend of man, the Lord of Death, who can extend his invitation to me at any time and put a stop to all this chatter on my part whether I agree or not.

I do not see any wrong in bodies or associations of men following my principles and giving their opinions on disputed questions by a majority vote when I am no more, or even now whilst I am alive. But as in the case of individuals so also in that of groups they must be inspired by the ideal of *dharma*.

The education in the Vidyapith is divided into three distinct stages: the primary, the secondary and the higher. How far would it be right to name these respectively as the education for the village, education for the city, and the education for those who would take up social service work?

I do not like the meanings suggested here by the correspondent to the primary, the secondary and the higher education respectively. Why should we want village people to be satisfied merely with primary education? They too have a right to receive secondary and higher education—those of them at least who want it. And the boys in the cities cannot do without primary education. The object of all the three should be the prosperity of the villages.

Why do you always attach so much importance to music?

It is said that the study of music is generally neglected in our country today. Without it, the entire educational system seems to me to be incomplete. Music brings sweetness to the individual and to the social life of the people. Even as *pranayam* is necessary for the regulation of breath, so is music for disciplining the voice. A dissemination of the knowledge of music among the people will greatly help in controlling and stopping the noise which is an usual feature of public meetings in this country. Music pacifies anger and its judicious use is highly helpful in leading a man to the vision of God. It does not mean shouting and shrieking a tune anyhow like a rigmarole, nor does it mean the singing of film songs. I have already referred to its ordinary meaning above, but its deeper meaning is that our whole life should be sweet and musical like a song.

It goes without saying that life cannot be made like that without the practice of virtues such as truth, honesty, etc. To make life musical means to make it one with God, to merge it into Him. He who has not rid himself of *raga* and *dwesha, i.e.*, likes and dislike, who has not tasted of the joy of service, cannot have any understanding of celestial music. A study of music, which does not take account of this deeper aspect of this divine art, has little or no value for me.

The art of painting means an expression of the emotions of the artist through line and colour. If this definition of painting were to be accepted, would you include painting as an essential part of the scheme of national education which should be universally taught to all?

Some people are of the view that such subjects as grammar, compound interest, higher geometry, etc., which the learners are apt to forget in after years should not be included in the courses to be framed for purposes of national education. Do you agree to this? If you do, why should not Urdu also be put in the same category? When Hindus and Muslims feel the urge to come into close contact with each other and to understand each other's cultures, then only will the knowledge of Sanskrit and Urdu prove useful and lasting. Knowledge of Urdu will be put to active use and hence increase only when there is respect for and a desire to learn the culture of which Urdu is the vehicle. Until then it is bound to remain no more than a religious rite like the worship of Ganesha—a formal affair without any practical value.

I do not understand why grammar, compound interest and higher geometry have all been classed together. I have always believed that grammar is absolutely necessary for the mastery of a language, and that grammar and higher geometry are highly interesting subjects. Both provide innocent intellectual entertainment. Besides, grammar is indispensable for the study of philology. I will, therefore, accord a place to both these subjects in the courses of study for national education. In the same way, he who wants to be good at accounts cannot do so without learning compound interest. Therefore, all the three things mentioned by the correspondent in the question will have their due place in the syllabus for national education.

The point is that there are things which are common to all schemes of education. Today, we have to differentiate between Government education and National education because the former is detrimental to national development. But there are many things in Government schools which will and must also be in our schools. Thus, though there are points of similarity between the two, the atmosphere in Government schools strengthens the bonds of slavery and is used at critical moments to suppress us. Therefore, such schools are to be renounced. Besides, as we have already seen, a portion, at least, of the education imparted there is wholly unnecessary; it is just a burden and nothing more. But I am moving away from the subject under discussion. I have thought it fit to offer this clarification under the impression that I might not have grasped the point behind this question.

Urdu stands apart from the above-mentioned subjects: the question of its study must be considered separately. Hindus and Muslims will ultimately unite but in our national schools we must continue to strive unremittingly to bring them closer together. For this, we must acquaint ourselves with each other's religion. If the students forget whatever little of Urdu they learn, evidently they are not serious about its study and must be learning it only because they must. But this can also be said about Hindi. Only God knows how interest in Hindi or Urdu can be created among the students, but there is no doubt in my mind that its knowledge is necessary for the progress of the nation. Students should have full freedom; there should be nothing which will obstruct their free growth; to achieve this objective the teachers should have no prejudices for or against anything; while they teach they should so conduct themselves as though they have no partiality for any particular rule or habit or principle: This ideal for a teacher is coming to be accepted in many places. Do you accept it?

What has been said above can be supported as well as opposed. If it does not help in preserving the real essence, is should be opposed, and if it does help, the students may well be allowed full freedom and the teachers remain as detached and neutral as they like. They may do what they wish with a view to securing the independence of the students, the only condition being that they must mix with the students to the extent of being one of them. In the language of Akha, I will say to them:

> *"Live in the world as you like, but keep constantly before your mind the aim of attaining to God at any cost."*

An ideal teacher never had nor should he ever have any other aim before him. *(Navajivan, 3 June–1 July 1928 (The Problem of Education, pp. 154–69))*

National University

The National University stands today as a protest against British injustice, and as a vindication of national honour. But it has come to stay. It draws its inspiration from the national ideals of a united India. It stands for a religion which is the Dharma of the Hindus and Islam of Mohammedans. It wants to rescue the Indian vernaculars from unmerited oblivion and make them the fountains of national regeneration and Indian culture. It holds that a systematic study of Asiatic cultures is no less essential than the study of Western sciences for a complete education for life. The vast treasures of Sanskrit and Arabic, Persian and Pali, and Magadhi have to be ransacked in order to discover wherein lies the source of strength for the nation.

It does not propose merely to feed on, or repeat, the ancient cultures. It rather hopes to build a new culture based on the traditions of the past, enriched by the experience of later times. It stands for the synthesis of the different cultures that have come to stay in India, that have influenced Indian life and that in their turn, have themselves been influenced by the spirit of the soil. This synthesis will naturally be of the Swadeshi type where each culture is assured its legitimate place, and not of American pattern, where one dominant culture absorbs the rest, and where the aim is not towards harmony, but towards an artificial and forced unity. That is why the University has desired a study of all the Indian religions by its students.

The Hindus may thus have an opportunity of studying the Koran and the Muslims of knowing what the Hindus Shastras contain. If the University has excluded anything, it is the spirit of exclusion that regards any section of humanity as permanently untouchable. The study of Hindustani, which is a national blend of Sanskrit, Hindi and Persianized Urdu, has been made compulsory. The spirit of independence will be fostered not only through Religion, Politics and History but through vocational training also, which alone can give the youths of the country economic independence and a backbone that comes out of a sense of self-respect. The University hopes to organize higher schools throughout the mofussil towns, so that education may be spread broadcast and filtered down to the masses as early as possible. The use of Gujarati as the medium of education will facilitate this process and, ere long, the suicidal cleavage between the educated and the non-educated will be bridged. And as an effect of industrial education to the genteel folks, and literary education for the industrial classes, the unequal distribution of wealth and the consequent social discontent will be considerably checked.

The greatest defect of the Government Universities has been their alien control and the false values they have created as regards 'careers'. The Gujarat Universities by non-co-operating with the Government has automatically eradicated both these evils from its own system. If the founders and promoters stick to this resolve till the Government becomes nationalized, it will help them to cultivate a clear perception of national ideals and national needs. *(Tagore, pp. 455–57; 17 November 1920 (CW 18, p. 481))*

College Education

I would revolutionize college education and relate it to national necessities. There would be degrees for mechanical and other engineers. They would be attached to the different industries which should pay for the training of the graduates they need. Thus the Tatas would be expected to run a college for training engineers under the supervision of the State, the mill associations would run among them a college for training graduates whom they need.

Similarly for the other industries that may be named. Commerce will have its college. There remain arts, medicine and agriculture. Several private arts colleges are today self-supporting. The State would, therefore, cease to run its own. Medical colleges would be attached to certified hospitals. As they are popular among moneyed men they may be expected by voluntary contributions to support medical colleges. And agricultural colleges to be worthy of the name must be self-supporting. I have a painful experience of some agricultural graduates. Their knowledge is superficial. They lack practical experience. But if they had their apprenticeship on farms which are self-sustained and answer the requirements of the country, they would not have to gain experience after getting their degrees and at the expense of their employers. *(Harijan, 31 July 1937 (CW 65, p. 451))*

State Universities

Higher education should be left to private enterprise and for meeting national requirements whether in the various industries, technical arts, belles-letters or fine arts.

The State Universities should be purely examining bodies, self-supporting through the fees charged for examinations.

Universities will look after the whole of the field of education and will prepare and approve courses of studies in the various departments of education. No private school should be run without the previous sanction of the respective Universities. University charters should be given liberally to any body of persons of proved worth and integrity, it being always understood that the Universities will not cost the State anything except that it will bear the cost of running a Central Education Department.

The foregoing scheme does not absolve the State from running such seminaries as may be required for supplying State needs. *(Harijan, 2 October 1937)*

Higher Education

1. I am not opposed to education even of the highest type attainable in the world.
2. The State must pay for it wherever it has definite use for it.
3. I am opposed to all higher education being paid for from the general revenue.
4. It is my firm conviction that the vast amount of the so-called education in arts, given in our colleges, is sheer waste and has resulted in unemployment among the educated classes. What is more, it has destroyed the health, both mental and physical, of the boys and girls who have the misfortune to go through the grind in our colleges.
5. The medium of a foreign language through which higher education has been imparted in India has caused incalculable intellectual and moral injury to the nation. We are too near our own times to judge the enormity of the damage done. And we who have received such

> education have both to be victims and judges—an almost impossible feat.

Thus I claim that I am not an enemy of Higher Education. But I am an enemy of Higher Education as it is given in this country. Under my scheme there will be more and better libraries, more and better laboratories, more and better research institutes. Under it we should have an army of chemists, engineers and other experts who will be real servants of the nation, and answer the varied and growing requirements of a people who are becoming increasingly conscious of their rights and wants. And all these experts will speak, not a foreign language, but the language of the people. The knowledge gained by them will be the common property of the people. There will be truly original work instead of mere imitation. And the cost will be evenly and justly distributed. *(Harijan, 9 July 1938 (CW 67, p. 158))*

Self-Supporting Universities

Your third conclusion about general revenue and claims of Higher Education and its corollary, *viz.* that Universities should be self-supporting, has left me unconvinced. I believe that every country to be a progressive country must have sufficient facilities for the pursuit of *all* branches of knowledge—not merely chemistry, medicine and engineering, but every kind of knowledge, literature, philosophy, history, sociology, both abstract and applied. All higher pursuits require many facilities which cannot be had without State support. A country depending *only* on voluntary effort for such pursuits is sure to fall behind and suffer.

It can never hope to be free and be able to maintain that freedom. The State must be jealously watchful over the position of higher education in *all* fields. Voluntary effort must be there and we must have our Nuffields and Rockfellers. But the State cannot and must not be allowed to remain a silent spectator. It must actively come forward to organize, help and direct. I wish you to clarify this aspect of the question.

You say at the end of your article: 'Under my scheme there will be more and better libraries.' I do not find *The Scheme* you speak of in your article, nor am I able to make out how 'more and better libraries and laboratories' will come into being thereunder.

I am of opinion that such libraries and laboratories must be maintained, and so long as donors and voluntary agencies are not coming forward in sufficient numbers, the State cannot divest itself of this responsibility.

My article is clear enough if the expression 'definite use' mentioned in it is given its extensive meaning. I have not pictured a poverty-stricken India containing ignorant millions. I have pictured to myself an India continually progressing along the lines best suited to her genius. I do not, however, picture it as a third class or even a first class copy of the dying civilization of the West. If my dream is fulfilled and every one of the seven lakhs of villages becomes a well-living republic in which there are no illiterates, in which no one is idle for want of work, in which everyone is usefully occupied and has nourishing food, well-ventilated dwellings, and sufficient Khadi for covering the body, and in which all the villagers know and observe the laws of hygiene and sanitation, such a State must have varied and increasing needs, which it must supply unless it would stagnate. I can therefore well imagine the State financing all the education my correspondent mentions and much more that I could add. And if the State has such requirements, surely it will have corresponding libraries.

What, however, according to my view the State will not have is an army of B.A.'s and M.A.'s with their brains sapped with too much cramming and minds almost paralyzed by the impossible attempt to speak and write English like Englishmen. The majority of these have no work, no employment. And when they have the latter, it is usually clerkships at which most of the knowledge gained during their twelve years of High Schools and Colleges is of no use whatsoever to them.

University training becomes self-supporting when it is utilized by the State. It is criminal to pay for a training which benefits neither the nation nor the individual. In my opinion there is no such thing as individual benefit which cannot be proved to be also national benefit. And since most of my critics seem to be agreed that the existing Higher Education, and for that matter both Primary and Secondary, are not connected with realities, it cannot be of benefit to the State. When it is directly based on realities and is wholly given through the mother tongue, I shall perhaps have nothing to say against it. To be based on realities is to be based on national, *i.e.*, State, requirements. And the State will pay for it. Even when that happy time comes, we shall find that many institutions will be conducted by voluntary contributions. They may or may not benefit the State. Much of what passes for education today in India belongs to that category and would therefore not be paid for from the general revenue, if I had the way. *(Harijan, 30 July 1938 (CW 67, pp. 210–12))*

Reorientation of University Education

Gandhiji remarked at the Conference of Education Ministers in Poona that what he had said about adult education applied to University education. It must be originally related to the Indian scene. It must therefore be an extension and continuation of the Basic Education course. That was the central point. If they did not see eye to eye with him on that point, he was afraid they would have little use for his advice. If, on the other hand, they agreed with him that the present University education did not fit them for independence but only enslaved them, they would be as impatient as he was to completely overhaul and scrap that system and remodel it on new lines consonant with the national requirement.

Today the youth educated in our universities either ran after the Government jobs or fell into devious ways and sought outlet for their frustration by fomenting unrest. They were not even ashamed to beg or sponge upon others. Such was their sad plight. The aim of University education should be to turn out true servants of the people, who would live and die for the country's freedom. He was therefore of opinion that University education should be coordinated and brought into line with Basic Education, by taking in teachers from the Talimi Sangh. *(Harijan, 25 August 1946)*

New Universities

There seems to be a mania for establishing new universities in the provinces. Gujarat wants one for Gujarati, Maharashtra for Marathi, Karnatic for Kannad, Orissa for Uriya, Assam for Assami and what not. I do believe that there should be such universities if these rich provincial languages and the people who speak them are to attain their full height.

At the same time I fear that we betray ourselves into undue haste in accomplishing the object. The first step should be linguistic political redistribution of provinces. Their separate administration will naturally lead to the establishment of universities where there are none. The province of Bombay absorbs three languages: Gujarati, Marathi and Kannad and, therefore, stunts their growth. Madras absorbs four: Tamil, Telugu, Malayalam and Kannad. Thus there is overlapping also. That Andradesh has an Andhra University is true. In my opinion it does not occupy the place it would, if Andhra was a separate administrative unit, free from foreign control. India attained that freedom only two months ago. The same thing can be said of the Annamalai University. Who can say that Tamil has come to its own in that University?

There should be a proper background for new universities. They should have feeders in the shape of schools and colleges which will impart instruction through the medium of their respective provincial languages. Then only can there be a proper milieu. University is at the top. A majestic top can only be sustained if there is a sound foundation.

Though we are politically free, we are hardly free from the subtle domination of the West. I have nothing to say to that school of politicians who believe that knowledge can only come from the West. Nor do I subscribe to the belief that nothing good can come out of the West. I do fear, however, that we are unable as yet to come to a correct decision in the matter. It is to be hoped that no one contends that because we seem to be politically free from foreign domination the mere fact gives us freedom from the more subtle influence of the foreign language and foreign thought.

Is it not wisdom, does not duty to the country dictate, that before we embark on new universities we should stop and fill our own lungs first with the ozone of our newly got freedom? A university never needs a pile of majestic buildings and treasures of gold and silver. What it does need most of all is the intelligent backing of public opinion. It should have a large reservoir of teachers to draw upon. Its founders should be farseeing.

In my opinion it is not for a democratic State to find money for founding universities. If the people want them they will supply the funds. Universities so founded will adorn the country which they represent. Where administration is in foreign hands, whatever comes to the people comes from the top and thus they become more and more dependent. Where it is broad-based on popular will, everything goes from bottom upward and hence it lasts.

It is good looking and strengthens the people. In such a democratic scheme money invested in the promotion of learning gives a tenfold return to the people even as a seed sown in good soil returns a luxuriant crop. Universities founded under foreign domination have run in the reverse direction. Any other result was perhaps impossible. Therefore, there is every reason for being cautious about founding new universities till India has digested the newly-acquired freedom.

Then take the Hindu–Muslim question. The poison has assumed dangerous proportions, such that it is difficult to forecast where it will land us. Assume that the unthinkable has happened and that not a single Muslim can remain in the Union safely and honourably and that neither Hindu nor Sikh can do likewise in Pakistan. Our education will then wear a poisonous form. If, on the other hand, Hindus, Muslims and all the others who may belong to different faiths can live in either dominion with perfect safety and honour, then in the nature of things our education will take a shape altogether pleasing.

Either people of different faiths having lived together in friendship have produced a beautiful blend of cultures, which we shall strive to perpetuate and increasingly strengthen and shape, or we shall cast about for the day when there was only one religion represented in Hindustan and retrace our steps to that exclusive culture.

It is just possible that we might not be able to find any such historical date and if we do and we retrace our steps, we shall throw our culture back to that ugly period and deservedly earn the execration of the universe. By way of example, if we make the vain attempt to obliterate the Muslim period, we shall have to forget that there was a mighty Juma Masjid in Delhi second to none in the world, or that there was a Muslim University in Aligarh, or that there was the Taj in Agra, one of the seven wonders of the world, or that there were the great forts of Delhi and Agra built during the Mughal period. We shall then have to rewrite our history with that end in view.

Surely, today we have not the atmosphere which will enable us to come to a right conclusion about the conflicting choices. Our two months' old freedom is struggling to get itself shaped. We do not know what shape it will ultimately take. Until we know this definitely, it should be enough if we make such changes as are possible in the existing universities and breathe in our existing educational institutions the quickening spirit of freedom.

The experience we will thus gain will be helpful when the time is ripe for founding new universities. *(Harijan, 2 November 1947 (CW 89, pp. 402–04))*

7

Gandhi on Objectives of Education

Nationalism

Education is just a means. If it is not accompanied by truthfulness, firmness, patience and other virtues, it remains sterile, and sometimes does harm instead of good. The object of education is not to be able to earn money, but to improve oneself and to serve the country. If this object is not realized, it must be taken that the money spent on education has been wasted. (*Indian Opinion,* 9 March 1907 (*CW* 6, p. 361)

Public Good

The Indian community has a moral to learn from this case. Without the right kind of education, the community will not only remain backward, but become increasingly so. Education in England, the study of English, world history and of the sciences—all these are essential in the world of today. Without them one is crippled. It is also necessary to learn how to put the knowledge thus acquired to proper use. In itself knowledge is only a means. It can be employed for good, for making money, and in the service of public causes. Knowledge is justified only when it is put to good use and employed in the public cause. Otherwise, as we pointed out once earlier and as everyone will readily admit, it is like poison. *(Indian Opinion, 4 April 1908 (CW 8, p. 171))*

Cardinal Virtues

If you practise the three virtues if they become part of your life so far as I am concerned, you will have completed your education—your training. Armed with them, believe me, you will earn your bread in any part of the world and you will have paved the way to acquire a true knowledge of the soul, yourself and God. This does not mean that you should not receive instruction in letters. That you should and you are doing. But it is a thing over which you need not fret yourself. You have plenty of time for it and after all you are to receive such instruction in order that your training may be of use to the others. *(Letter to Manilal Gandhi, 25 March 1909 (CW 9, p. 205))*

Not Mere Employment

You—the students of Madras as well as students all over India—are you receiving an education which will make you worthy to realise that ideal and which will draw the best out of you, or is it an education which has become a factory for making Government employees or clerks in commercial offices? Is the goal of the education that you are receiving that of mere employment whether in the Government departments or other departments? If that be the goal of your education, if that is the goal that you have set before yourselves, I feel and I fear that the vision which the poet pictured for himself is far from being realised. *(Speech at Y.M.C.A., Madras, 27 April 1915 (CW 13, p. 65))*

National Service

Pupils are to receive education which will incline them to do nothing but national service when their studies are over. If, on growing up, they leave the Ashram, the education will have failed to that extent. Should any occasion of the kind arise, the student will be free [to follow his inclination]. It is not the aim, however, that the students should return to their parents and get lost in the sea of practical affairs. *(Letter to Ranchhodlal Patwari, 10 June 1915 (CW 13, p. 105))*

Thinking and Becoming

But I am afraid that most of the students do not pay any regard to the real aim of education. They go to school merely because it is the custom to do so. Some go to be able to obtain employment later on. In my opinion, to think of education as a means of earning a living betrays an unworthy disposition of mind. The body is the means of earning a living while the school is the place for building character. To regard the latter as the means of fulfilling one's bodily needs is like killing a buffalo for a small piece of hide. The body should be maintained through doing physical work. How can the *atma*, the spirit, be employed for this purpose? You earn your bread by the sweat of your brow—this is one of the most significant sayings of Christ. The Gita also seems to say the same.

Students who attend school without taking thought as to the true aim of education, should first make sure what it should be. Such a student may resolve this very day that, henceforth, he will regard school as a place for building character. I am sure that he will effect a change for the better in his character in the course of a month and that his companions will also bear witness to his having done so. The shastras assert that we become what we think. *(Speech at Bihar Students' Conference, Bhagalpur, 19 July 1917—(CW 14, pp. 134–35))*

Knowing the Self

As I have earlier pointed out, most of the students look listless and devoid of energy. Many have asked me what they should do to overcome lethargy and serve the country? What should they do to earn their living? I have the impression that they are anxious about this matter. Before answering these questions it is necessary to find out the aim of education. Huxley has said that the aim of education is the building up of character. Our seers aver that, if in spite of his knowledge of the Vedas and shastras, a man fails to know himself and acquire the power to liberate himself from all bonds, his knowledge is useless. They have also said: "He who has known the Self knows all." Knowledge of the Self is possible without any literary education. Prophet Mohammed was an illiterate man. Christ too did not attend school.

But it would be impudent to deny that these great men had acquired knowledge of the Self. Though they did not pass any examination, yet we hold them in high esteem and worship them.

They were in possession of all the fruits of learning. They were *mahatmas*—men of great spiritual attainment. *(Speech at Bihar Students' Conference, Bhagalpur, 19 July 1917 (CW 14, p. 133))*

Building Character

All education must aim at building character. I cannot see how this can be done except through religion. We are yet to realize that gradually we are being reduced to a state in which we shall have lost our own without having acquired the new. I cannot go more into this, but I have met hundreds of teachers and they sighed in pain as they told me of their experiences... If pupils in schools lose their character, everything will have been lost. *(Speech at Gujarat Educational Conference, Broach, 20 October 1917 (CW 14, p. 29))*

Manliness and Self-Respect

If education is to be bought at the price of manliness and self-respect, the price is too heavy. "Man does not live by bread alone." Self-respect and character are above means of livelihood or a career. I am sorry that so many students have taken their expulsion so much to heart. The parents as well as students must revise their ideas about education. Education is treated merely as a means of earning a livelihood and acquiring a status in society. These are not unworthy ambitions. But they are not everything in life. There are many other honourable means of acquiring wealth and status.

There are many independent activities in life which one may undertake without having to contemplate loss of self-respect. And there is no better or cleaner passport to status in society than honesty and selfless service of fellow-beings. If, therefore, after due effort, the college door remains banged in the students' faces, they should not lose heart but seek other means of livelihood. And if the other students will empty the recalcitrant colleges as a matter of respectful protest, they and India will not be losers, but both will be considerable gainers. *(Young India, 1 October 1919 (CW 16, pp. 175–76))*

Kindness to All

He said the essence of all education was kindness—kindness to all, friends, foes, men and beasts. The chief object of education was the building of character which could be done by strict observance of *Brahmacharya.* Mr. Gandhi then explained to the students the necessity of learning Hindi and spinning and said that if the whole younger generation was educated in the manner in which they were trained in national schools then there would not have been any difficulty in getting swaraj. *(Speech at National College, Bombay – The Bombay Chronicle, 17 March 1921 (CW 14, p. 441))*

Knowledge to Character

That is certainly what we mean. Even imparting knowledge should aim at character-building. Knowledge is the means and character-building is the end. *(Navajivan, 20 October 1921 (CW 21, p. 327))*

Reaching the Ideal

In my humble opinion, knowledge should never be used for acquiring wealth. Business should be the only means of doing so. The means of livelihood should be labour, *i.e.,* weaving, carpentry, tailoring and such other occupations essential for maintaining human life. I believe that one of the chief reasons for our moral fall is that doctors, lawyers, teachers and others acquire their knowledge mainly for getting money and, in fact, use it for that purpose. What I have set out is, of course, an ideal, which we cannot attain. I have no doubt, however, that the nearer we get to it, the better for us. *(Navajivan, 1 July 1924 (CW 24, p. 174))*

Making a True Student

The education that you are receiving is intended for swaraj. I have taken up the responsibilities of a chancellor in Gujarat. That too I have done in my capacity as a fighter for freedom and with the intention of training students to be fighters for freedom. I landed in England on 4th of August, 1914. What did I see there? As the War spread, the Inns of Courts went on closing.

Many faculties in Oxford and Cambridge were also closed. During the War, they allotted a minor role to education. And why should they not? The outcome of education is that the student becomes an ideal citizen, an ideal patriot and an ornament to his family, his community and his nation. *(Convocation address at Tilak Mahavidyalaya, Poona, 4 September 1924 (CW 25, p. 89))*

Service of Humanity

In asking them to study the lives of lawyers like Ghose, Mahatma Gandhi asked them not merely to be satisfied with the heritage those great lawyers had left for them, but wished the present generation to do better. They should become the poor man's friend in every sense and then alone would they be able to justify the legal profession. Their end was not to get more than a decent livelihood or how to shine in life, but to serve humanity in order to serve the motherland. They ought not to become lawyers in order to increase cases.

The education they received ought not to be prostituted to the base use of earning a livelihood, it ought to be used to promote moral growth to enable them to realize themselves, to understand that there was the Maker who saw everything and registered all thoughts, pure and impure, and the learning they derived should be dedicated to a vigorous self-analysis and not prostituted. *(Speech at Law College, Trivandrum, 14 March 1925 (CW 26, p. 307))*

Fearlessness

The little boys of the school had all been waiting in the sun with the handsome purse they had collected and they had the lesson of fearlessness from Gandhiji's lips:

> *Fearlessness is the foundation of all education, the beginning and not the end. If you do not build on that foundation, the edifice of all your education will topple over.*

And to send the lesson home to them he told them the story of Prahalda and exhorted them to declare the truth courteously and bravely without regard for the consequences as the twelve-year-old Prahalda did. *(Speech at Boys' Meeting, Kolhapur, Young India, 31 March 1927 (CW 33, p. 192))*

Purity of Personal Life

Purity of personal life is the one indispensable condition for building a sound education. And my meetings with thousands of students and the correspondence which I continuously have with the students in which they pour out their innermost feelings and take me into their confidence show me quite clearly that there is much left to be desired. I am sure that all of you understand thoroughly what I mean. In our languages, there is a beautiful word, equivalent for the word student, that is, *Brahmachari. Vidyarthi* is a coined word and a poor equivalent for *Brahmachari*. And I hope you know what the word *Brahmachari* means.

It means searcher after God, one who conducts himself so as to bring himself nearest to God in the least possible time. And all the great religions of the world, however much they may differ, are absolutely one on this fundamental thing that no man or woman with an impure heart can possibly appear before the Great White Throne. All our learning or recitation of the Vedas, correct knowledge of Sanskrit, Latin, Greek and what not will avail us nothing if they do not enable us to cultivate absolute purity of heart. The end of all knowledge must be building of character. *(Speech at Voorhee's College, Vellore, 30 August 1927 (CW 34, pp. 422-23))*

Freedom from Bondage

You have asked for my blessings. Them you certainly have. But you have them on the condition that you impart lustre to this Vidyalaya and its name. The Patidars also should benefit by it and should disgrace neither the Vallabh Vidyalaya nor my name. I do not care for the sort of Vidyalaya which may prove a millstone round my neck and be a burden to me. Education liberates us, frees us from bondage, helps us to shine, adds to the country's wealth, enriches character: our boys and girls become smart and intelligent thereby. This Vidyalaya has been established with this end in view. May this end be realized. *(Speech at Vallabh Vidyalaya Bochasan, 10 May 1931 (CW 46, p. 101))*

Quest for Truth

True education is that which helps us to know the *atman*, our true self, God and Truth. To acquire this knowledge, some persons may feel the need for a study of literature, some for a study of physical sciences and some others for art. But every branch of knowledge should have as its goal, knowledge of the self. That is so in the Ashram. We carry on numerous activities with that aim in view. All of them are, in my sense of the term, true education. Those activities can also be carried on without any reference to the goal of knowledge of the self. When they are so carried on, they may serve as a means of livelihood or of something else, but they are not education.

In an activity carried on as education, a proper understanding of its meaning, devotion to duty and the spirit of service are necessary. The first necessarily brings about development of the intellect. In doing any piece of work, however small, we should be inspired by a holy aim and, while doing it, we should try to understand the purpose which it will serve and the scientific method of doing it. There is a science of every type of work—whether it be cooking, sanitation, carpentry or spinning. Everybody who does his work with the attitude of a student knows its science or discovers it. *(From a microfilm of the Gujarati: M.M.U./II, 10 July 1932 (CW 50, p. 182))*

Sparing the Rod

Our aim is not just to impart education to children or teach them discipline, but to build character in them. Education, discipline, etc., are means to that end. If the result of building character in them is that education and discipline are neglected, let that be so. I understand your arguments, though. I also see that there is no ill will behind your use of the rod. But there are certainly anger and impatience behind them. May I make a suggestion? Call a meeting of the children. If any of them, say, "You may punish us, and in this manner, if we play mischief or disobey you", you may punish them in the manner which they suggest. *(Letter to Premabehn Kantak, 14 December 1930 (CW 44, p. 380))*

Selfless Service

Studies should be undertaken only with the aim of equipping oneself for service. Since, however, service of others gives one the highest joy, one may say that studies are for joy. I have not heard of anyone, however, who found unbroken joy in life through literary pursuits alone without devoting himself to service. *(Letter to Premabehn Kantak, 3 August 1932 (CW 50, p. 326))*

National Character

What is your goal in education when India obtains self-rule?

Character-building. I would try to develop courage, strength, virtue, the ability to forget oneself in working towards great aims. This is more important than literacy, academic learning is only a means to this greater end. That is why India's great lack of literacy, deplorable as it is, does not appeal to me nor make me feel that India is unfit for self-rule.

Would you try to bring about any specific kind of social organisation through education.

I would feel that if we succeed in building the character of the individual, society will take care of itself. I would be quite willing to trust the organisation of society to individuals so developed.

In developing the new national spirit in India would you like to make patriotic feelings so strong that duty to one's country would be a higher good than obeying one's personal conscience?

I hope that will never be. One's own inner convictions come first always. But in a nation where character is developed in all individuals, there can be no conflict between the dictates of one's own conscience and those of the State. *(Remakers of Mankind, 1932, pp. 104–05)*

Self Control

The true aim of education is spiritual development. One should, therefore, go in for such kind of education as will bring it about. It need not be of one fixed type. Hence it is not necessary to say anything on that subject. One should lead a life of self-control. *(Letter to Bhogilal, 20 February 1933 (CW 53, p. 366))*

Humility

With this introduction I would like to tell the students, boys and girls, that humility is the primary thing to be acquired. One who is not humble cannot put one's learning to proper use. What does it matter if he has obtained double first class or has stood first? One does not achieve everything by just passing an examination. It is possible that it may help in securing a good job or a good marriage alliance. But, if learning is to be put to proper use, if it is to be used only for the sake of service, one should acquire more and more humility every day. No service is possible without it. *(Speech at Dayaram Jethamal College, Karachi, 10 July 1934 (CW 58, p. 164))*

Developing Independent Thinking

At present, the minds of the students become dull there. They can only imitate. Instead of this, they must acquire the power of independent thinking. We are born into this world not for indulging in sensuous activities but for sacrifice, for restraint. The purpose of education is that we know God and progress towards the ideal, and get closer to Him. It is the strict law of God that anyone who desires to be close to Him should renounce the world and yet be in it. This is what the first *mantra* of the *Ishopanishad* exhorts us to do. This thing is difficult and yet easy at the same time. It is easy if we believe that we have to live for service. We acquire learning not for sensuous pleasures and for earning but for *mukti*. Education is considered necessary to save ourselves from darkness, sensuous pleasures and capricious behaviour. *(Speech at students' meeting, Lahore, 13 July 1934 (CW 58, p. 183))*

Wholesome Educational Environment

That boy will grow into a courageous, healthy and service-minded boy, provided he gets a wholesome, environment. His body as well as his mind will develop in right proportion. He will be free of any fraud or immorality. Staying in the village he will serve the villagers and will be content to live on the subsistence provided by the villagers. Through his service and the knowledge acquired by him he will provide proper guidance to the people around him and thus train more young men. I expect that a student trained under the Nayee Taleem would develop on these lines. *(Talk with Manu Gandhi, Biharni Komi Agman (Translated from Gujarati), 21 April 1947, p. 238 (CW 87, p. 326))*

8

The Gandhian Experiments

Shantiniketan

From Rajkot I proceeded to Shantiniketan. The teachers and students overwhelmed me with affection. The reception was a beautiful combination of simplicity, art and love.

The Phoenix family had been assigned separate quarters at Shantiniketan. Maganlal Gandhi was at their head, and he had made it his business to see that all the rules of the Phoenix Ashram should be scrupulously observed. I saw that, by dint of his love, knowledge and perseverance, he had made his fragrance felt in the whole of Shantiniketan.

Andrews was there, and also Pearson. Amongst the Bengali teachers with whom we came in fairly close contact were Jagadanandbabu, Nepalbabu, Santoshbabu, Kshitimohanbabu, Nagenbabu, Sharadbabu and Kalibabu.

As is my wont, I quickly mixed with the teachers and students, and engaged them in a discussion on self-help. I put it to the teachers that, if they and the boys dispensed with the services of paid cooks and cooked their food themselves, it would enable the teachers to control the kitchen from the point of view the boys' physical and moral health, and it would afford to the students an object-lesson in self-help. One or two of them were inclined to shake their heads. Some of them strongly approved of the proposal. The boys welcomed it, if only because of their instinctive taste for novelty. So we launched the experiment. When I invited the Poet to express his opinion, he said that he did not mind it provided the teachers were favourable. To the boys he said, ' The experiment contains the key to Swaraj.'

Pearson began to wear away his body in making the experiment a success. He threw himself into it with zest. A batch was formed to cut vegetables, another to clean the grain, and so on. Nagenbabu and others undertook to see the sanitary cleaning of the kitchen and its surroundings. It was a delight to me to see them working spade in hand.

But it was too much to expect the hundred and twenty-five boys with their teachers to take to this work of physical labour like ducks to water. There used to be daily discussion. Some began early to show fatigue. But Pearson was not the man to be tired. One would always find him with his smiling face doing something or other in or about the kitchen. He had taken upon himself the cleaning of the bigger utensils. A party of students played on their sitar before this cleaning party in order to beguile the tedium of the operation. All alike took the thing up with zest and Shantiniketan became a busy hive. Changes like these when once begun always develop. Not only was the Phoenix party's kitchen self-conducted, but the food cooked in it was of the simplest. Condiments were eschewed. Rice, dal, vegetables and even wheat flour were all cooked at one and the same time in a steam cooker. And Shantiniketan boys started a similar kitchen with a view to introducing reform in the Bengali kitchen. One or two teachers and some students ran this kitchen.

The experiment was, however, dropped after some time. I am of opinion that the famous institution lost nothing by having conducted the experiment for a brief interval, and some of the experiences gained could not but be of help to the teachers. *(An Autobiography Vol. II, p. 565)*

Satyagraha Ashram, Kochrab

The Ashram experiment in education was a trial for us as nothing else was.

We saw at once that the women and children in the Ashram should be taught to read and write, and a little later on that there should be similar facilities for even the illiterate men that came to the Ashram. Those who had already joined the Ashram could not undertake to teach. If capable teachers were to be attracted to the Ashram, the rule of Brahmacharya had to be relaxed in their case. The Ashram was therefore divided into two sections, the 'teachers' quarters and the Ashram proper.

Human beings cannot overcome their weakness all at once. As soon as the two sections came into being, a feeling of superiority and inferiority poisoned the Ashram atmosphere in spite of all our efforts to scotch it. The Ashramites developed spiritual pride, which the teachers could not tolerate. This pride was an obstacle in the attainment of the Ashram ideal and therefore an aspect of untruth as well. If Brahmacharya was to be observed in its perfection, the division was inevitable. But the brahmacharis had no reason to think too highly of themselves. It may be that the brahmacharis who sinned mentally in spite of themselves were retrogressing while those who did not claim to be brahmacharis but liked Brahmacharya were making progress. This was clear to the intellect but it was not easy for all of us to put it into practice.

Then again there were differences of opinion as regards the method of education which gave rise to difficulties in administration. There were bitter discussions, but at last all calmed down and learned the lesson of forbearance. This was in my view a triumph of truth, the goal of all Ashram endeavour. Those who held divergent views harboured no evil intentions in their minds, and were indeed grieved at the divergence. They wished to practise truth as they saw it. Their partiality for their own standpoint came in the way of their giving due weight to the arguments of their opponents. Hence the quarrels which put our charity to a severe test.

I have my own perhaps peculiar views on education which have not been accepted by my colleagues in full, and here they are:

1. Young boys and girls should have coeducation till they are eight years of age.
2. Their education should mainly consist in manual training under the supervision of an educationist.

3. The special aptitudes of each child should be recognized in determining the kind of work he or she should do.
4. The reasons for every process should be explained when the process is being carried.
5. General knowledge should be imparted to each child as he begins to understand things. Learning to read or write should come later.
6. The child should first be taught to draw simple geometrical figures, and when he has learnt to draw these with ease, he should be taught to write the alphabet. If this is done he will write a good hand from the very first.
7. Reading should come before writing. The letters should be treated as pictures to be recognized and later on to be copied.
8. A child taught on these lines will have acquired considerable knowledge according to his capacity by the time he is eight.
9. Nothing should be taught to a child by force.
10. He should be interested in everything taught to him.
11. Education should appear to the child like play. Play is an essential part of education.
12. All education should be imparted through the mother tongue.
13. The child should be taught Hindi-Urdu as the national language, before he learns letters.
14. Religious education is indispensable and the child should get it by watching the teacher's conduct and by hearing him talk about it.
15. Nine to sixteen constitutes the second stage in the child's education.
16. It is desirable that boys and girls should have coeducation during the second stage also as far as possible.
17. Hindu children should now be taught Sanskrit, and Muslim children Arabic.

18. Manual training should be continued during the second stage. Literary education should be allotted more time according to necessity.
19. The boys during this stage should be taught their parents' vocation in such a way that they will by their own choice obtain their livelihood by practising the hereditary craft. This does not apply to the girls.
20. During this stage the child should acquire a general knowledge of world history and geography, botany, astronomy, arithmetic, geometry and algebra.
21. Each child should now be taught to sew and to cook.
22. Sixteen to twenty-five is the third stage, during which every young person should have an education according to his or her wishes and circumstances.
23. During the second stage (9–16) education should be self-supporting; that is, the child, all the time that he is learning, is working upon some industry, the proceeds of which will meet the expenditure of the school.
24. Production starts from the very beginning, but during the first stage it does not still catch up with the expenditure.
25. Teachers should be paid not very high salaries but only a living wage. They should be inspired by a spirit of service. It is a despicable thing to take any Tom, Dick or Harry as a teacher in the primary stage. All teachers should be men of character.
26. Big and expensive buildings are not necessary for educational institutions.
27. English should be taught only as one of several languages. As Hindi is the national language, English is to be used in dealing with other nations and international commerce.

As for women's education I am not sure whether it should be different from men's and when it should begin. But I am strongly of opinion that women should have the same facilities as men and even special facilities where necessary.

There should be night schools for illiterate adults. But I do not think that they must be taught the three R's; they must be helped to acquire general knowledge through lectures, etc., and if they wish, we should arrange to teach them the three R's also.

Experiments in the Ashram have convinced us of one thing, *viz.*, that industry in general and spinning in particular should have pride of place in education, which must be largely self-supporting as well as related to and tending to the betterment of rural life.

In these experiments we have achieved the largest measure of success with the women, who have imbibed the spirit of freedom and self-confidence as no other class of women have done to my knowledge. This success is due to the Ashram atmosphere.

Women in the Ashram are not subject to any restraint which is not imposed on the men as well. They are placed on a footing of absolute equality with the men in all activities. Not a single Ashram task is assigned to the women to the exclusion of the men. Cooking is attended to by both. Women are of course exempted from work which is beyond their strength; otherwise men and women work together everywhere. There is no such thing as purdah or laj in the Ashram. No matter from where she has come, a woman, as soon as she enters the Ashram, breathes the air of freedom and casts out all fear from her mind. And I believe that the Ashram observance of Brahmacharya has made a big contribution to this state of things. Adult girls live in the Ashram as virgins. We are aware that this experiment is fraught with risk but we feel that no awakening among women is possible without incurring it.

Women cannot make any progress so long as there are child marriages. All girls are supposed to be in duty bound to marry and that too before menstruation commences, and widow remarriage is not permitted. Women, therefore, when they join the Ashram, are told that these social customs are wrong and irreligious. But they are not shocked as they find the Ashram practising what it preaches.

Not much of what is usually called education will be observed in the Ashram. Still we find that the old as well as the young, women as well as men are eager to acquire knowledge and complain that they have no time for it. This is a good sign.

Real education begins after a child has left school. One who has appreciated the value of studies is a student all his life. His knowledge must increase from day to day while he is discharging his duty in a conscientious manner. And this is well understood in the Ashram.

The superstition that no education is possible without a teacher is an obstacle in the path of educational progress. A man's real teacher is himself. And nowadays there numerous aids available for self-education. A diligent person can easily acquire knowledge about many things by himself and obtain the assistance of a teacher when it is needed. Experience is the biggest of all schools. Quite a number of crafts cannot be learnt at school but only in the workshop. Knowledge of these acquired at school is often only parrotlike. Other subjects can be learnt with the help of books. Therefore what adults need is not so much a school as a thirst for knowledge, diligence and self-confidence.

The education of children is primarily a duty to be discharged by the parents. Therefore the creation of a vital educational atmosphere is more important than the foundation of numerous schools. When once this atmosphere has been established on a firm footing the schools will come in due course. *(History of the Satyagraha Ashram, 11 July 1932 (CW 50, pp. 232–36))*

National Gujarati School

For many years past, several friends and I have felt that our present education is not national and that in consequence people do not get from it the benefit they ought to. Our children languish as a result of this education. They become incapable of any great achievement and the knowledge they acquire does not spread among the masses—not even in their families. Nor do the young people have any aim in mind in taking this modern education except to get a job and make money. It is one of the fundamental principles of education that it should be planned with a view to the needs of the people. This idea finds no place at all in our schools. Wherever I have travelled in India, I have discussed this question with the leaders and, without exception, almost every one has admitted that our educational system must change.

To look to the Government for this will be sheer waste of time. The Government will wait on public opinion and, being foreign, move very timidly; it cannot understand our needs, its advisers may be ill-informed or they may have interests of their own to serve. For a variety of such reasons, it will probably be quite long before there is any serious change in the present system; the time that passes meanwhile is so much loss to the people.

It is, however, not intended to suggest here that we should not try to get the Government to move. Let petitions be made to it and let public opinion be ascertained. But the best petition to the Government will be an actual demonstration by us and this will also be the easiest way of cultivating public opinion. It has accordingly been decided, in consultation with some educated gentlemen, to start a national school.

Basic principle: The education will be physical, intellectual and religious.

For physical education, there will be training in agriculture and hand-weaving and in the use of carpenter's and blacksmith's tools incidental to these. That will provide sufficient exercise for the pupils. In addition, they will be given drill, which is both an entertainment [and a practical utility] and, as part of this, they will be taught how to march in squads and how each one may work with quiet efficiency in case of accidents such as fire.

They will have instruction on how to preserve health and on home remedies for ordinary ailments, with as much of physiology and botany as may be necessary for the purpose.

For intellectual training, they will study Gujarati, Marathi, Hindi and Sanskrit as compulsory subjects. Urdu, Tamil and Bengali will also be taught.

There will be no teaching of English during the first three years.

In addition, the pupils will be taught Mathematics (Arithmetic, Algebra and Geometry). Instruction in multiplication tables, Indian book-keeping and the measures, weights, etc., currently in use will begin at once and the rest of the curriculum will be covered progressively.

There will be instruction in History, Geography, Elements of Astronomy and Elements of Chemistry.

By way of instruction in religion, pupils will be taught general ethical principles and we are hopeful that the teachers will demonstrate by their conduct that the essence of religion is good character.

All teaching will be through Gujarati, right up to the highest stage, and most of it will be oral during the first few years. The intention is to put across to the children, before they learn to read and write, quite a few things orally by way of stories, as was the practice in old days, and so help their minds to grow, and to give them some general knowledge as they play about, rather than repress them by doing nothing more than remarking, "Oh dear, dear! How dirty", and so on.

Explanation

The aim at present is that after a few years of such education, the student's equipment will approximate to that of a well-informed graduate. That is, he will have a reduced load by way of learning English and, during the time so saved, he will be given all the useful knowledge a graduate acquires. He will be freed from the fear of examinations. All the students will be tested from time to time, but that will be by the teachers of the school itself. The use to which the student puts his abilities after leaving school will be the true measure of the worth of his education.

Every opportunity will be taken to rid his mind of the fallacious notion that the aim of education is to get employment. And, finally, every pupil joining this school is likely to develop such self-confidence in a few years that he will not be troubled with doubts or fears about how he will make a living. A pupil who has been in the school for five years will be fixed up, if he so desires, in some work in the school itself and be paid for it. The school will make arrangements with some factories, etc., so that they provide training in vocations and give a start to those who wish to set themselves up independently. If, after ten years of study, anyone wants to pursue a subject further, necessary arrangements for the purpose are left to the future.

Free Education

No fees will be charged in this school, the expenses being met from donations received.

Teachers

Paid teachers will be engaged and will be, all of them, grown-up men who have reached the college level or possess equivalent attainments. The idea is that children should have the best teachers in the early stages.

Objects of School

1. To adopt a new method of education.
2. To pay special attention to character-building, the aim being that ten per cent of the pupils at any rate get trained for national service.
3. To raise the status of the Gujarati language.
4. To work for the spread of the national language, Hindi.
5. To open schools of the new pattern in every place, and make this school a model for them, and for Government as well, to copy. The aim is to have teachers trained in this school who will then go to villages and run schools there.
6. To get the new pattern adopted by the Government.

Requirements for Teachers

1. Knowledge of Hindi and Marathi
2. Proficiency in weaving
3. Well-preserved health
4. Travel in India
5. Readiness for other work besides that in the school, that is, for work in the Ashram or as secretary to Bapu

Work to be Attended to by Teachers, Apart from Teaching

1. Textbooks
2. Vocabulary of technical terms

Co-Education

I am myself in favour of coeducation, but I don't insist on it if the teachers hold a different opinion. I am not in favour of common residence. Girls should not be kept in a hostel. I am of the view that they must live under the constant supervision of their mothers and nowhere else. There should be holidays in summer and the school should be shifted to a cooler place. This, I believe, will enable the teachers and the pupils to work very much better at other times. The teachers and the pupils should spend the holidays together.

English should be an optional subject. One should know good, at any rate correct, English. It would be excellent if we could get an English teacher for the purpose, but I can think of no one at present except Miss Schlesin. If only she would come, we could want nothing better. She is a very capable person. A pupil of the school should be able to talk in English with any Englishman without being nervous. Drawing will be taught not as a fine art but because the pupil should be able to draw for practical purposes, draw maps, for instance, and straight lines, have a good handwriting and should know memory drawing.

Rules should be framed for discipline in the school, but no compulsion should be used to enforce obedience to them; they [the pupil] should feel inclined to obey them on their own. One should keep a watch on them whether they do. If any of them does not, we should express our disapproval and advise him. To start with, 100 pupils should be admitted to the school, all of whom can pay for their own expenses. Nothing may be spent from the School Fund for any of the pupils. If there is a good but poor student, we may secure help for him from one of our friends and beg of another for his fees; but the School Fund cannot be used for the purpose.

History, Geography, Science and Hygiene can be part of Gujarati.

We have necessarily to come into contact with people from the South, and this is to our benefit too; everyone should, therefore, know Marathi. *(After 18 January 1917; 23 June 1917 (CW 13, pp. 332–34, 447–48))*

True National Education

Our teachers must be men of high moral character. Conditions must be created to enable the poorest Indian to receive the best possible education. There must be a happy union of literary knowledge and Dharma. Education must be related to the conditions of life in our country. And the heavy burden on the minds of our young men resulting from the use of an alien language as the medium of instruction must be removed. Unless we reshape our education so as to fulfil the foregoing the level of the life of our people cannot be raised.

True national education should be imparted through the language of each province. The teachers must be men of high ability. The school should be located at a place where students would get clean drinking water, pure air and a peaceful atmosphere. The surroundings must be perfectly healthy. The scheme of education must provide for securing to the students a knowledge of the main occupations and religions of India.

[Except]... the first five years of a child's life, the rest of his education is given through a foreign language. Besides, in the first five years, which are in some respects the most useful and of the greatest importance, education is usually imparted by the most ordinary type of teachers. Then begins English. At this stage the boys pass as if into a different world altogether. The education which is given to them has no relation to the life at home. The boys who till then were quite happy to do their lessons sitting on the ground now have benches. At home, even today, the prevailing custom in most homes is to sit on the floor. Until then, the boy, if he was a Hindu, was content to wear a dhoti, a kurta and the angarakha and, if a Muslim, to wear the payjamas instead of the dhoti; but now he uses a coat and trousers.

Until then, he could do with the homely kalam, but now he has a pen with a steel nib. Thus, many significant changes take place in his outer living and a wide gulf divides the home and the school. Gradually, but definitely, this change begins to enter his inner life too. How are these changes in the outer life and the inner mental make-up of the boy going to affect his home and the way his people live at home? His parents have no idea at all as to what sort of education the boy is getting and their faith in that education is negligible.

Parents only know that it will help the boy to earn money. And this satisfies them. If this situation lasts long, we might all become foreigners! What is worse even the Swaraj for which we are struggling may become foreign in character when we finally get it, with the result that the very burden under which we are crushed today may continue even after Swaraj. There is only one way to escape this danger. It is to change and overhaul our system of education. In the national education to be evolved:

1. Education must be imparted through the mother-tongue.
2. There must be accord between the education a child receives at school and the environment of the home.
3. It must be so planned as to meet the needs of the majority of the people.
4. The teachers in primary classes must be competent men of good character right from the first class.
5. Education must be free.
6. Overall control must be in the hands of the people.

Education must be imparted through the mother-tongue. It is a pity that we are required to prove this self-evident truth. If we had not been dazzled by the lure of English, there should have been no need to prove this most obvious truth. The advocates of English say:

1. It is through English that an awakening has been created in the country.
2. English literature is so rich and vast that to give it up would be a great misfortune. It is not possible to translate it all into our language.
3. We can achieve unity only through English. To try to encourage and promote the different languages of India would amount to disrupting this unity and retarding the growing feeling that we are one nation.
4. English is the language of the rulers.

These are the main arguments of the advocates of English. They have many other things to say, but they have no more substance or importance than is included in the above.

To say that all the awakening we see in the country has been brought about through English is only a half-truth. The fact is that all the education in the country is being imparted through English. And because the Hindus are not absolute blockheads they have imbibed and utilized the good they have found in it. And yet the overall result which this education has yielded has been disappointing. Everybody admits that the present system of education suffers from some grave defects. We have not received from it the results which we are entitled to expect of an education which has now lasted for more than fifty years. Why is it so?

If it had been imparted from the beginning through the mother-tongue it would have produced much good by this time. What only a few English-knowing people know at present would have spread and reached crores of our people – who would have shown the spirit and the strength which is now shown only by the English-knowing handful. At present, our young men, when they pass out of the college, appear to be devoid of all energy and just wander about in search of jobs. Instead, if they had been educated through the mother-tongue, then having been spared the strain of cramming, they would have been stronger both in body and mind and would have therefore rejected Government service as something inferior.

No one suggests that English literature should be given up. We should have translated what is precious in it into our different languages. Japan and South Africa have done it. In Japan, they taught German and French to some who then translated good books from German and French into Japanese. It is not that German has nothing to borrow from English. Even so, not all Germans learn English. No German receives his education through English. Only a few Germans learn English and then translate into German whatever they think will be of value to their nation, and thus serve their mother-tongue. We should do the same.

As to the assumption that we have received a sense of unity by using English, the fact is that we become sharply aware of the illusion of our separateness from one another only after this alien language was introduced into our country, though it may be admitted that once we had seen through that illusion we strove to throw it off and regain our national solidarity. We observe that in many countries the oneness of the people is not always due to the oneness of the language. There are two languages in South Africa. But the people are striving to achieve unity because their interests are the same. Similar is the case with Canada. In England, Scotland and Wales they still speak three different languages. Mr. Lloyd George is making great efforts to revive Welsh, the language of Wales. And, yet, in all the three parts of Great Britain there is a strong feeling that they are one nation. Development of the regional languages of our country will produce social, political and economic awakening amongst our people.

They will have a better appreciation of their condition and position in the picture of the wider whole of the country. They will know that though belonging to different provinces they are sailing in the same boat. Thus they will forget differences of language, appreciate the unity of their interests and be ready to fight for it, and protect it from dangers. Besides, the better educated amongst us will have to learn Hindi—as the common medium of speech. The effort required to learn Hindi is as nothing compared to that needed to learn English.

That English is the language of the rulers proves nothing beyond the fact that some of us have to master this alien tongue. I do not dislike English; I am only pleading that it be put in its proper place. Then, we can truly appreciate its merits, and derive such benefit as we can. It cannot, however, continue to be the medium of our education; nor can it be the language of interprovincial communication. In our schools and colleges we must provide for imparting even the highest education through the mother-tongue.

There must be accord between the education given in the school and the home. The reason for this is obvious. Today, there is no such accord between the two. In national education, we must see that such accord is achieved and maintained.

We will now pass on to the third attribute of national education, namely, that it should be so designed as to meet the needs of the majority of the people. The great bulk of our people are peasants. So, if our boys had been given, from the very beginning, a knowledge of agriculture and weaving and if they had cultivated an appreciation of the needs of these two classes, and if these classes had received the scientific training in these vocations, our peasants today would have been happy and prosperous. Our cattle would not have been weak and diseased as they are today. Our peasants would not have been crushed with the weight of debt—incurred by poverty. Our produce would not have first gone to foreign countries as raw material and then brought back to us in the shape of finished goods to drain us of wealth. Today, we feel ashamed of such a state of affairs. We could not have paid England 85 crores rupees a year for cotton cloth. The prevailing system of education has made slaves of us instead of masters.

In the lower stages of primary education teachers must be men of high character. There is a proverb in English: 'The child is the father of the man.' We have a similar proverb: 'A child, even while in the cradle, shows signs of what he is going to be in the future.' If we entrust our children, in their most impressionable years, to incompetent teachers, we have no right to expect that they will grow to be men of good and strong character. That would be as absurd as to sow the seeds of kauvach and expect from them the flowers of mogra. We must procure the best teachers for our children whatever it may cost. In ancient times, our children received their education from learned and wise Rishis and Munis.

The fifth requirement of national education is that it should be free. Education should not be made to depend on money. Just as the sun gives light to all equally and rain pours down for all, even so learning must be made available to all.

Lastly, the people themselves must have control over the planning and carrying out of education. In the exercise of this control lies education too. People will then have faith in the education meted out to their children, and feel their responsibility towards it. When this stage is reached and education occupies an important place in the life of our people, it will be possible for us to obtain Swaraj with no trouble at all. Therefore, it is our duty to initiate such education. It is also our right to ask the Government for it. But we can approach the Government about this matter only after we start the ball rolling ourselves. However, it is beyond the scope of this article to discuss the steps we should take for organizing such a type of national education. Let people first accept the view expressed herein. *(Atmoddhar – a Marathi Monthly, True Education, pp. 39–44)*

National Higher Education

I have done a good many things in my life; some of them I feel proud of, though some others I regret. A few of them were very responsible undertakings. But I should like to state here – I am sure I am guilty of no exaggeration – that nothing I have done so far can stand comparison with what we are about to do today. I am aware of a great risk in this undertaking, but not because I fear that it may prove harmful to the nation; what pains me, or rather the incongruity I feel, is this that I am not fit for the task I have undertaken. I do not say this as a matter of formality, I speak from the heart.

If I knew that the present undertaking related to education in the real sense of the term, this preface would not have been necessary. This Mahavidyalaya is not being established with the sole object of imparting education; it [also] aims at helping the student to acquire a means of livelihood and when, in this respect, I compare it with Gujarat College and other similar institutions, I simply shudder.

In this, too, I am not exaggerating. What comparison is possible between Gujarat College and other similar colleges, on the one hand, and this small Mahavidyalaya of ours? To my mind, of course, it is great, but I am afraid that in your eyes, as you compare this Vidyalaya with the colleges you have in India, this Mahavidyalaya probably appears an Anuvidyalaya. You are very likely thinking in terms of brick and mortar. Of this, to be sure, I see more in Gujarat College.

Today, not an inch of the ground is ours. Everything belongs to the Government. This land, these trees, everything belongs to Government, even this body, and I have now begun to doubt whether our soul also is ours. Placed in this pitiable condition, why go looking for good buildings to house our Mahavidyalaya? How can we afford to wait till we had found men of great learning? Even if the most ignorant of ignorant men, a mere simpleton, were to come forward and could succeed in convincing us that our atman had been starved, that this country had lost its light—its knowledge of things of the spirit—I would appoint him as the principal. I am not sure that you would be ready to appoint a shepherd as principal and so we have had to find Shri Gidwani. I have not been attracted by the position he occupied. Perhaps you do not know him apart from that position. I should, however, like you to adopt a different criterion, some another touchstone, for judging the worth of this Vidyalaya if you test it on the common touchstone, it will seem to be brass but it will be found to be gold if you test it on the touchstone of character.

The coming together of [talented] men for educational work here is like the holy confluence of rivers. We have men of character assembled here. Fine men from Sind, Maharashtra and Gujarat have banded together here. How could we have, ordinarily, secured this?

I shall first address my prayer to the sisters and brothers who have come here for the function. You are witnesses to the establishment of this Mahavidyalaya. If there are any among you who feel that what is taking place is a farce, I would ask them not to be so conscientious and sit through the function. They should remain only if they wish to give their blessings. With the blessings of you all, the Mahavidyalaya will earn a name as a great institution. But they should not be blessings merely uttered with the lips; bless it from your heart. This you can do only by offering your sons and daughters to the institution. People in India have plenty of capacity to contribute money. In no field is progress held up for lack of funds. It is held up for want of men—of teachers or leaders, or if a leader is forthcoming, for want of pupils, *i.e.*, soldiers. It is my belief that, if the leader is worthy, there will be no lack of soldiers. A carpenter will not quarrel with his tools, however bad they may be. He will handle the bluntest of them with the utmost ease. Likewise, if the leader is a real artisan, whatever the quality of the material, he will produce gold from it, will produce gold from the country's clay. This is my prayer to the principal.

You, principal and teachers, have been inspired by one ideal only in joining this institution. You have undertaken to secure freedom through the miracle not of learning but of character, secure it not by meeting the Government, sword against its shining sword, but with peaceful, spiritual effort—howsoever imperfect it be—against its aggressive, Satanic way. We want just now to sow the seed of freedom and afterwards we will water the plant and rear it into a tree. This tree can be raised only through character, with pure, spiritual strength.

So long as the principal and the teachers go on working with their eyes on this one aim, we shall never be put to shame. May God justify in your experience the faith which is mine. Were it not for this unshakable faith of mine, I would not at all have accepted the sacred position of chancellor. I am ready to live and die for this cause, thinking that to die in this cause is to live; it is because I know that this is also true of you that I live among you and have accepted this exalted position.

We are establishing this Vidyalaya, not with an educational, but with a national aim in view. Advising that students be taught to cultivate strength and character, I have been saying everywhere that in the measure we succeed with them we shall make ourselves fit for Swaraj in the country. Swaraj cannot be secured in any other way. No amount of money we can spend or strength of character we can employ to ensure the success of such colleges will be enough.

This is a time not for words but for action. I have placed my thoughts before you as they came. I asked of you what you could give. Now I shall ask something of the students as well. There is no doubt at all that they have in them the courage which takes risks. I shall not look upon them-upon those who have already joined—as mere students and, therefore, I will not treat them as being free from responsibility. Those who have registered their names here are half teachers. It is they who have provided the foundation for the Mahavidyalaya.

It is on them that the structure of the institution has been raised. Had they not joined, this Mahavidyalaya could not have been started. They also, therefore, share equal responsibility. You are equal partners in this and, if you do not play your part well, no efforts on the part of the teachers will succeed or, at any rate, succeed completely. Students who have left their colleges should understand why they have joined here and what they should expect to gain. May God grant them the strength to go on with their work, no matter how long this grim war continues. If they do, I am sure that, even if they are a mere handful, this Mahavidyalaya will shine forth and be a model institution for the whole country.

The reason will not be that Gujarat has wealth or that it has learning; it will be rather, that noncooperation had its origin here. The seed was sown and watered here, the required tapascharaya was performed here. Do not think from this that I am a conceited man to speak in this manner, or that all the tapascharaya has been mine and the seed was sown by me. I merely gave the mantra, I fulfilled the function of a rishi, if a Vanik's son can do so.

I have done nothing more than this. The planting was done by my co-workers. It is because their faith was greater than mine that we have succeeded. I claim the knowledge which comes from direct perception. Even if the gods came down and tried to persuade me to the contrary, my faith would not be shaken. As surely as I see, with my eyes, the trees in front of me, so surely I know that there is no salvation for India except through nonviolent noncooperation. As for my co-workers, however, they have believed this through logic or reasoning or accepted it on faith.

My co-workers have laid the foundation. Many of them are Gujaratis; there are Maharashtrians, too, but having been in Gujarat, they have become half or three-quarters Gujaratis or, perhaps, more Gujaratis than the Gujaratis themselves. They have made this a weapon of shining strength. We have not yet seen all its miraculous power. Within six months, you will see more of the miraculous power of this programme for which young girls handed over their bangles to me. But the source of it all—the visible image—is this Mahavidyalaya. Hindus are worshippers of images and we are proud of being so. This image has its various limbs: one of them is the chancellor and that is myself. The teachers, the principal and the students are other limbs. I am, myself, an old man, a withering leaf, and busy with other work. The falling away of such a leaf as I am can do no harm to a tree. The principal and the teachers, too, are no more than leaves, though green leaves as yet. In a short while, they also will grow old and, perhaps, fall off. The students, however, are the branches of this beautiful tree and it is on them that principals and teachers will grow as leaves.

I request them to put the same faith in their teachers as they do in me. Should they, however, see that the principal or any of the teachers is weak, let them burn him to ashes with the fire which was Prahlad's and go ahead with their work. This is my prayer to God and my blessings to the students.

I shall end with a prayer to God and I want you all to say "amen" to it. Join me in my prayer, all of you, with a pure heart, "God! Make this Mahavidyalaya of such worth that through it we may win the freedom for which we offer prayers day and night and grant it that, through that freedom, not only India but the entire world, in which India is but a dot, may be happy." *(Inaugural speech at the setting up of Gujarat Vidyapith, 15 November 1920 Navajivan, 18 November 1920 (CW 18, pp. 463–68) (Translated from Gujarati))*

National Institutions

Since some of the staunchest supporters of noncooperation have lost faith in it and since the numbers attending national institutions are dwindling, what is the use of holding on to these tottering schools and colleges and wasting good money after bad institutions?

My believing eye detects a flaw in this argument. My faith in noncooperation remaining as staunch as ever, I can find it possible to reconcile myself to the existing national institutions even though the attendance may be reduced to half a dozen. For the half a dozen will be the makers of Swaraj whenever it comes. When virgins are required to perform certain sacred ceremonies, others are not accepted as substitute if no virgin is found. And even one virgin if found is enough to save the situation. So will it be with the planting of the Swaraj flag-post. The flags will be unfurled with the unsullied hands of those, be they ever so few, who have remained true to their original creed.

I do not therefore regard it as waste of money to continue the national institutions. They are so many oases in the desert. They give the water of life to the souls thirsting for freedom. In writing this I cast no reflection upon those who attend or otherwise support Government schools. They are entitled to hold the view if they choose that theirs is the only way or also a way to freedom. National institutions are meant for those whose thirst for freedom is not satisfied by the ones managed or patronized by the Government. Few as they are, insignificant though they may appear, they supply a felt want and contain in them the seeds, as it appears to non-co-operators, of true and lasting freedom.

The final success of these institutions depends upon the worth of the teachers. "But they are deserting the national schools and colleges," says the critic. So some of them are. It tries the faith of the survivors. Have they the courage to stand alone? Are there enough monied men to support the surviving national institutions? On the correct answer to these questions depends the future of the national institutions and with them the freedom of the country, and so far as I can judge, there are teachers enough to stand the severest test and there are monied men enough to support them. I know no organisation that has died for want of funds. Organisations die always for want of men, *i.e.*, honesty, efficiency and self-sacrifice. And it is my certain knowledge that where there are teachers, pupils are not wanting.

But the pupils have perhaps the largest share of responsibility on their shoulders. The future depends upon their ability, integrity, application, and patriotism. The teachers cannot give what the pupils have not. The teachers can help to 'draw out' in the pupils what they have. If it were otherwise, if the teachers were capable of putting something into their pupils, all the latter receiving instruction under them will be alike, whereas we know as a matter of fact that no two pupils have been yet known to be alike. The pupils must therefore have initiative. They must cease to be mere imitators. They must learn to think and act for themselves and yet be thoroughly obedient and disciplined. The highest form of freedom carries with it the greatest measure of discipline and humility. Freedom that comes from discipline and humility cannot be denied; unbridled licence is a sign of vulgarity injurious alike to self and one's neighbours. *(Young India, 3 June 1926 (CW 30, pp. 519–20)*

Non-Co-operation Movement's First University

Kakasaheb is writing about what Gujarat Vidyapith has done and what it is trying to achieve. There is one bit of criticism, however, to which he cannot reply. Some say that the Vidyapith has met with disaster since he took charge of it. If it has been ruined, I am responsible for it, not Kakasaheb. This is because so long as the people are enamoured of me or are fond of me and largely accept my advice, I am responsible for the changes that have been made in the Vidyapith. I was primarily responsible for the boycott of Government schools and for formulating a policy for national education. This I must humbly say or admit.

It was I who brought over Acharya Gidwani and it is I who asked him to step down. Kakasaheb was connected with the Vidyapith ever since its inception. Again, it was I who took him away from the Vidyapith. During Acharya Gidwani's term of office, the Vidyapith attracted students, land was bought for it and buildings were erected. Perhaps the Vidyapith would not be there if there were no Acharya Gidwani. He had promised me twice that he would readily come over whenever I summoned him. I received Vallabhabhai's telegram in Bhiwani in which he had suggested that Acharya Gidwani should take charge of the Vidyapith. He immediately agreed to do so. And in a few days, the first noncooperation university in India was launched.

The treaty that was made between Gujarat and Sind by bringing him over to the former place is still there. I withdrew Acharya Gidwani because of a difference of opinion that arose in the Vidyapith. That did not imply any slur on anyone. It is my conviction that even today, Acharya Gidwani belongs to Gujarat. He went over to Prem Mahavidyalaya because Gujarat sent him there. And today he is in Karachi, only as a delegate from Gujarat. At all the three places, it is hoped, the national viewpoint will be fostered. At all the three places, there will certainly be propaganda for Khadi.

Acharya Kripalani was borrowed from the Kashi Ashram, which is his own creation. I relieved him as I had promised to do so. Under his leadership, too, the Vidyapith has not taken a retrograde step. At the time of the students' strike, we saw that he had stolen the hearts of the students. Acharya Kripalani was a second gift that Sind gave to Gujarat. Even today, he belongs to Gujarat. In my opinion, under his leadership also the Vidyapith has progressed. Although all may have a common ideal, there is naturally a difference in the work and character of every man.

And, it is in accordance with this that an institution which is in charge of a particular person develops and takes on a distinct colour. However, in regard to the Vidyapith, I have felt that this variety has been as beautiful as the variety in the colours of a rainbow. Whereas one principal has strengthened one aspect of it, another has done the same for another aspect of it. The result has only been good. At present the rudder is in the hands of Kakasaheb. He has been moulding the Vidyapith.

The Vidyapith has not crumbled; it is going ahead. So long as Kakasaheb is at the helm, all that needs to be said with regard to it is that anyone who has any doubts about it should go there and inspect it. Just as all the three principals have been complementary to one another, the periods to which they belonged also stand in the same relationship to one another. As all the three are fruits of the same tree, there is a continuity hidden behind their work. Not even one of them has wiped out what had been achieved before, but has added to the sum total of its achievements. The present state of the Vidyapith, itself bears testimony to this. At the very inception of the Vidyapith, I had suggested a test for judging it; that holds good even today.

The Vidyapith is going to be judged neither by its buildings nor by the number of its students, nor again by the knowledge of English that its students possess. It is going to be judged by the patriotism of its students, by their capacity to give to others the knowledge of the subjects which they have learnt, by their knowledge of Hindi by their knowledge of the science of the spinning-wheel, by the strength of character of its students and teachers, and by their turning towards the villages. Judged by these standards, it is my confirmed belief that the Vidyapith has taken forward strides and anyone who wishes to ascertain this can do so by going over to examine it. Just as a tree is judged by its fruit, the Vidyapith can be examined in a similar manner. It is not a distant institution about which an investigator would need a testimonial from me or from anyone else. Moreover, it is fair to scrutinize a thing personally, wherever this is possible and where such a scrutiny is necessary. After conducting this inquiry if it is felt that the Vidyapith has made continuous progress and has augmented its capacity to serve, it is only fitting that contributions should flow in to its doors. *(Navajivan, 29 December 1929 (CW 42, pp. 327–29) (Translated from Gujarati))*

Salt Satyagraha

It has been often said that the money spent on national education in general and the Gujarat Vidyapith in particular has been so much waste. In my opinion the Gujarat Vidyapith by its supreme sacrifice has more than justified its existence, the hopes entertained by its authors and the grants made to it by donors. For the Vidyapith has suspended its literary activities save for boys under 16 who are already under training there. The teachers and students of over 15 years of age have offered their services as volunteers and nearly forty students with the teachers are already in the field.

A class for giving fifteen days' emergency training in connection with Satyagraha has been opened for the sake of those who may need such training. I congratulate the students and the teachers on the promptitude with which they have acted. I may state that twenty of these are with me on the march. They are divided into two parties, both preceding the 80 pilgrims to make preparations in advance and assisting the villagers. They are under orders not to offer civil resistance till the 80 are arrested and immediately to replace them as soon as they are arrested.

I am sure that every national educational institution will copy the noble example of the Gujarat Vidyapith which was the first to come into being in response to the call of noncooperation in 1920. And I hope that the Government and aided institutions will also copy the example. Every revolution of modern times has found students in the forefront. This, because it is peaceful, ought not to offer less attraction to the students. *(Young India, 20 March 1930 (CW 43, pp. 109–10))*

Freedom Struggle

I learnt what happened in India after my arrest in Karadi only through the newspapers. Later on, after my release, I also heard about it from the people. I have heard so much about the part that the Vidyapiths—our national schools and colleges—have played in the movement that I am really overwhelmed with joy. I have come to know more about the Gujarat Vidyapith as also of the Bihar and Kashi Vidyapiths. It is no small matter that the teachers and students from all these three institutions cast aside their books and came to join the fight for freedom. When the history of this fight comes to be written the world will be glad to know of the great part played in it by the students and the national Vidyapiths. While in jail, whenever I read anything in the newspapers about the students and the teachers, I would at once make a comparison between them and those in Government schools. As a result of which it became clear to me how correct we were in launching the programme of the boycott of Government schools in 1920.

It is true that the Government schools are yet as crowded with students as they used to be. And it is even more tragic that the students are so eager to enter them that they ask for pardon, pay fines and somehow secure admission into them. This so far emboldens the heads of the colleges, or the authorities of the education department, that they send circulars that before admitting the students who have taken a direct or indirect part in the fight or who have gone to jail the matter should first be referred to the head of the education department. It is he who is to permit their admission after studying their cases. What are we to think of students who thus seek entrance into Government schools and colleges at the cost of their self-respect, and what of the authorities of the education department who insist on such conditions?

So much about the achievement of our college section. Let me now draw your attention to Appendix III of the Report of the Vidyapith. It mentions the names of the teachers and students who had gone to jail. Kakasaheb has said that what the students have learnt in the past one year, they had never learnt before, though the Vidyapith was the same; it was no less national then, and yet we did not then achieve as much as in the past year. And in future too whenever there is a call for the fight and we fill the jails, we will again have the satisfaction of having done our duty which is the greatest gift of knowledge. We believe that when we do so we shall be true teachers and students.

The point is that the Snataka and Gramseva-Dikshitas should not think that they are the product of any ordinary school. What can we do; we too have to earn a living; fate has brought us to the Vidyapith, so willy-nilly we must act as we are asked to! You should never entertain such thoughts in your mind even for a moment. Even though superficially you may appear to be only a handful, really you are like a sea, while the others, though they may appear to be as big as a sea, are really a phantom which has no existence. It is difficult, if not impossible, to instil in them the courage and the power to win Swaraj. As to the cultivation of that power in national schools, we can see it in these students. Those who have seen their work will bear witness to the fact that we have not lost anything in setting up these Vidyapiths. On the contrary, we have fully recovered with interest the money gifted for it. *(Navajivan, 3 May 1931 (CW 45, pp. 407–08))*

The Spinning Wheel Message

The real work of the Vidyapith lies in the villages. I have been stressing this point ever since the inception of the Vidyapith, but until a couple of years ago, when it was declared an illegal organisation and most of our professors and boys were imprisoned, we laboured under the impression that the work could be carried on only through a central institute situated in the capital town of Gujarat. But under the altered conditions and now that we have some breathing time to put our heads together and to collect our thoughts, we shall do well to hark back to the original conception and think of our future work in its terms. Each member of a live institution must be a living embodiment of the ideals of the institution, wherever he may be, and when such a state of things is brought about, it is the same thing whether the institution has a habitation and a corporate existence or not.

I would, therefore, expect every one of you who has cherished the ideals of the Vidyapith and who is pledged to serve it to go straight to the villages and start living those ideals there. Each one of you will thus be a peripatetic Vidyapith, teaching the ideals by means of his own personal example. It is quite conceivable that a host of workers, after having lived the life in the villages according to the ideals of the Vidyapith, re-establish the central institute in a village. But we are not in that position today. We have yet to gain all that experience on which alone you can build the new Vidyapith.

The centre of this village worker's life will be the spinning-wheel. I am sorry I have not been able yet to bring home to anyone the message of the spinning-wheel in all its implication. The reason is that my life itself is not a true echo of the message. But it came home to me again and again during my nine months' peregrinations in India. We have not yet sufficiently realized that hand-spinning is a supplementary industry of universal application and scope in India. The village weaver cannot live but for the spinning-wheel. He gets his yarn no doubt from the mills, but he is doomed to destruction, if he is to remain for ever dependent on the mills. Today, the spinning-wheel has established itself in our economic life only to the extent that it is needed to minister to the clothing needs of the new class of khadi weavers that has sprung up during the past decade.

But a large body like the Spinners' Association cannot justify its existence to fulfil that limited object. The idea at the back of khadi is that it is an industry supplementary to agriculture and coextensive with it, that it is the life-breath of millions of Harijan weavers who derive their sustenance from it. The spinning-wheel cannot be said to have been established in its own proper place in our life, until we can banish idleness from our villages and make every village home a busy hive. Unemployment and idleness of millions must lead to bloody strife. Khadi is the only alternative to this and not the so called socialism, which presupposes industrialism. The socialism that India can assimilate is the socialism of the spinning-wheel. Let the village worker, therefore, make the wheel the central point of his activities.

The worker will not be spinning regularly but will be working for his bread with the adze or the spade or the last, as the case may be. All his hours minus the eight hours of sleep and rest will be fully occupied with some work. He will have no time to waste. He will allow himself no laziness and allow others none. His life will be a constant lesson to his neighbours in ceaseless and joy-giving industry. Bodily sustenance should come from body labour, and intellectual labour is necessary for the culture of the mind.

Division of labour there will necessarily be, but it will be a division into various species of body labour and not a division into intellectual labour to be confined to one class and body labour to be confined to another class. Our compulsory or voluntary idleness has to go. If it does not go, no panacea will be of any avail, and semi-starvation will remain the eternal problem that it is. He who eats two grains must produce four. Unless the law is accepted as universal, no amount of reduction in population would serve to solve the problem. If the law is accepted and observed, we have room enough to accommodate millions more to come.

The village worker will thus be a living embodiment of industry. He will master all the process of khadi, from cotton-sowing and picking to weaving, and will devote all his thought to perfecting them. If he treats it as a science, it won't jar on him, but he will derive fresh joy from it everyday, as he realizes more and more its great possibilities. If he will go to the village as a teacher, he will go there no less as a learner. He will soon find that he has much to learn from the simple villagers. He will enter into every detail of village life, he will discover the village handicrafts and investigate the possibilities of their growth and their improvement. He may find the villagers completely apathetic to the message of khadi, but he will, by his life of service compel interest and attention. Of course, he will not forget his limitations and will not engage in, for him, the futile task of solving the problem of agricultural indebtedness.

Sanitation and hygiene will engage a good part of his attention. His home and his surroundings will not only be a model of cleanliness, but he will help to promote sanitation in the whole village by taking the broom and the basket round.

He will not attempt to setup a village dispensary or to become the village doctor. These are traps which must be avoided. I happened during my Harijan tour to come across a village where one of our workers who should have known better had built a pretentious building in which he had housed a dispensary and was distributing free medicine to the villages around. In fact, the medicines were being taken from home to home by volunteers and the dispensary was described as boasting a register of 1,200 patients a month! I had naturally to criticize this severely. That was not the way to do village work, I told him. His duty was to inculcate lessons of hygiene and sanitation in the village folk and thus to show them the way of preventing illness, rather than attempt to cure them. I asked him to leave the palace-like building and to hire it out to the Local Board and to settle in thatched huts. All that one need stock in the way of drugs is quinine, castor oil and iodine and the like. The worker should concentrate more on helping people realize the value of personal and village cleanliness and maintaining it at all cost.

Then he will interest himself in the welfare of the village Harijans. His home will be open to them. In fact, they will turn to him naturally for help in their troubles and difficulties. If the village folk will not suffer him to have the Harijan friends in his house situated in their midst, he must take up his residence in the Harijan quarters.

A word about the knowledge of the alphabet. It has its place, but I should warn you against a misplaced emphasis on it. Do not proceed on the assumption that you cannot proceed with rural instruction without first teaching the children or adults how to read and write. Lots of useful information on current affairs, history, geography and elementary arithmetic, can be given by word of mouth before the alphabet is touched. The eyes, the ears and the tongue come before the hand. Reading comes before writing and drawing before tracing the letters of the alphabet. If this natural method is followed, the understanding of the children will have a much better opportunity of development than when it is under check by beginning the children's training with the alphabet.

The worker's life will be in tune with the village life. He will not pose as a literature buried in his book, loath to listen to details of humdrum life. On the contrary, the people, whenever they see him, will find him busy with his tools—spinning-wheel, loom, adze, spade, etc.—and always responsive to their meanest inquiries. He will always insist on working for his bread. God has given to everyone the capacity of producing more than his daily needs and, if he will only use his resourcefulness, he will not be in want of an occupation suited to his capacities, however poor they may be. It is more likely than not that the people will gladly maintain him, but it is not improbable that in some places he may be given a cold shoulder. He will still plod on. It is likely that in some villages he may be boycotted for his pro-Harijan proclivities. Let him in that case approach the Harijans and look to them to provide him with food. The labourer is always worthy of his hire and, if he conscientiously serves them, let him not hesitate to accept his food from the Harijans always, provided that he gives more than he takes. In the very early stages of course, he will draw his meagre allowance from a central fund where such is possible.

I have deliberately left out the question of the cow. The village worker will find it difficult to tackle the question and will not attempt it, except to the extent of educating the people in the theory of it. We have not yet hit upon the best way of curing dead cattle's hide and dyeing it, as also the best means of protecting the cow. In Gujarat the buffalo problem complicates the situation. We have got to make people realize that to encourage the buffalo is to allow the cow to die. But more of this some other time.

Remember that our weapons are spiritual. It is a force that works irresistibly, if imperceptibly. Its progress is geometrical rather than arithmetical. It never ceases so long as there is a propeller behind. The background of all your activities has therefore, to be spiritual. Hence the necessity for the strictest purity of conduct and character.

You will not tell me that this is an impossible programme, that you have not the qualifications for it. That you have not fulfilled it so far should be no impediment in your way. If it appeals to your reason and your heart, you must not hesitate. Do not fight shy of the experiment. The experiment will itself provide the momentum for more and more effort. *(Harijan, 31 August 1934 (CW 58, pp. 305–9))*

Village Schools

"The cruelest irony of the new Reforms lies in the fact that we are left with nothing but the liquor revenue to fall back upon in order to give our children education," said Gandhiji in one of the numerous talks he has been giving on the subject, ever since the Congress Ministers took up office. "That is the educational puzzle but it should not baffle us. We have to solve it and the solution must not involve the compromise of our ideal of prohibition cost whatever else it may.

It must be shameful and humiliating to think that unless we got the drink revenue, our children would be starved of their education. But if it comes to it, we should prefer it as a lesser evil. If only we will refuse to be obsessed by the figures and by the supposed necessity of giving our children the exact kind of education that they get today, the problem should not baffle us." That explains Gandhiji's emphasis on our educationists putting their heads together in order to evolve a system of education which is at once inexpensive and also in consonance with the needs of our vast rural population.

"Then you would really abolish what is called secondary education and give the whole education up to matriculation in the village schools?" asked a questioner in great surprise.

"Certainly. What is your secondary education but compelling the poor boys to learn in a foreign language in seven years what they should learn in the course of a couple of years in their own mother-tongue? If you can but make up your minds to free the children from the incubus of learning their subjects in a foreign tongue, and if you teach them to use their hands and feet profitably, the educational puzzle is solved. You can sacrifice without compunction the whole of the drink revenue. But you must resolve to sacrifice this revenue first, and think of the ways and means about education later. Make the beginning by taking the big step." *(Harijan, 21 August 1937 (CW 66, p. 57))*

Self-supporting Education

In spite of the weak state of his health and the quantities of rest that he needs, Gandhiji has shown his readiness to discuss his theory of self-supporting education with anyone who has thought about the subject and wants to contribute his share to making the new experiment a success. The discussions have been, in view of his health, necessarily few and brief, but every now and then something new has emerged, and whenever he has talked, he has had some fresh suggestion to make and fresh light to throw. Thus on one occasion he sounded a warning against the assumption that the idea of self-supporting education sprang from the necessity of achieving total prohibition as soon as possible. "Both are independent necessities," he said. "You have to start with the conviction that total prohibition has to be achieved revenue or no revenue, education or no education. Similarly, you have to start with the conviction that looking to the needs of the villages of India our rural education ought to be made self-supporting if it is to be compulsory."

"I have the first conviction deep down in me," said an educationist who carried on the discussion. "Prohibition to me is an end in itself, and I regard it as a great education in itself. I should, therefore, sacrifice education altogether to make prohibition a success. But the other conviction is lacking. I cannot yet believe that education can be made self-supporting."

"There, too, I want you to start with the conviction. The ways and means will come as you begin to work it out. I regret that I woke up to the necessity of this at this very late age. Otherwise I should have made the experiment my self. Even now, God willing, I shall do what I can to show that it can be self-supporting. But my time has been taken up by other things all these years, equally important perhaps; but it is this stay in Segaon that brought the conviction home to me. We have up to now concentrated on stuffing children's minds with all kinds of information, without ever thinking of stimulating and developing them. Let us now cry a halt and concentrate on educating the child properly through manual work, not as a side activity, but as the prime means of intellectual training."

"I see that too. But why should it also support the school?"

"That will be the test of its value. The child at the age of 14, that is, after finishing a seven years' course, should be discharged as an earning unit. Even now the poor people's children automatically lend a helping hand to their parents—the feeling at the back of their minds being, what shall my parents eat and what shall they give me to eat if I do not also work with them? That is an education in itself. Even so the State takes charge of the child at seven and returns it to the family as an earning unit. You impart education and simultaneously cut at the root of unemployment. You have to train the boys in one occupation or another. Round this special occupation you will train up his mind, his body, his writing, his artistic sense, and so on. He will be master of the craft he learns."

"But supposing a boy takes up the art and science of making Khadi. Do you think it must occupy him all the seven years to master the craft?"

"Yes. It must, if he will not learn it mechanically. Why do we give years to the study of history or to the study of languages? Is a craft any the less important than these subjects which have been up to now given an artificial importance?"

"But as you have been mainly thinking of spinning and weaving, evidently you are thinking of making of these schools so many weaving schools. A child may have no aptitude for weaving and may have it for something else."

"Quite so. Then we will teach him some other craft. But you must know that one school will not teach many crafts. The idea is that we should have one teacher for twenty-five boys, and you may have as many classes or schools of twenty-five boys as you have teachers available, and have each of these schools specializing in a separate craft—carpentry, smithy, tanning or shoe-making. Only you must bear in mind the fact that you develop the child's mind through each of these crafts. And I would emphasize one more thing. You must forget the cities and concentrate on the villages. They are an ocean. The cities are a mere drop in the ocean. That is why you cannot think of subjects like brick-making. If they must be civil and mechanical engineers, they will after the seven years' course go to the special colleges meant for these higher and specialized courses.

"And let me emphasize one more fact. We are apt to think lightly of the village crafts because we have divorced educational from manual training. Manual work has been regarded as something inferior, and owing to the wretched distortion of the varna we came to regard spinners and weavers and carpenters and shoemakers as belonging to the inferior castes, the proletariat. We have had no Cromptons and Hargreaves because of this vicious system of considering the crafts as something inferior, divorced from the skilled.

If they had been regarded as callings having an independent status that learning enjoyed, we should have had great inventors from among our craftsmen. Of course the 'Spinning Jenny' led on to the discovery of water-power and other things which made the mill displace the labour of thousands of people. That was, in my view, a monstrosity. We will by concentrating on the villages see that the inventive skill that an intensive learning of the craft will stimulate will subserve the needs of the villages as a whole." *(Harijan, 18 September 1937 (CW 66, pp. 137–9))*

The Best System

At the end of the Educational conference held at Wardha, (1937), Gandhiji remarked in the course of a talk with the members of the Executive Committee," I have given many things to India. But this system of education together with its technique is, I feel, the best of them. I do not think I will have anything better to offer to the country." *(Problem of Education, 'Introduction', p. v.)*

Nayee Taleem

This work of basic education is the last work of my life. If, by the grace of God, it is completed, Hindustan will be totally transformed. The present system of education is useless. Those boys who get their education in schools and colleges, they get only literacy, but over and above literacy something more is needed. If that literacy renders our other parts of the body inactive, I would say I don't need such literacy. We need blacksmiths, carpenters, oil millers, masons, carders, spinners and labourers. In essence, we need persons ready to do all sorts of physical work and along with that literacy for all is also necessary. Knowledge that is confined to a handful of individuals is not useful to me. Now the question is, how could that knowledge be available to all? Nai Taleem has emerged from this consideration.

I say that Nai Taleem should start with the conception by the mother rather than at the age of seven years. Please try to understand its mystery. If mother would be the one inclined to do physical labour, be thoughtful, be systematic, be under self-restraint, her child would inherit her qualities from the time of his very conception.

My definition of Nayee Taleem is that if the person who has received Nayee Taleem, is enthroned, he would not feel vanity of power, on the other hand, if he is given a broom, he will not feel ashamed. For him both the jobs will be of equal importance. There would be no place to vain rejoicing in his life. None of his actions will be unproductive or useless. No student of Nayee Taleem shall be dull, because each part of his body would be active and he would have nice neuromuscular coordination.

When the people would do manual labour, there would be no unemployment or starvation. My Nayee Taleem and the village industries are mutually complementary. When they both will be a success, we will attain true Swaraj. *(Bapuni Chaayaman, pp. 157–158 (Translated from Gujarati))*

Newness and Originality

It is necessary to understand the newness or originality in the Nai Taleem. Whatever good there is in the old education will of course, be retained in the Nayee Taleem; but there will be enough of the new element besides. If Nayee Taleem is really new it should lead to the following results: Our sense of frustration should give place to hope; our penury and starvation to a sufficiency of means to maintain ourselves; unemployment to industry and work; discord to concord.

It should enable our sons and daughters to learn to read and write and know along with it a craft through which they will acquire knowledge. *(Utmanzai, 14 October 1938 (CW 67, p. 438))*

Education Through Craft

Speaking about education through a craft Gandhiji said:

"If such education is given, the direct result will be that it will be self-supporting. But the test of success is not its self-supporting character, but that the whole man has been drawn out through the teaching of the handicraft in a scientific manner. In fact I would reject a teacher who would promise to make it self-supporting under any circumstances. The self-supporting part will be the logical corollary of the fact that the pupil has learnt the use of every one of his faculties. If a boy who works at a handicraft for three hours a day will surely earn his keep, how much more a boy who adds to the work a development of his mind and soul!" (Harijan, 11 June 1938 (CW 67, p. 115))

Basic Education

This Basic Education has grown out of the atmosphere surrounding us in the country and is in response to it. It is, therefore, designed to cope with that atmosphere. This atmosphere pervades India's seven hundred thousand villages and its millions of inhabitants. Forget them and you forget India. India is not to be found in her cities. It is in her innumerable villages.

The following are the fundamentals of Basic Education:

1. All education to be true must be self-supporting, that is to say, in the end it will pay its expenses excepting the capital which will remain intact.
2. In it the cunning of the hand will be utilized even up to the final stage, that is to say, hands of the pupils will be skilfully working at some industry for some period during the day.
3. All education must be imparted through the medium of the provincial language.
4. In this there is no room for giving sectional religious training. Fundamental universal ethics will have full scope.
5. This education, whether it is confined to children or adults, male or female, will find its way to the homes of the pupils.

6. Since millions of students receiving this education will consider themselves as of the whole of India, they must learn an interprovincial language. This common interprovincial speech can only be Hindustani written in Nagari or Urdu script. Therefore, pupils have to master both the scripts. *(Harijan, 2 November 1947 (CW 89, pp. 404–05))*

Intellectual Development

During my recent wanderings in Travancore and Madras I found that most of the students and 'intellectuals' who came into touch with me were an instance of intellectual dissipation rather than intellectual development. The fault lies in the modern system of education which encourages this vicious tendency, misdirects the mind, and thereby hinders its development instead of helping it. My experiments in Segaon have only confirmed this impression. But they are as yet too incomplete to be cited as evidence. The views on education that I am now going to set forth have been held by me right from the time of the founding of the Phoenix Settlement in South Africa in the year 1904.

I hold that true education of the intellect can only come through a proper exercise and training of the bodily organs, *e.g.* hands, feet, eyes, ears, nose, etc. In other words, an intelligent use of the bodily organs in a child provides the best and quickest way of developing his intellect. But unless the development of the mind and body goes hand in hand with a corresponding awakening of the soul, the former alone would prove to be a poor lopsided affair. By spiritual training I mean education of the heart. A proper and all-round development of the mind, therefore, can take place only when it proceeds pari passu with the education of the physical and spiritual faculties of the child. They constitute an indivisible whole. According to this theory, therefore, it would be a gross fallacy to suppose that they can be developed piecemeal or independently of one another.

The baneful effects of absence of proper coordination and harmony among the various faculties of body, mind and soul respectively are obvious. They are all around us; only we have lost perception of them owing to our present perverse associations.

Take the case of our village folk. From their childhood upward they toil and labour in their fields, from morning till night, like their cattle in the midst of whom they live. Their existence is a weary endless round of mechanical drudgery unrelieved by a spark of intelligence or higher graces of life. Deprived of all scope for developing their mind and soul, they have sunk to the level of the beast. Life to them is a sorry bungle which they muddle through anyhow. On the other hand, what goes by the name of education in our schools and colleges in the cities today is in reality only intellectual dissipation.

Intellectual training is there looked upon as something altogether unrelated to manual or physical work. But since the body must have some sort of physical exercise to keep it in health, they vainly try to attain that end by means of an artificial and otherwise barren system of physical culture which would be ridiculous beyond words if the result was not so tragic. The young man who emerges from this system can in no way compete in physical endurance with an ordinary labourer. The slightest physical exertion gives him a headache; a mild exposure to the sun is enough to cause him giddiness. And what is more, all this is looked upon as quite 'natural'. As for the faculties of the heart, they are simply allowed to run to seed or to grow anyhow in a wild undisciplined manner. The result is moral and spiritual anarchy. And it is regarded as something laudable!

As against this, take the case of a child in whom the education of the heart is attended to from the very beginning. Supposing he is set to some useful occupation like spinning, carpentry, agriculture, etc., for his education and in that connection is given a thorough comprehensive knowledge relating to the theory of the various operations that he is to perform and the use and construction of the tools that he would be wielding. He would not only develop a fine healthy body but also a sound, vigorous intellect that is not merely academic but is firmly rooted in and is tested from day to day by experience. His intellectual education would include a knowledge of mathematics and various other sciences that are useful for an intelligent and efficient exercise of his avocation.

If to this is added literature by way of recreation, it would give him a perfect well-balanced, all-round education in which the intellect, the body and the spirit have all full play and develop together into a natural, harmonious whole. Man is neither mere intellect, nor the gross animal body, nor the heart of soul alone. A proper and harmonious combination of all the three is required for the making of the whole man and constitutes the true economics of education. To say that this kind of education can only be given after we have attained our independence would, I am afraid, be like putting the cart before the horse.

The advent of independence would be incredibly hastened if we could educate millions of our people through an intelligent exercise of their respective vocations like this and teach them that they live for the common good of all. *(Harijan, 8 May 1937 (CW 65, pp. 73–75))*

Just Social Order

What kinds of vocations are the fittest for being taught to children in urban schools? There is no hard and fast rule about it. But my reply is clear. I want to resuscitate the villages of India. Today our villages have become a mere appendage to the cities. They exist, as it were, to be exploited by the latter and depend on the latter's sufferance. This is unnatural. It is only when the cities realize the duty of making an adequate return to the villages for the strength and sustenance which they derive from them, instead of selfishly exploiting them, that a healthy and moral relationship between the two will spring up.

And if the city children are to play their part in this great and noble work of social reconstruction, the vocations through which they are to achieve their education ought to be directly related to the requirements of the villages. So far as I can see, the various processes of cotton manufacture from ginning and cleaning of cotton to the spinning of yarn, answer this test as nothing else does. Even today the cotton is grown in the villages and is ginned and spun and converted into cloth in the cities. But the chain of processes which cotton undergoes in the mills from the beginning to the end constitutes a huge tragedy of waste in men, materials and mechanical power.

My plan to impart primary education through the medium of village handicrafts like spinning and carding, etc. is thus conceived as the spearhead of a silent social revolution fraught with the most far-reaching consequences. It will provide a healthy and moral basis of relationship between the city and the village and thus go a long way towards eradicating some of the worst evils of the present social insecurity and poisoned relationship between the classes. It will check the progressive decay of our villages and lay the foundation of a juster social order in which there is no unnatural division between the 'haves' and the 'have-nots' and everybody is assured of a living wage and the right to freedom.

And all this would be accomplished without the horror of a bloody class war or a colossal capital expenditure such as would be involved in the mechanisation of a vast continent like India. Nor would it entail a helpless dependence on foreign imported machinery or technical skill. Lastly, by obviating the necessity for highly specialized talent, it would place the destiny of the masses, as it were, in their own hands. But who will bell the cat? Will the city-folk listen to me at all? Or, will mine remain a mere cry in the wilderness? Replies to these and similar questions will depend more on lovers of education like my correspondent living in cities than on me. *(Harijan, 9 October 1937)*

Manual Labour

"One of the complaints that has been made by one of you," Gandhiji remarked, "is that too much emphasis is laid here on manual work. I am a firm believer in the educative value of manual work. Our present educational system is meant for strengthening and perpetuating the imperialist power in India. Those of you who have been brought up under it have naturally developed a taste for it and so find labour irksome. No one in Government schools or colleges bothers to teach the students, how to clean the roads or latrines. Here, cleanliness and sanitation form the very alpha and omega of your training. Scavenging is a fine art you should take pains to learn. Persistent questioning and healthy inquisitiveness are the first requisite for acquiring learning of any kind. Inquisitiveness should be tempered by humility and respectful regard for the teacher. It must not degenerate into impudence. The latter is the enemy of the receptivity of mind. There can be no knowledge without humility and the will to learn.

"Useful manual labour, intelligently performed, is the means par excellence for developing the intellect. One may develop a sharp intellect otherwise too. But then it will not be a balanced growth but an unbalanced, distorted abortion. It might easily make of one a rogue and a rascal. A balanced intellect presupposes a harmonious growth of body, mind and soul. That is why we give to manual labour the central place in our curriculum of training here. An intellect that is developed through the medium of socially useful labour will be an instrument for service and will not easily be led astray or fall into devious paths. The latter can well be a scourge. If you grasp that essential point, the money spent by your respective governments in sending you here for training will have been well-spent." *(Harijan, 8 September 1946 (CW 85, pp. 199–200))*

Basic School Product

Shri Aryanayakam brought nine boys of the 7th class to meet Gandhiji. These had all practically completed their seven years' course in the Sevagram Basic School. They were village lads from Sevagram and the neighbouring villages. Compared to those whom one sees working in the fields and who have never been to school, they were a heartening result of a first endeavour. They were clean, well-groomed, disciplined well-mannered. Gandhiji cracked a few jokes with them which they entered into with merry laughter. One of them had the temerity to ask Gandhiji what type of boys of fourteen he expected to be turned out after a seven years' course at a Basic School? Gandhiji seized the opportunity of telling them that if the school had done its duty by them, boys of fourteen should be truthful, pure and healthy.

They should be village-minded. Their brains and hands should have been equally developed. There would be no guile in them. Their intelligence would be keen but they would not be worried about earning money. They would be able to turn their hands to any honest task that came their way. They would not want to go into the cities. Having learnt the lessons of cooperation and service in the school, they would infect their surroundings with the same spirit. They would never be beggars or parasites. *(Harijan, 8 September 1946 (CW 85, pp. 199–200))*

Craft and Curriculum

This is a libel on me. It is true I have said that all instruction must be linked with some basic craft. When you are imparting knowledge to a child of 7 or 10 through the medium of an industry, you should, to begin with, exclude all those subjects which cannot be linked with the craft. By doing so from day to day you will discover ways and means of linking with the craft many things which you had excluded in the beginning. You will save your own energy and the pupils' if you follow this process of exclusion to begin with.

We have today no books to go by, no precedents to guide us. Therefore we have to go slow. The main thing is that the teacher should retain his freshness of mind. If you come across something that you cannot correlate with the craft, do not fret over it and get disheartened. Leave it and go ahead with the subjects that you can correlate. May be another teacher will hit upon the right way and show how it can be correlated. And when you have pooled the experience of many, you will have books to guide you, so that the work of those who follow you will become easier.

How long, you will ask, are we to go on with this process of exclusion? My reply is, for the whole lifetime. At the end you will find that you have included many things that you had excluded at first, that practically all that was worth including has been included, and whatever you have been obliged to exclude till the end was something very superficial that deserved exclusion. This has been my experience of life. I would not have been able to do many things that I have done if I had not excluded an equal number.

Shrimati Asha Devi asked Gandhiji to explain to them how the mind could be trained through the hands.

The old idea was to add a handicraft to the ordinary curriculum of education followed in the schools. That is to say, the craft was to be taken in hand wholly separately from education. To me that seems a fatal mistake. The teacher must learn the craft and correlate his knowledge to the craft, so that he will impart all that knowledge to his pupils through the medium of the particular craft that he chooses.

Take the instance of spinning. Unless I know arithmetic I cannot report how many yards of yarn I have produced on the takli, or how many standard rounds it will make, or what is the count of the yarn that I have spun. I must learn figures to be able to do so, and I also must learn addition and subtraction and multiplication and division. In dealing with complicated sums I shall have to use symbols and so I get my algebra. Even here, I would insist on the use of Hindustani letters instead of Roman.

Take geometry next. What can be a better demonstration of a circle than the disc of the takli? I can teach all about circles in this way, without even mentioning the name of Euclid.

Again, you may ask how I can teach my child geography and history through spinning. Some time ago I came across a book called Cotton—The Story of Mankind. It thrilled me. It read like a romance.

It began with the history of ancient times, how and when cotton was first grown, the stages of its development, the cotton trade between the different Countries, and so on. As I mention the different countries to the child, I shall naturally tell him something about the history and geography of these countries. Under whose reign the different commercial treaties were signed during the different periods? Why has cotton to be imported by some countries and cloth by others? Why can every country not grow the cotton it requires? That will lead me into economics and elements of agriculture. I shall teach him to know the different varieties of cotton, in what kind of soil they grow, how to grow them, from where to get them, and so on.

Thus takli-spinning leads me into the whole history of the East India Company, what brought them here, how they destroyed our spinning industry, how the economic motive that brought them to India led them later to entertain political aspirations, how it became a causative factor in the downfall of the Moguls and the Marathas, in the establishment of the English Raj, and then again in the awakening of the masses in our times. There is thus no end to the educative possibilities of this new scheme. And how much quicker the child will learn all that, without putting an unnecessary tax on his mind and memory.

Let me further elaborate the idea. Just as a biologist, in order to become a good biologist, must learn many other sciences besides biology, the basic education, if it is treated as a science, takes us into interminable channels of learning. To extend the example of the takli a pupil teacher, who rivets his attention not merely on the mechanical process of spinning, which of course he must master, but on the spirit of the thing, will concentrate on the takli and its various aspects. He will ask himself why the takli is made out of a brass disc and has a steel spindle.

The original takli had its disc made anyhow. The still more primitive takli consisted of a wooden spindle with a disc of slate or clay. The takli has been developed scientifically, and there is a reason for making the disc out of brass and the spindle out of steel. He must find out that reason. Then, the teacher must ask himself why the disc has that particular diameter, no more and no less. When he has solved these questions satisfactorily and has gone into the mathematics of the thing, your pupil becomes a good engineer. The takli becomes his Kamadhenu – the 'Cow of plenty'. There is no limit to the possibilities of knowledge that can be imparted through this medium. It will be limited only by the energy and conviction with which you work. You have been here for three weeks. You will have spent them usefully if it has enabled you to take to this scheme seriously, so that you will say to yourself, 'I shall either do or die.'

I am elaborating the instance of spinning because I know it. If I were a carpenter, I would teach my child all these things through carpentry, or through cardboard work if I were a worker in cardboard.

In training pupil teachers, would it not be better if they are first taught a craft separately and then given a sound exposition of the method of teaching through the medium of that craft? As it is, they are advised to imagine themselves to be of the age of 7 and relearn everything through a craft. In this way it will take them years before they can master the new technique and become competent teachers.

No, it would not take them years. Let us imagine that the teacher when he comes to me has a working knowledge of mathematics and history and other subjects. I teach him to make cardboard boxes or to spin. While he is at it I show him how he could have derived his knowledge of mathematics, history and geography through the particular craft. He thus learns how to link his knowledge to the craft. It should not take him long to do so. Take another instance. Suppose I go with my boy of 7 to a basic school. We both learn spinning and I get all my previous knowledge linked with spinning. To the boy it is all new. For the 70-year-old father it is all repetition but he will have his old knowledge in a new setting. He should not take more than a few weeks for the process. Thus, unless the teacher develops the receptivity and eagerness of the child of 7, he will end up by becoming a mere mechanical spinner, which would not fit him for the new method.

A boy who has passed his matriculation can go to college if he wishes to. Will a child who has gone through the basic education syllabus too be able to do so?

Between the boy who has passed his matriculation and the boy who has gone through basic education, the latter will give a better account of himself because his faculties have been developed. He would not feel helpless when he goes to college as matriculates often do. Seven has been put down as the minimum age for admission of children to a basic education school. Is it to be a chronological or mental age?

Seven should be the average minimum age, but there will be some children of a higher and some of a lower age as well. There is physical as well as mental age to be considered. One child at the age of 7 may have attained sufficient physical development to handle a craft. Another one may not be able to do so even at 7. One cannot therefore lay down any hard and fast rules. All the factors have to be taken into consideration.

Many questions show that many of you are filled with doubts. This is the wrong way of going about the work. You should have robust faith. If you have the conviction that I have, that Wardha education is the thing required to give training for life to millions of our children, your work will flourish. If you have not that faith, there is something wrong with those in charge of your training. They should be able to imbue you with this faith, whatever else they may or may not give you.

The basic education scheme is supposed to be for the villages. Is there no way out for the city-dwellers? Are they to go along the old rut?

This is a pertinent question and a good one, but I have answered it already in the columns of Harijan. Sufficient for the day is the good thereof. As it is, we have a big enough morsel to bite. If we can solve the educational problem of seven lakhs of villages, it will be enough for the present. No doubt educationists are thinking of the cities too. But if we take up the question of the cities along with that of the villages, we will fritter away our energies.

Supposing in a village there were three schools with a different craft in each, the scope for learning may be wider in one than in the other. To which school out of these should the child go?

Such overlapping should not occur. For the majority of our villages are too small to have more than one school. But a big village may have more. Here the craft taught in both should be the same. But I should lay down no hard and fast rule. Experience in such matters would be the best guide. The capacity of various crafts to become popular, their ability to draw out the faculties of the student, should be studied. The idea is that whatever craft you choose, it should draw out the faculties of the child fully and equally. It should be a village craft and it should be useful.

Why should a child waste 7 years on learning a craft when his real profession is going to be something else, *e.g.*, why should a banker's son, who is expected to take to banking later on, learn spinning for 7 years?

The question betrays gross ignorance of the new scheme of education. The boy under the scheme of basic education does not go to school merely to learn a craft. He goes there to receive his primary education, to train his mind through the craft. I claim that the boy who has gone through the new course of primary education for seven years, will make a better banker than the one who has gone through the seven years of ordinary schooling. The latter when he goes to a banking school will be ill at ease because all his faculties will not have been trained. Prejudices die hard. I will have done a good day's work if I have made you realize this one central fact that the new education scheme is not a little of literary education and a little of craft. It is full education up to the primary stage through the medium of a craft.

Would it not be better to teach more than one craft in every school? The children might begin to feel bored of doing the same thing from month to month and year to year.

If I find a teacher who becomes dull to his students after a month's spinning, I should dismiss him. There will be newness in every lesson such as there can be new music on the same instrument. By changing over from one craft to another a child tends to become like a monkey jumping from branch to branch with abode nowhere. But I have shown already in the course of our discussion that teaching spinning in a scientific spirit involves learning many things besides spinning. The child will be taught to make his own takli and his own winder soon. Therefore, to go back to what I began with, if the teacher takes up the craft in a scientific spirit, he will speak to his pupils through many channels, all of which will contribute to the development of all his faculties. *(Harijan, 18 February 1939 and 4 March 1939 (CW 68, pp. 372–77))*

Nayee Taleem and Medical Education

Being engrossed in her work and being considerate of my time, Ashadevi never takes it unnecessarily. She did, however, come to me for five minutes the day before my departure for Delhi, to ask whether, in my opinion, there was need for teachers in the Talimi Sangh to study medicine and whether she herself should have the same four or five years' course that doctors have.

I at once realized that in spite of utmost trying, it is difficult for one like Ashadevi who has taken her M.A. under the old system of education to break away completely from its influence.

I have no degrees to boast of. And I forgot long ago to attach any value to the little knowledge I acquired in a high school. And I have drunk deep at the fountain of nature cure. So I said to her:

> *"You say that the first lesson our children have to learn is how to keep fit and how to keep themselves and their surroundings, clean in every respect. I say to you that all the medical knowledge you require comes into this. Our education is conceived for the crores of villagers, it is for their benefit. They live close to*

nature, but even so they do not know the laws of nature. What little they know they do not carry out. Nayee Taleem is derived from our knowledge of the piteous condition of the villagers. We cannot, therefore, know much about this Nayee Taleem from books. What we have hitherto acquired is from the book of nature. In the same way, we have to learn village doctoring from nature too. The essence of nature cure is that we learn the principles of hygiene and sanitation and abide by those laws as well as the laws relating to proper nutrition. Thus does every one become his own doctor. The man who eats to live, who is friends with the five powers, earth, water, ether, sun and air, and who is a servant of God, the Creator of all these, ought not to fall ill. If he does, he will remain calm relying on God and die in peace, if need be. If there are any medical herbs in the fields of his village he may make use of them. Crores live and die like this without a murmur.

They have not so much as heard of a doctor, much less seen one face to face. Let us become really village-minded. Village children and adults come to us. Let us teach them how to live truly. Doctors aver that 99 per cent of the patients suffer from diseases due to insanitation, eating the wrong food and undernourishment. If we can teach this 99 per cent the art of living, we can afford to forget the 1 per cent. They may find a philanthropic doctor like Dr. Sushila Nayyar to look after them. We need not worry about them. Today pure water, good earth, fresh air, are unknown to us. We do not know the inestimable value of ether and the sun. If we make wise use of these five powers and if we eat the proper and balanced diet, we shall have done the work of ages. For acquiring this knowledge, we need neither degrees nor crores of money. What we need are a living faith in God, a zeal for service, an acquaintance with the five powers of nature and a knowledge of dietetics. All this can be acquired without wasting time in schools and colleges." (Harijan, 1 September 1946 (CW 85, pp. 212–3))

Agriculture as a Basic Craft

"Some people ask me why agriculture could not be a basic craft. The answer is that it has not the educational potentialities of spinning. It cannot, for example, develop deftness as in spinning.

The function of Nayee Taleem is not merely to teach an occupation, but through it to develop the whole man."

"But though I do not begin with agriculture, it is bound to come in ultimately. For, the field of New Education is comprehensive. The pupils and teachers of the school of my conception will together have to make provision for all they need. A teacher of Nayee Taleem will have to be a first-class craftsman. All the children of the village will be themselves drawn to the school. In this way, education would automatically become free and universal."

"Today, the condition of India is that vegetables grown in a village are not available for the use of the villagers themselves. The villagers of Travancore cannot use the cocoanuts that are grown there. They are collected at one place and sent to the towns. This anomaly will disappear where basic schools come into existence. Again, today we cultivate money crops such as opium, tobacco, cotton, etc. Those trained in Nayee Taleem will cultivate food crops which they themselves need." *(Harijan, 9 November 1947)*

9

Gandhian Philosophy for Teachers and Students

Students' Dharma

Many students feel that it is not necessary to pay much attention to the body. This is a great mistake. Regular exercise for the body is absolutely necessary. What can be expected of a student who has not the wealth of the body? Just as milk cannot be kept for long in a paper or cardboard container, so also education is not likely to remain for long in the paper-like (delicate) bodies of our students.

The body being the abode of the spirit, is holy. We must protect it. Walking regularly and zestfully for an hour and a half in the morning and for the same period in the evening keeps it healthy, and the mind fresh. The time thus devoted is not wasted. Exercise and rest invigorate both the body and the intellect, enabling one to learn things more quickly. I think expensive games like hockey and cricket are not advisable for a poor country like India. We have a number of inexpensive and interesting games of our own.

The daily life of the student also should be above reproach. He alone can experience true delight whose mind is pure. Indeed, to ask him to seek delight in worldly pleasures is to deprive him of the real delight which is his. He who has resolved to rise higher does indeed rise higher. Ramachandra wished for the moon and he got it because his mind was pure.

Looked at in one way the world appears illusory; in another, quite solid and real. Students should regard it as the latter because they have to use their energy for the good of humanity and do brave deeds in this world. He who declares the world to be illusory without getting at the real truth, claims to have renounced it and then acts as he likes in disregard of moral laws, is not a *jnani;* he is merely a self-deluded fool even though he may be a Sannyasi.

Now I come to *Dharma.* Where there is no *dharma,* there can be no knowledge, wealth, health, etc. Where there is no *dharma,* life is totally barren. There can be no progress. In our present scheme of education there is no place for the teaching of *dharma.* It is like a *barat* (wedding party) without the bridegroom. Students cannot experience pure joy without a knowledge of *dharma.* In order to have this experience it is necessary to study the *shastras,* to reflect over their teaching and to act thoughtfully. Smoking a cigarette or indulging in useless gossip as soon as one gets up in the morning does good to nobody. Nazir has said that even the birds sing the name of the Lord morning and evening, but we waste our time in sleeping.

It is the duty of every student to somehow acquire the knowledge of *dharma*. Whether this is taught in schools or not, it is my prayer that students will try to introduce the substance of *dharma* in their life. What exactly is *dharma?* What should be the concrete method of imparting knowledge concerning it? We cannot discuss these questions here for lack of time. However, from experience, let me tell you to read the Gita and Ramayana with understanding, for you have a real jewel in the latter. Make use of its teachings. But remember that you have to study these two books in order to learn the secret of *dharma.*

The seers who wrote these works had no intention of writing history. They desired only to impart teaching of *dharma* and *neeti, i.e.,* the rules of good conduct. Crores of people read these books and try to pattern their lives upon them. They study them with a pure heart and carry on their work sustained by the strength and joy which they derive from these two books. For Muslim students, the Koran is the best book in this respect. They should study it in a spirit of religious humility, and try to understand its message. I also recommend that both Hindus and Muslims study each other's religious scriptures with humility and try to understand them, for this in turn will create a better understandings of one community by the other.

From this most absorbing question I shall pass on to topics of more worldly interest. I have often been asked whether students should take part in politics or not. I will let you know my opinion about it without going into the reasons. Politics may be divided into two parts; first, the study of its science; second, political action. It is certainly necessary for students to study the former, but dangerous to embark on the latter. Students may attend political meetings or the sessions of the Congress in order to learn the science of politics, since they are useful in giving them object-lessons in the subject of their study. Students should have complete freedom to attend such meetings and conferences, and efforts should be made to remove the bans which have recently been placed on attending these. Students should, however, refrain from speaking or giving their opinion on the questions discussed at such assemblies.

But they may serve as volunteers if this does not interfere with their studies. No student can afford to miss the opportunity of serving Malaviyaji if it comes his way. Students should avoid party politics. They should observe neutrality and not align themselves with this or that group, and should also cultivate respect for all leaders without any distinction. It is not for students to discuss their merits and demerits, and assess their comparative worth and importance. Students are concerned only with seeking and acquiring virtues wherever they can find them; they have to learn to worship the virtues.

It is the duty of students to respect elders, to consider what they say, and follow their advice whenever possible. He who has not learnt to respect others cannot hope for respect from them. An attitude of insolence ill becomes students. Here, I should like to point out a phenomenon which is taking place in the India of today. Older folk are disregarding the standard of conduct expected of them. They seem to be oblivious of the fact that in their behaviour and conduct they set a model for the younger generation. What are the students to do in the circumstances? I cherish the hope that they will cultivate and acquire the spirit of *dharma*.

When confronted with a clash between their loyalty to *dharma* and obedience or respect to elders, students should remember Prahlad. Placed in certain circumstances which were distasteful to him, this boy respectfully disobeyed the commands of his father. In the same way, we can also respectfully refuse to obey the elders if the circumstances warrant it. But any disrespect shown to them beyond this will be wrong. Disrespect to elders leads to the ruin of the community. The right of the elders to respect does not depend merely on age, but also on knowledge, experience and wisdom. Where the latter are absent the right depends simply on age. But nobody worships mere age.

Another question is: How can students serve the country? First, by carefully acquiring knowledge and, while doing so, keeping up their health, for both these will be needed in the service of our country. If a student does this he certainly serves his country. We can easily do much useful work without any great effort on our part if we would just try to live a good and useful life. I shall now tell you of one job which all of you can do quite easily. You must have seen my letter in the newspapers about the difficulties of the third class passengers. I suppose most of you travel third.

You must have then noticed that these passengers spit in the compartment; they also expectorate betel leaves and tobacco which they go on chewing; throw the skins of oranges and bannanas and other leavings on the floor of the carriage; do not use the latrine carefully and foul it, and smoke *bidis* and *cigarettes* without any regard for the inconvenience of fellow-passengers. Students should explain to such passengers, when they travel, that doing these things is not only bad manners, but also unhygienic. You can explain the ill effect of creating this filth. Most passengers respect students and listen to what they have to say with attention.

They should not then miss these opportunities of explaining the rules of hygiene to our masses. The eatables sold at stations by vendors are often dirty. It is the duty of students, when they see any such uncleanliness, to draw the attention of the traffic manager to it. And take care that you write to him in Hindi. It may be that the traffic manager will ignore your request. But when he receives many such letters, he will be forced to pay attention to it. This can be done without much effort, but it will yield important results.

I have spoken about the habits of chewing betel leaves and tobacco. In my opinion, both are harmful and unclean. Large numbers of Indian men and women have become the slaves of these evil habits. We have to get rid of this slavery. A stranger visiting India would surely feel that we go on eating some thing or the other throughout the day. That the betel leaf, possibly, helps to digest food may be conceded, but food taken in accordance with the laws of health gets digested without any help from it. Moreover, there is hardly any agreeable taste in the betel leaf. And tobacco-chewing must be given up as well. Students should always practise self-control.

The problem of smoking is a difficult one to tackle. Our rulers have set a bad example in this matter. They are used to smoking irrespective of time and place. This has led us to consider it a fashion, and to turn our mouths into chimneys for ejecting the smoke. There are many books by competent writers to show that smoking of tobacco does great harm. We call this age Kaliyuga. Christians believe that Christ will reincarnate Himself when such evils as selfishness, immorality, addiction to drugs and drink, etc. becomes rife in the life of human beings. I do not say how far we can concur in this belief. Yet, I do feel that the world is suffering a great deal from such evils as drink, tobacco, opium, *ganja, bhang (hemp)*, etc. We cannot exactly assess the harm which these are doing to us, because almost all of us are caught in their widespread snares. It is my fervent prayer that you, the students, keep away from them.

The purpose in my making and your hearing these speeches is that you should learn something from them and put it into practice. How many of you following Smt. Besant's advice, have adopted the Indian mode of dress, simplified your food and given up unclean habits? Or acting on Prof. Jadunath Sirkar's advice, how many of your have spent your summar vacation in teaching poor students without any charge? Many such questions may be asked. I do not want a reply now. But you may reply these questions to your conscience.

The value of your learning is judged not by what you know intellectually but how you act. You may receive some monetary reward for filling your mind with book learning, but the value of the good work you do will be many times greater than that. The value of the learning you have acquired is really equal only to that of the work you do. The rest is an useless burden. My request to you is that you practise what you learn and what appears to you to be right. That is the only way to progress. *(Presidential Speech, 17th Session of the Bihar Students' Conference, Bhagalpur, 1917, (CW 14, pp. 137–39))*

Students' Life

The life of students is similar to that of *Sannyasis*. You must therefore live in complete purity and celibacy as befits a *Brahmachari*. The two civilizations—the old and the modern—are at present vying with each other or for supremacy over the student community. The old civilization lays stress on self-control. It proclaims that the more a man reduces his wants consciously and with full understanding of what it means, the greater is his progress towards higher living. Whereas modern civilization holds that progress lies in increasing one's wants. There is the same difference between control and abandonment as between *dharma* and *adharma* or the right and wrong way of living. The method advocating control accords an inferior status to the trappings of material living, and rightly gives more importance to the quality of our thoughts and emotions or spiritual and mental well-being. There is the danger, at present, of our people being carried away by the lure of the newer civilization and throwing away the older one. Students can do a lot in warding off this danger. For instance, the students of this University will be judged not by what they know but by what they do.

Therefore, teaching and practice of *dharma* should be given prior consideration in the scheme of education at this University.

Students should offer their wholehearted cooperation in achieving this object. I, personally, feel that we shall not derive any real benefit from political reforms unless we first arrive at a clear conception of *dharma,* or the right way of individual and social life for us in India. For it is not these reforms which will create and establish *dharma* but *dharma* which will show up the defects of the former and help us in removing them. *(Speech delivered before the students of the Hindu University, Navajivan, 29 January 1920 (True Education, pp. 208–09))*

Students' Faith

I have come in contact with thousands of students during the last ten years. They have confided their innermost secrets to me and have given me the right to enter their hearts. I know therefore all your difficulties and every one of your weaknesses. I do not know whether I can render any effective help to you. I can but be your friend and guide, attempt to share your sorrows and give you the benefit of my experience, though you must know that the only help of the helpless is God. There is no greater punishment or misery for man than that his faith in God should be blasted. And I confess to a deep sense of sorrow that faith is gradually disappearing in the student world. When I suggest to a Hindu boy to have recourse to *Ramanama,* he stares at me and wonders who Rama may be; when I ask a Musalman boy to read the Koran and fear God, he confesses his inability to read the Koran and Allah is a mere lip-profession. How can I convince such boys that the first step to a true education is a pure heart? If the education you get turns you away from God, I do not know how it is going to help you and how you are going to help the world. *(Young India, 4 August 1927 (True Education, p. 225))*

No Intoxicants Please

In response to the request of a Calicut professor I shall now proceed to say something about cigarette smoking and coffee and tea drinking. These are not necessities of life. There are some who manage to take ten cups of coffee a day. Is it necessary for their healthy development and for keeping them awake for the performance of their duties? If it is necessary to take coffee or tea to keep them awake, let them not drink coffee or tea but go to sleep. We must not become slaves to these things. But the majority of the people who drink coffee or tea are slaves to them. Cigars and cigarettes, whether foreign or indigenous, must be avoided. Cigarette smoking is like an opiate and the cigars that you smoke have a touch of opium about them. They get to your nerves and you cannot leave them afterwards. How can a single student foul his mouth by converting it into a chimney? If you give up these habits of smoking cigars and cigarettes and drinking coffee and tea you will find out for yourselves how much you are able to save. A drunkard in Tolstoy's story is hesitating to execute his design of murder so long as he has not smoked his cigar. But he puffs it, and then gets up smiling and saying, 'What a coward am I,' takes the dagger and does the deed. Tolstoy spoke from experience. He has written nothing without having had personal experience of it. And he is much more against cigars and cigarettes than against drink. But do not make the mistake that between drink and tobacco drink is a lesser evil. No, if cigarette is Beelzebub, then drink is Satan. *(Young India, 15 September 1927 (True Education, pp. 234–35))*

Gain Courage to Ask Questions

Three students write: "We desire to serve the country. Kindly tell us through the columns of the *Navajivan* how we can do so without having to leave our native place or our studies." These students have given their names, age and addresses. They say, "Please do not disclose our names and addresses. Nor should you write to us direct to our addresses. The conditions in which we are living are such that we cannot even send for letters." I consider it difficult to give any advice to such students. What can I say to those who have not the freedom even to receive replies to their letters?

However, I can say this much: Self-purification is the best service one can render to the country. Have these students attempted such self-purification? Are their hearts pure? Have they been able to keep away from the evils prevailing amongst students? Do they observe the vow of truth? Seeing that they are afraid even to get a reply to their letters, there appears to be something gravely wrong in this situation.

The students should cast out fear. They must learn to put their views to their elders firmly and courageously. Do they use Khadi? Do they spin? If they spin and use Khadi they may be said to be taking part in the service of the country. Do they attend on an ailing neighbour in their leisure hours? Do they, if things are messy about them, or streets dirty around their home, snatch time from their work and clean them with their own hands? Many more such questions could be asked and if they can answer them satisfactorily, they may be said to be serving the country even now. *(Navajivan, 8 July 1928 (True Education, pp. 238–39))*

Utilize Vacations for Social Service

As to the use of the vacation by students, if they will approach the work with zeal, they can undoubtedly do many things. I enumerate a few of them:

1. Conduct night and day schools with just a short course, well-conceived, to last for the period of the vacation.
2. Visit Harijan quarters and clean them, taking the assistance of Harijans if they would give it.
3. Taking Harijan children for excursions, showing them sights near their villages and teaching them how to study nature, and generally interesting them in their surroundings, giving them by the way a working knowledge of geography and history.
4. Reading to them simple stories from the Ramayana and the Mahabharata.
5. Teaching them simple *bhajans.*
6. Cleaning the Harijan boys of all the dirt that they would find about their persons and giving both the grown-ups and the children simple lessons in hygiene.
7. Taking a detailed census in selected areas of the condition of Harijans.
8. Taking medical aid to the ailing Harijans.

This is but a sample of what is possible to do among the Harijans. It is a list hurriedly made, but a thoughtful student will, I have no doubt, add many other items. I have so far confined my attention to the service of Harijans, but there is a service no less necessary to be rendered to caste-Hindus. The students can often in the gentlest manner possible carry the message of anti-untouchability to them in spite of themselves. There is so much ignorance which can be easily dispelled by a judicious distribution of clean authentic literature. The students can make a survey of those who are for abolishing untouchability and who are against and, whilst they are making this survey, they may take note of wells, schools, ponds and temples open to Harijans and of those closed to them.

If they will do all these things in a methodical and persistent manner, they will find the results to be startling. Every student should keep a log-book in which he should enter the details of his work, and at the end of the vacation a comprehensive but brief report of the results of their labours could be prepared and sent by them to the Servants of Untouchables Society of their province. Whether other students accept all or any of the suggestions made here, I shall expect my correspondent to give me a report of what he and his associates have done. *(Harijan, 1 April 1933 (True Education, pp. 246–47))*

Be Humble

The first thing the students had to learn was humility, without which they could not make a good use of their attainments. They might achieve academic distinction and secure high office, but if they would devote their learning to the service of man, humility was absolutely necessary. There was a vast number of bright students among them but they scarcely existed for the poor long-suffering Indian villager. The ideal all the world over was that man's intellectual and spiritual gifts were designed for service and that he should use his hands and feet in order to obtain his livelihood.

In ancient times, jurisconsults charged their clients nothing for their advice, and even now barristers could not sue a client for fees, which were called their honorarium. If the students wished to serve the country, it would not do for them to become imitation *sahebs,* like the jackdaw in the fable, dressed up in peacock's feathers. They should realize that they had to serve a nation whose average income per head was 40 rupees, according to Lord Curzon. They could render this service only if they were satisfied with a coarse piece of Khadi and gave up all ambition of living in expensive European style. They should, as men of culture, also be ashamed of exacting large sums of money as dowry from their prospective father-in-law. *(Speech delivered to students at Karachi – Harijan, 27 July 1934)*

Pay for Your Own Education

When it is difficult for millions even to make the two ends meet, when millions are dying of starvation, it is monstrous to think of giving our relatives a costly education. Expansion of the mind will come from hard experience, not necessarily in the college or the school-room. When some of us deny ourselves and ours the so-called Higher Education, we shall find the true means of giving and receiving a really Higher Education. Is there not, may there not be, a way of each boy paying for his own education? There may be no such way. Whether there is or there is not such a way is irrelevant.

But there is no doubt that when we deny ourselves the way of expensive education, seeing that aspiration after Higher Education is a laudable end, we shall find out a way of fulfilling it more in accord with our surroundings. The golden rule to apply in all such cases is resolutely to refuse to have what millions cannot. This ability to refuse will not descend upon us all of a sudden. The first thing is to cultivate the mental attitude that will not have possessions or facilities denied to millions, and the next immediate thing is to rearrange our lives as fast as possible in accordance with that mentality. *(Young India, 24 June 1926 (Towards New Education, pp. 100–01))*

Self-study

It is a gross superstition to suppose that knowledge can be obtained only by going to schools and colleges. The world produced brilliant students before schools and colleges came into being. There is nothing so ennobling or lasting as self-study. Schools and colleges make most of us mere receptacles for holding the superfluities of knowledge. Wheat is left out and mere husk is taken in. I do not wish to decry schools and colleges as such. They have their use. But we are making altogether too much of them. They are but one of the many means of gaining knowledge. *(Young India, 25 May 1931 (Towards New Education, pp. 101–02))*

Dignity of Labour

A student asks:

What should a matriculate or an undergraduate who is unfortunately father of two or three children do in order to produce a living wage, and what should he do when he is forced to marry against his will and before even the age of twenty-five?

The simplest answer that occurs to me is that a student who does not know how to support his wife or children or who marries against his will has studied to no purpose. But that is past history for him. The perplexed student deserves a helpful answer. He does not say what his requirement is. If he does not pitch it high because he is a matriculate and will put himself in level with an ordinary labourer, he should have no difficulty in earning a livelihood. His intelligence should help his hands and feet and enable him to do better than the labourer who has had no opportunity of developing his intelligence.

This is not to say that the labourer who has never learnt English is devoid of intelligence. Unfortunately labour has never been helped to develop the mind, and those who pass through schools do have their minds opened even though under a handicap not to be found in any part of the world. Even this mental equipment is counterbalanced by false notions of dignity inculcated during school and college days. And so students think that they can earn their living only at the desk. The inquirer has therefore to realize the dignity of labour and seek the maintenance of himself and his family in that field.

And there is no reason why his wife should not add to the family income by utilizing her spare hours. Similarly if the children are at all able to do any work, they too should be inspanned for productive work. The utterly false idea that intelligence can be developed only through book reading should give place to the truth that the quickest development of the mind can be achieved by the artisan's work being learnt in a scientific manner. True development of the mind commences immediately the apprentice is taught at every step why a particular manipulation of the hand or a tool is required. The problem of the unemployment of students can be solved without difficulty, if they will rank themselves among the common labourers. *(Harijan, 9 January 1937)*

Foreign Studies

I have never been an advocate of our students going abroad. My experience tells me that such, on return, find themselves to be square pegs in round holes. That experience is the richest and contributes most to growth which springs from the soil. *(Harijan, 8 September 1946)*

Help Educational Reconstruction

If there is one compact students' organization, it can become a mighty instrument of service. Their objective can only be one: Never for the purpose of finding a lucrative career but fitting themselves for the service of the motherland. If they were to do so, their knowledge would attain a great height. Agitation is only for those who have completed their studies. While studying, the only occupation of students must be to increase their knowledge. The education, as it is prescribed today, is detrimental, conceived in terms of masses of India. It is possible to show that the present education has been of some use to the country. I regard it as negligible. Let no one be deceived by it. The acid test of its usefulness is this: Does it make, as it should, an effective contribution to the production of food and clothing? What part does the student world play in allaying the present senseless slaughter? All education in a country has got to be demonstrably in promotion of the progress of the country in which it is given.

Who will deny that education in India has not served that purpose? Hence, one purpose of the organization should be to discover the defects of the present education and seek to remove them, so far as possible in their own persons. By their correct conduct they will be able to convert to their view the heads of education. If they do so, they will never be entangled in party politics. In the revised scheme, constructive and creative programme will naturally have its due place. Indirectly, their action will keep the politics of the country free of the spirit of exploitation. *(Harijan, 7 September 1947)*

No Party Politics

Gandhiji referred to a letter by some students saying that the proposed students' strike on the 9th was being organized by the Communist students, not Congress students. Gandhiji said that while he congratulated the Congress students who had dissociated themselves from the proposed strike, he would reiterate what he had already said about such strikes, *viz.* that for students there should be no party politics. There should be no Socialist, Communist, Congress and other groups among students. They should be all students first and last determined to gather as much knowledge as possible and that for the sake of the service of the people, not for the sake of getting jobs. *(Harijan, 18 January 1948)*

Improve Teaching Methods

My ideas about education are very exacting. If we want to pour our souls into the pupils, we should constantly exercise our mind on how to teach them. We should not get angry with them. Passing on to them in the best possible language from day to day whatever we wish to give them, will take up much of our time. Moreover, we must for the present think of teaching methods as well. Everything will have to be taught in a new way.

The teachers will have to come together at least once a week to exchange ideas and make such changes as may be called for. The intelligent students should be consulted and their suggestions invited about methods of teaching.

The students' health is the collective responsibility of the teachers; the main responsibility, however, will rest on the teacher in charge of hygiene.

The teachers should read up the subjects in the curriculum which they do not know. Especially Hindi. I can see from my work here how very essential Hindi is. I find that I shall have to ask for volunteers from other places. Difficulties will arise about those of them who do not know Hindi. I see it proved every day that education is altogether incomplete without Hindi. *(Letter to Narahari Parikh, 17 May 1917 (CW 13, p. 399))*

Build National Education

So long as education in the country is not imparted by persons of integrity and conditions are not created in which the highest knowledge will be available to the poorest of Indians, so long as a perfect confluence of education and *dharma* has not taken place and education has not been brought into relation with conditions in India, so long as the intolerable burden imposed on the minds of the young by imparting education through a foreign medium has not been lifted, so long will there be no upsurge of national life; there is no denying this. Purely national education should be imparted in the regional language. The teachers must be of a high calibre. The school should be situated in surroundings where the student has fresh air and water, where he enjoys peace, where the building and the adjoining land are object lessons in healthful living; and the educational pattern must be one which will instruct (the pupil) in the main professions and religions of India. *(Navajivan, 21 September 1919 (CW 16, p. 156))*

Cultivate the Spirit of Sacrifice

As the second condition for the success of national education we need teachers of good character. I congratulate the head master and other teachers of this high school who have made a sacrifice for the sake of their *dharma* and their country, and I ask of them that in their work henceforth they show the same spirit which has prompted their self-sacrifice. Once you are absorbed in your work, money will come in of itself. Your executive committee will be able to raise funds with ease. Even if they have nothing else than clean ground to sit on, the boys of national schools will be able to hold their own against other boys and, if their teachers are men of character, will acquire a greater spirit of manliness than the pupils of the more pretentious Government schools. *(Navajivan, 10 November 1920 (CW 18, p. 419))*

Be Makers of New India

You are embarking upon a new career. You are turning over a new leaf. You are shouldering a great responsibility. You are counting yourselves among the makers of India of the future. And if you realize this responsibility, I have no doubt, you will dispel all these fears which have been expressed in other parts of India. Those who know Bengal well are in the position also to testify that Bengalis on many an occasion have not been found wanting; and for my part I shall certainly decline to believe that those students who have responded and who will join this institution will be found wanting.

I shall hope also that the professors and the teachers will prove true to their trust. What I said in all humility to the professors and teachers at the time of performing the opening ceremony of the Gujarat National College, I am tempted to repeat here; that the success and failure of this institution will very largely depend upon the honest exertion that the professors and teachers may put forth. At this critical moment in the history of our dear country every one of us, who intends to mould the young mind of the country, has a serious responsibility, and if the professors and the teachers are found asleep, if they are overtaken with doubt, if they are overtaken with fear as to the future, God help the students who come under their charge. And I shall pray to the Almighty that he may bless the professors and teachers with wisdom, with courage, with faith and hope. *(Young India, 9 February 1921 (CW 19, p. 320))*

Develop Positive Outlook

This conference was held and is now over. It should be regarded as an important conference from the point of view of teachers and the general public too. But these are not days when either of them would attach importance to it. The value of teachers is recognized neither by the public nor by the teachers themselves. They are valued according to their salary. A teacher is paid less than an ordinary clerk. Hence, in practice, a teacher is valued less than a clerk. Is it for this reason that we refer to a teacher as *Mehtaji?*

If it is so, how can we expect that the teachers' worth will ever rise? Can anyone raise the salaries of seven lakh teachers in seven lakh villages? If the salaries of so many teachers do not rise and if it is considered necessary to raise them, we should rest content with employing high-paid teachers in a few villages and allowing the rest to go without education. We have been doing this since the establishment of British rule. We realize that this practice is wrong. Hence let us find out a scheme which can cover all villages. Under this scheme, teachers will not be valued according to their salaries and work.

Teachers themselves will place more value on their teaching work than on their salaries. In short, teaching should be regarded as the teachers' *dharma*. The teacher who takes his food without performing the sacrifice should be looked upon as a thief. If that is done, there will be no shortage of teachers and yet they will be valued a million times higher than millionaires. By changing his outlook, every teacher can enjoy that position even today.

It is up to the teachers to make a success or failure of this conference. The key to success lies in the teachers' pledge.

If the teachers would forget the question of their livelihood and think only of their duty, the schools will come to have new vitality and become truly national, and then alone will they be of use to the national movement. It is the first lesson for the young and the old, for men and women, that they should remain loyal to a pledge once they have accepted it. *(Navajivan, 10 August 1924 (CW 24, p. 542) (Translated from Gujarati))*

Make Teaching Absorbing

Experience shows that students' interest in a subject is sustained not by the subject-matter but by the teacher. My own experience has been that one teacher used to bore me to sleep while teaching chemistry, whereas another teacher kept me wide awake and interested in the same subject. The former, who talked and talked without clarifying the topic, was not liked while, as the other teacher elucidated the theme, one wished that his period should never end. The topic was the same as well as the students. Instruction by one, however, was absorbing and by the other insipid. The spinning-wheel holds a jar or nectar. In the Dakshinamurti Bhavan, it appears, there are teachers who can reveal this. *(Navajivan, 17 August 1924 (CW 25, p. 5) (Translated from Gujarati))*

Working for Livelihood

As this teacher has answered his own questions, my task is simplified. What I had said could not possibly mean that ten teachers or a single teacher should rest after teaching only one child. My contention is that not merely ten but even twenty teachers should not forsake a solitary student or leave a school but should try to increase their number. When plenty of students are available, the teacher should draw an allowance sufficient for his living, but his true test lies in his ability to accept nothing and starve to death if the need arises, and let his dependents also starve to death. Such a teacher sacrifices his relations, his parents, his children, his all for his work. What do those who practise other professions do when they incur heavy losses? If a person does not find a job despite all possible efforts, he lets his dependents starve along with himself; this should be the case with the teachers in national schools. This would make our dependents work for their livelihood. When teachers are idle for want of students, they should, of course, take up some other activity, but even while doing so, they must try to revive the school. *(Navajivan, 15 March 1925 (CW 26, p. 315))*

Build Heart to Heart Contact

I ask their teachers to cultivate their hearts and establish with the students a heart-contact. I have felt that the teachers' work lies more outside than inside the lecture-room. In this workaday life where teachers and professors work for the wages they get they have no time to give to the students outside the classroom, and that is the greatest stumbling-block in the development of the life and character of students today. But unless the teachers are prepared to give all their time outside the classroom to their students, not much can be done. Let them fashion their hearts rather than their brains. Let them help them to erase every word out of their dictionary which means disappointment and despair. *(Young India, 4 April 1929 (CW 40, p. 120))*

Freedom for All-round Growth

The students' minds must not be caged nor for that matter those of the teachers. The teachers can only point to their pupils what they or the State considers is the best way. Having done so they have no right to curb their pupils' thoughts and feelings. This does not mean that they are not to be subject to any discipline. No school can be run without it. But discipline has nothing to do with artificial restraint upon the students' all-round growth. This is impossible where they are subjected to espionage. The fact is that hitherto they have been in an atmosphere subtly anti-national where it has not been openly that. This should now be dispelled. The students should know that the cultivation of nationalism is not a crime but a virtue. *(Harijan, 18 September 1937 (CW 66, p. 141))*

Use all Resources to be Constructive and Creative

What we need is educationists with originality, fired with true zeal, who will think out from day to day what they are going to teach their pupils. The teacher cannot get this knowledge through musty volumes. He has to use his own faculties of observation and thinking and impart his knowledge to the children through his lips, with the help of a craft. This means a revolution in the method of teaching, a revolution in the teachers' outlook. Up till now you have been guided by inspector's reports. You wanted to do what the inspector might like, so that you might get more money yet for your institutions or higher salaries for yourselves. But the new teacher will not care for all that. He will say, 'I have done my duty to my pupil if I have made him a better man and in doing so I have used all my resources. That is enough for me. *(Harijan, 18 February 1939 (CW 68, pp. 374–75))*

Develop Sense of Belonging

How to teach in the best possible manner?

You can teach best by identifying yourself with your students. In order to do so, the teacher must prepare himself fully in the subject he has to teach. *(Navajivan, 11 April 1926 (CW 30, p. 322))*

Establish Spiritual Relationship

The suggestion which the writer has made to teachers is certainly sound. But where there are forty to fifty children in a class and the relationship of the teacher with the pupils is confined to class-work lessons, how will it be possible for the teacher, even if he so wishes, to establish any spiritual relationship with so many children? Again, when six or seven teachers teach six or seven different subjects, which of them can assume the responsibility to give them moral instruction? Lastly, how many teachers can we come across who will guide the children along the path of morality or win their confidence? This indeed raises the whole question of education, but it cannot be discussed here. *(Navajivan, 26 September 1926 (CW 31, p. 454))*

Make Schools Ideal

To teachers, Gandhiji said that they must not make any use of books for imparting education, as books spoiled eyes and blunted the intellect. He himself had experienced that. He understood that in Russia they were conducting one thousand schools for peasants and that they were giving education without the aid of books by making all possible use of the senses. He asked them to clean their own houses and streets themselves and not to depend on others for doing the same. Concluding, Mahatmaji asked them to make their schools ideal in every way, so that the boys and girls of the mill-owners might envy them and the mill-owners might be tempted to send their children to the labour schools. On truth depended the foundation of education, and they must always resort to truth. *(The Hindu, 31 March 1928 (CW 36, p. 166))*

Develop Motherly Love

I have made no use in this article of the word 'teacher'. A teacher is a mother. She who cannot take the place of a mother can never become a teacher. A child should not feel that it is receiving education. The child whose mother's eyes follow it everywhere is receiving education all the twenty-four hours. A child who sits six hours in a school may not be receiving any education at all. In this topsy-turvy life, perhaps we may not find women-teachers. It may well be that child education is practicable at present only through men-teachers. Then the men-teachers will have to acquire the noble status of a mother and ultimately the mothers will have to get ready for this job. But if my concept is right, any mother if she has love in her heart can become fit with a little assistance. And while preparing herself she will prepare the children as well. *(Navajivan, 2 June 1929 (CW 41, p. 9) (Translated from Gujarati))*

Develop Proper Relationship

If a student develops contempt for national education whom would you hold responsible? Generally, the teachers and the students both are responsible, but more often the teachers. Should a teacher marry a girl who is his student? Likewise, should a boy marry a girl studying in his class?

I at any rate would consider both very improper. A girl who is my student should be as safe (with me) as my daughter, and a girl in my class as safe as a sister. That pure brother-and-sister relationship is the only proper relationship between boys and girls studying together. This is all I should like to say in reply to this question, but it is an important enough question for a fuller discussion. I have no doubt in my mind about the correctness of my reply to the first question. With regard to the second, however, I see some difficulties in these modern times when thousands of boys and girls attend the same school. In any case, in every institution that I have managed I have insisted on the foregoing rule being followed and the results have always been happy. *(Navajivan, 20 October 1921 (CW 21, pp. 328–29))*

Teaching for the Love of It

However, the teachers have asked for advice and I can but place it before them so that each may then respond to the best of his ability. The unfortunate position is that educated Indians take to teaching not for the love of it, but because they have nothing better and nothing else for giving them a livelihood. Many of them even enter the teaching profession with a view to preparing for what they regard as a better thing. The wonder is that in spite of this self-imposed initial handicap so many teachers are not worse than they are. By well-ordered agitation, no doubt they may better their pecuniary prospects, but I see no chance even under a swaraj government of the scale of salary being raised much higher than it is today. I believe in the ancient idea of teachers teaching for the love of it and receiving the barest maintenance.

The Roman Catholics have retained that idea and they are responsible for some of the best educational institutions in the world. The *rishis* of old did even better. They made their pupils members of their families, but in those days that class of teaching which they imparted was not intended for the masses. They simply brought up a race of real teachers of mankind in India. The masses got their training in their homes and in their hereditary occupations. It was a good enough ideal for those times. Circumstances have now changed. There is a general insistent demand for literary training. The masses claim the same attention as the classes. How far it is possible and beneficial to mankind generally cannot be discussed here. *(Young India, 6 August 1925 (CW 28, pp. 34–35))*

Be Affectionate

Students must not be given corporal punishment. But there should be such a rapport between the teacher and the taught that if the teacher punishes himself in some way the children, because of their affection for him, should feel sorry, their hearts should melt and they should change for the better. I am not talking in the air. This has been my personal experience. Mothers also can reform their children in the same way. In South Africa I had looked after Hindu, Muslim and Parsi boys and girls. During those days I remember having only once beaten a pupil. But it was my experience that my nonviolent method was more successful. If the children have affection for their teacher they are bound to feel sorry when they find the teachers suffering on their account. That would soften them. But if in spite of that there is a difficult pupil, we should non-co-operate with him. But that is another method. The former is the better method. *(Letter to a Teacher, 15 April 1947 – Biharni Komi Agman, pp. 202–03 (CW 87, pp. 283–84) (Translated from Gujarati))*

Strive Continuously to Improve

I am a teacher in a school. I have not as much character, love of truth and *Brahmacharya* as a teacher should have, though I am striving to achieve them. Under the circumstances, would you advise me to resign?

I believe that in the absence of sufficient strength of character it is well to resign your post as teacher. But, discrimination is necessary. Resignation is not necessary if the defects are likely to be overcome. No one is perfect. Character in teachers is not much in evidence today. One may well feel satisfied if one remains watchful in one's work and continuously strives to improve oneself. But there can be no single rule which would cover all such cases. Everyone must think for himself and do what is best. *(Navajivan, 27 September 1925)*

Inculcate Sense of Honour

We have to fall back upon the voluntary assistance of teachers, but when I look for teachers, they are very few, especially, teachers of the type wanted, in order to draw the best from the children through understanding, through studying their individuality and then putting the child on its own resources, as it were, on its own honour. And believe me from my experience of hundreds, I was going to say thousands, of children—I know that they have perhaps a finer sense of honour than you and I have.

The greatest lessons in life—if we would but stoop and humble ourselves, we would learn not from grown-up learned men, but from the so-called ignorant children. Jesus never uttered a loftier or a grander truth than when he said that wisdom cometh out of the mouths of babes. I believe it, I have noticed it in my own experience that, if we would approach babes in humility and in innocence, we would learn wisdom from them. *(Speech at Montessori Training College, London, 28 October 1931 – (CW 48, pp. 239–40))*

Follow Golden Rule

If the teachers have secret relations with their girl students and later when such relations can no longer be kept concealed legalize them with marriage, this cannot be said to have sanctified those relations. It is my firm belief that just as a brother and a sister cannot have a husband–wife relation even so a teacher and his girl-student too cannot have a husband–wife relation. This is a golden rule and its non-observance can only result in the destruction of the institution. This rule serves as guarantee for the protection of the girls from their teachers. The teacher's is a high office and it enables him to exercise great influence upon the boys and girls in his charge. They regard what he says as gospel truth. They are not likely to suspect him of any illicit designs and he must, therefore, observe these essential rules. Where the welfare of the soul as distinct from the body is of greater importance such relations (as marriage between the teacher and his girl-student) are inadmissible and must be so regarded. *(Harijanbandhu, 29 November 1936 (CW 64, p. 91))*

Be a Student of Students

A teacher who establishes rapport with the taught, becomes one with them, learns more from them than he teaches them. He who learns nothing from his disciples is, in my opinion, worthless. Whenever I talk with someone I learn from him. I take from him more than I give him. In this way, a true teacher regards himself as a student of his students. If you will teach your pupils with this attitude, you will benefit much from them. *(Talk to Khadi Vidyalaya Students, Sevagram – Harijan Sevak, 15 February 1942 (CW 75, p. 269))*

10

Nayee Taleem—A Method of Teaching

Mahatma Gandhi came up with a novel manner of imparting education. Even though, the system of education in the country was too nervous to experiment with his ideas at the national level, in pockets his method, called Nayee Taleem is being followed to yield impressive results. Two introductions need to be made. The first one is easy. Meet Mohandas Karamchand Gandhi, the greatest leader of the twentieth century. The second one is to the method of teaching as enunciated by him. He called it Nayee Taleem, which literally translated means New Education. As you go through the ideas that form the basis of Nayee Taleem, you realize, Gandhi had indeed loved and understood children and the learning process.

I will begin my relating my first encounter with Nayee Taleem. I had gone to Kausani. This is a small quiet hill station in the state of Uttar Pradesh, northeast of Delhi. The majestic Himalayas as the backdrop and valleys hurling down as surprises were filled with stories of dynamic enterprising village women. They had protested against the opening of a liquor shop at one village. At another they had resisted deforestation. And the women were as conversant with the written as well as the spoken word.

The most revealing encounter was on one of our treks. We met two young women who had come in the traditional attire including the scarf on their heads. They also carried with them was carrying some bramble too. With the spirit of reformation high in city-bred me, I asked them if they were literate. They said they were not and that they did not see why they should study. For one hour I explained to them why. At the end of it, they casually revealed they were doing their Masters in Sociology. They were home on vacation! Imagine my shock and a feeling of utter foolishness. It took some time to reflect on the fact that all their education had not alienated them from their roots.

As I followed the source of such spirit in these women I was led to an uphill climb. No vehicle went up, you just had to trek it. It went up so many steps that I felt I would soon reach the heavens, and in a sense I did. I was at Laxmi Ashram at Kasauni. It was set up in 1946 by Katherine Helliman, better known in India as Sarla Behn, an ardent follower of Gandhi. Working with the people while building awareness for the fight for independence, Sarla Behn noticed the amount of hardship a woman from that region underwent. She decided, under Gandhi's encouragement and insistence, that this was where an institution based on Nayee Taleem should be set up. Beginning with three students, Lakshmi Ashram began imparting education to the people along Gandhian lines. Today the names of some of our major reformers and grass root workers figure in the school's alumni.

When we entered the complex that is spread over many acres of open land, we saw some students and their teachers preparing a bed for vegetable sowing. One student, far out across the hill, was out grazing cows. A few others were in the kitchen making breakfast. Within half hour when we had gone around the neat but Spartan complex, we came across yet another student. This time she was with a teacher trying to record the temperature from a barometer. The diverse activities wee too distracting to the mind that went to see an ordinary school. So I sat down to hear and read about Nayee Taleem, which was what the school was all about.

Gandhi, on his return to India from South Africa, was struck by the failure of the modern system of education. He argued that beginning with the language in which children were and continue to be taught, the school syllabus based on Macaulays system, was irrelevant to the country's context. After accessing that kind of education, it alienated the student from his or her motherland and culture. Yet it did not make him vocationally any worthier. The student community that dominated the thinker leader's mind comprised eighty percent of India's rural folk.

As he ruminated the problem in his mind, he decided the way to go about education, true education, was to give literary training through vocational training. Quoting Gandhi, I hold that true education of the intellect can only come through a proper exercise and training of the bodily organs. In other words, the intelligent use of the bodily organs in a child provides the best and quickest way of developing his intellect. He went on to elaborate his idea with the example of a takli. The takli is the most primitive form of the spinning wheel. It is actually a tool that must have been fashioned before the discovery of the wheel. The use of the wheel for spinning came later in history. The initial taklis could have been fashioned out of clay or wet flour, dried and a bamboo splinter passed through it. In some parts of Bengal and Bihar, this kind of tool is spin is still used. Most cloth in India was made of the takli yarn and the cottage industries still uses it for finer counts of textiles.

There you are-that was just Gandhi's idea. Talk about the takli and you have perforce to talk of the wheel, science, the coming of mill cloth, the dying out of taklis, the regional variations of taklis, the areas where cotton is grown and so on. History, geography, science and arithmetic are all taught through practical experience.

The education system should go to the people, should lure them for its value, both economic and intellectual. He argued that primary education should be spread across seven years and should contain the entire syllabus that children study till they leave school. In addition they will pick up one vocational skill. The takli was an example, it could be anything. Another quote from Gandhi's writings would be in order: Then as to primary education, my confirmed opinion is that the commencement of training by teaching the alphabet and reading and writing, hampers their intellectual growth. I would not teach them the alphabet till they have had an elementary knowledge of history, geography, mental arithmetic and art.

Through these three I should develop their intelligence. Question may be asked how intelligence can be developed through the takli or the spinning wheel. It can to a marvellous degree if it is not taught mechanically. When you tell a child the reason for each process, when you explain the mechanism of the takli, when you give him/her the history of cotton and its connection with civilization itself and take him to the village field where it is grown and teach him to the village field where it is grown and teach him to the village field where it is grown and teach him to count the rounds he spins and the method of finding the evenness and strength of the yarn, you hold his interest and simultaneously train his eyes, hands and mind. I should give six months to this preliminary training. The child is now probably ready for learning how to read the alphabet and, when he is able to do so rapidly he is ready to learn simple drawing and when he has learnt to draw geometric figures and the figures if birds, etc., he will draw not scrawl the figures of the alphabet. I consider writing as a fine art. We kill it by imposing the alphabet on little children and making it the beginning of learning.

Gradually vocation should serve a dual process; it should pay for the student's course and also develop his skill. Land, building and equipment are not to be covered by the student's labour. All crafts that are widely practiced in India can be taught with minimal investment. The self-supporting aspect of Gandhi's New Education formula was in his opinion the only way to carry education to the crores of children in India awaiting education.

Higher education should be left to private enterprises and for meeting national requirements. The state universities should be purely examining bodies.

So when I looked up and saw the child returning from grazing the cows, I wondered what she would have associated with it-different types of greenery, love towards animals, the food cycle, milk, dairy farming… or the young women emerging from the kitchen, what would they have learnt about fire, cooking, nourishment, nutrition, agriculture and the growth of rice and pulses. A new desire seemed to sprout in me. I wished I could go back in time and sit amidst nature to learn.

British Education in India

As has been noted by numerous scholars of British rule in India, the physical presence of the British in India was not significant. Yet, for almost two centuries, the British were able to rule two-thirds of the subcontinent directly, and exercise considerable leverage over the Princely States that accounted for the remaining one-third. While the strategy of divide and conquer was used most effectively, an important aspect of British rule in India was the psychological indoctrination of an elite layer within Indian society who were artfully tutored into becoming model British subjects. This English-educated layer of Indian society was craftily encouraged in absorbing values and notions about themselves and their land of birth that would be conducive to the British occupation of India, and furthering British goals of looting India's physical wealth and exploiting it's labour.

In 1835, Thomas Macaulay articulated the goals of British colonial imperialism most succinctly: *"We must do our best to form a class who may be interpreters between us and the millions whom we govern, a class of persons Indian in blood and colour, but English in taste, in opinions, words and intellect."* As the architect of Colonial Britain's Educational Policy in India, Thomas Macaulay was to set the tone for what educated Indians were going to learn about themselves, their civilization, and their view of Britain and the world around them. An arch-racist, Thomas Macaulay had nothing but scornful disdain for Indian history and civilization. In his infamous minute of 1835, he wrote that he had *"never found one among them (speaking of Orientalists, an opposing political faction) who could deny that a single shelf of a good European library was worth the whole native literature of India and Arabia". "It is, no exaggeration to say, that all the historical information which has been collected from all the books written in Sanskrit language is less valuable than what may be found in the most paltry abridgments used at preparatory schools in England".*

As a contrast to such unabashed contempt for Indian civilization, we find glowing references to India in the writings of pre-colonial Europeans quoted by Swami Vivekananda: *"All history points to India as the mother of science and art,"* wrote William Macintosh. *"This country was anciently so renowned for knowledge and wisdom that the philosophers of Greece did not disdain to travel thither for their improvement."* Pierre Sonnerat, a French naturalist, concurred: *"We find among the Indians the vestiges of the most remote antiquity.... We know that all peoples came there to draw the elements of their knowledge.... India, in her splendour, gave religions and laws to all the other peoples; Egypt and Greece owed to her both their fables and their wisdom.*

But colonial exploitation had created a new imperative for the colonial lords. It could no longer be truthfully acknowledged that India had a rich civilization of its own-that its philosophical and scientific contributions may have influenced European scholars-or helped in shaping the European Renaissance. Britain needed a class of intellectuals meek and docile in their attitude towards the British, but full of hatred towards their fellow citizens. It was thus important to emphasize the negative aspects of the Indian tradition, and obliterate or obscure the positive. Indians were to be taught that they were a deeply conservative and fatalist people-genetically predisposed to irrational superstitions and mystic belief systems.

That they had no concept of nation, national feelings or a history. If they had any culture, it had been brought to them by invaders-that they themselves lacked the creative energy to achieve anything by themselves. But the British, on the other hand epitomized modernity-they were the harbingers of all that was rational and scientific in the world. With their unique organizational skills and energetic zeal, they would raise India from the morass of casteism and religious bigotry. These and other such ideas were repeatedly filled in the minds of the young Indians who received instruction in the British schools.

All manner of conscious (and subconscious) British (and European) agents would henceforth embark on a journey to rape and conquer the Indian mind. Within a matter of years, J.N Farquhar (a contemporary of Macaulay) was to write: *"The new educational policy of the Government created during these years the modern educated class of India. These are men who think and speak in English habitually, who are proud of their citizenship in the British Empire, who are devoted to English literature, and whose intellectual life has been almost entirely formed by the thought of the West, large numbers of them enter government services, while the rest practice law, medicine or teaching, or take to journalism or business."*

Macaulay's strategem could not have yielded greater dividends. Charles E. Trevelyan, brother-in-law of Macaulay, stated: " *Familiarly acquainted with us by means of our literature, the Indian youth almost cease to regard us as foreigners. They speak of "great" men with the same enthusiasm as we do. Educated in the same way, interested in the same objects, engaged in the same pursuits with ourselves, they become more English than Hindoos, just as the Roman provincial became more Romans than Gauls or Italians.."*

That this was no benign process, but intimately related to British colonial goals was expressed quite candidly by Charles Trevelyan in his testimony before the Select Committee of the House of Lords on the Government of Indian Territories on 23rd June, 1853: *"..... the effect of training in European learning is to give an entirely new turn to the native mind. The young men educated in this way cease to strive after independence according to the original Native model, and aim at, improving the institutions of the country according to the English model, with the ultimate result of establishing constitutional self-government. They cease to regard us as enemies and usurpers, and they look upon us as friends and patrons, and powerful beneficent persons, under whose protection the regeneration of their country will gradually be worked out......"*

Much of the indoctrination of the Indian mind actually took place outside the formal classrooms and through the sale of British literature to the English-educated Indian who developed a voracious appetite for the British novel and British writings on a host of popular subjects. In a speech before the Edinburgh Philosophical Society in 1846, Thomas Babington (1800-1859), shortly to become Baron Macaulay, offered a toast: *"To the literature of Britain... which has exercised an influence wider than that of our commerce and mightier than that of our arms...before the light of which impious and cruel superstitions are fast taking flight on the Banks of the Ganges!"*

However, the British were not content to influence Indian thinking just through books written in the English language.

Realizing the danger of Indians discovering their real heritage through the medium of Sanskrit, Christian missionaries such as William Carey anticipated the need for British educators to learn Sanskrit and transcribe and interpret Sanskrit texts in a manner compatible with colonial aims. That Carey's aims were thoroughly duplicitous is brought out in this quote cited by Richard Fox Young: *"To gain the ear of those who are thus deceived it is necessary for them to believe that the speaker has a superior knowledge of the subject. In these circumstances a knowledge of Sanskrit is valuable. As the person thus misled, perhaps a Brahman, deems this a most important part of knowledge, if the advocate of truth be deficient therein, he labours against the hill; presumption is altogether against him."*

In this manner, India's awareness of it's history and culture was manipulated in the hands of colonial ideologies. Domestic and external views of India were shaped by authors whose attitudes towards all things Indian were shaped either by subconscious prejudice or worse by barely concealed racism. For instance, William Carey (who bemoaned how so few Indians had converted to Christianity in spite of his best efforts) had little respect or sympathy for Indian traditions. In one of his letters, he described Indian music as *"disgusting"*, bringing to mind *"practices dishonorable to God"*. Charles Grant, who exercised tremendous influence in colonial evangelical circles, published his *"Observations"* in 1797 in which he attacked almost every aspect of Indian society and religion, describing Indians as morally depraved, *"lacking in truth, honesty and good faith" (p.103)*. British Governor General Cornwallis asserted *"Every native of Hindostan, I verily believe, is corrupt"*.

Victorian writer and important art critic of his time, John Ruskin dismissed all Indian art with ill-concealed contempt: *"..the Indian will not draw a form of nature but an amalgamation of monstrous objects"*. Adding: *"To all facts and forms of nature it wilfully and resolutely opposes itself; it will not draw a man but an eight armed monster, it will not draw a flower but only a spiral or a zig zag"*. Others such as George Birdwood (who took some interest in Indian decorative art) nevertheless opined: *"...painting and sculpture as fine art did not exist in India."*

Several British and European historians attempted to portray India as a society that had made no civilizational progress for several centuries. William Jones asserted that Hindu society had been stationary for so long that *"in beholding the Hindus of the present day, we are beholding the Hindus of many ages past"*. James Mill, author of the three-volume History of British India (1818) essentially concurred with William Jones as did Henry Maine. This view of India, as an essentially unchanging society where there was no intellectual debate, or technological innovation-where a hidebound caste system had existed without challenge or reform-where social mobility or class struggle were unheard of, became especially popular with European scholars and intellectuals of the colonial era.

It allowed influential philosophers such as Hegel to posit ethnocentric and self-serving justifications of colonization. Arguing that Europe was *"absolutely the end of universal history"*, he saw Asia as only the beginning of history, where history soon came to a standstill. *"If we had formerly the satisfaction of believing in the antiquity of the Indian wisdom and holding it in respect, we now have ascertained through being acquainted with the great astronomical works of the Indians, the inaccuracy of all figures quoted. Nothing can be more confused, nothing more imperfect than the chronology of the Indians; no people which attained to culture in astronomy, mathematics, etc., is as incapable for history; in it they have neither stability nor coherence."* With such distorted views of India, it was a small step to argue that *"The British, or rather the East India Company, are the masters of India because it is the fatal destiny of Asian empires to subject themselves to the Europeans."*

Hegel's racist consciousness comes out most explicitly in his descriptions of Africans: *"It is characteristic of the blacks that their consciousness has not yet even arrived at the intuition of any objectivity, as for example, of God or the law, in which humanity relates to the world and intuits its essence....He [the black person] is a human being in the rough."*

Such ideas also shaped the views of later German authors such Max Weber famous for his *"The Protestant Ethic and the Spirit of Capitalism,"* (1930) who in his descriptions of Indian religion and philosophy focused exclusively on *"material renunciation"* and the *"world denying character"* of Indian philosophical systems, ignoring completely the rich heritage of scientific realism and rational analysis that had in fact imbued much of Indian thought. Weber discounted the existence of any rational doctrines in the East, insisting that: *"Neither scientific, artistic, governmental, nor economic evolution has led to the modes of rationalization proper to the Occident."* Whether it was ignorance or prejudice that determined his views, such views were not uninfluential, and exemplified the euro-centric undercurrent that pervaded most British and European scholarship of that time.

Naturally, British-educated Indians absorbed and internalized such characterizations of themselves and their past. Amongst those most affected by such diminution of the Indian character was the young Gandhi, who when in South Africa, wished to meet General Smuts and offer the cooperation of the South African Indian population for the Boer war effort. In a conversation with the General, Gandhi appears as just the sort of colonized sycophant the British education system had hoped to create: *"General Smuts, sir we Indians would like to strengthen the hands of the government in the war. However, our efforts have been rebuffed. Could you inform us about our vices so we would reform and be better citizens of this land?"* to which Gen. Smuts replied: *"Mr. Gandhi, we are not afraid of your vices, We are afraid of your virtues".* (Although Gandhi eventually went through a slow and very gradual nationalist transformation, in 1914 he campaigned for the British war efforts in World War I, and was one of the last of the national leaders to call for complete independence from British rule.)

British-educated Indians grew up learning about Pythagoras, Archimedes, Galileo and Newton without ever learning about Panini, Aryabhatta, Bhaskar or Bhaskaracharya. The logic and epistemology of the Nyaya Sutras, the rationality of the early Buddhists or the intriguing philosophical systems of the Jains were generally unknown to the them. Neither was there any awareness of the numerous examples of dialectics in nature that are to be found in Indian texts. They may have read Homer or Dickens but not the Panchatantra, the Jataka tales or anything from the Indian epics. Schooled in the aesthetic and literary theories of the West, many felt embarrassed in acknowledging Indian contributions in the arts and literature. What was important to

Western civilization was deemed universal, but everything Indian was dismissed as either backward and anachronistic, or at best tolerated as idiosyncratic oddity. Little did the Westernized Indian know what debt "Western Science and Civilization" owed (directly or indirectly) to Indian scientific discoveries and scholarly texts.

Dilip K. Chakrabarti (Colonial Indology) thus summarized the situation: *"The model of the Indian past...was foisted on Indians by the hegemonic books written by Western Indologists concerned with language, literature and philosophy who were and perhaps have always been paternalistic at their best and racists at their worst.."*

Elaborating on the phenomenon of cultural colonization, Priya Joshi (Culture and Consumption: Fiction, the Reading Public, and the British Novel in Colonial India) writes: *"Often, the implementation of a new education system leaves those who are colonized with a lack of identity and a limited sense of their past. The indigenous history and customs once practiced and observed slowly slip away. The colonized become hybrids of two vastly different cultural systems. Colonial education creates a blurring that makes it difficult to differentiate between the new, enforced ideas of the colonizers and the formerly accepted native practices."*

Ngugi Wa Thiong'o, (Kenya, Decolonising the Mind), displaying anger toward the isolationist feelings colonial education causes, asserted that the process *"...annihilates a peoples belief in their names, in their languages, in their environment, in their heritage of struggle, in their unity, in their capacities and ultimately in themselves. It makes them see their past as one wasteland of non-achievement and it makes them want to distance themselves from that wasteland. It makes them want to identify with that which is furthest removed from themselves".*

Strong traces of such thinking continue to infect young Indians, especially those that migrate to the West. Elements of such mental insecurity and alienation also had an impact on the consciousness of the British-educated Indians who participated in the freedom struggle. In contemporary academic circles, various false theories continue to percolate. While some write as if Indian civilization has made no substantial progress since the Vedic period, for others the clock stopped with Ashoka, or with the "classical age" of the Guptas. Some Islamic scholars have attempted to construct a more positive view of the Islamic reigns in India, but continue to concur with colonial scholars in seeing pre-Islamic India as socially and culturally moribund and technologically backward. A range of scholars persist in basing their studies on views of Indian history that not only concentrate exclusively on its negative traits, but also fail to situate the negative aspects of Indian history in historical context. Few have attempted to make serious and objective comparisons of Indian social institutions and cultural attributes with those of other nations. Often the Indian historical record is unfavourably compared with European achievements that in fact took place many centuries later.

Unable to rise above the colonial paradigms, many post-independence scholars of Indian history and civilization continue to fumble with colonially inspired doctrines that run counter to the emerging historical record. Others more conscious of British distortions and frustrated by the hypercritical assessment of some Indian scholars, go to the other extreme of presenting the Indian historical record without any critical analysis whatsoever. Some have even attempted to construct artificially hyped views of Indian history where there is little attempt to distinguish myth from fact. Strong communal biases continue to prevail, as do xenophobic rejections of even potentially useful and valid Western constructs, even as Western-imposed hegemonic economic systems and exploitative economic models continue to dominate the Indian economic landscape and often find unquestioning acceptance.

Thus, one of the most difficult tasks facing the Indian subcontinent is to free all scholarship concerning its development and its relationship to the world from the biased formulations and distortions of colonially-influenced authors. At the same time, Indian authors also need to study the West and other civilizations with dispassionate objectivity-eschewing both craven and uncritical admiration and xenophobic skepticism and distrust of the scientific and cultural achievements made by others.

Gandhi's Concept on Education and its Relevance in the Present Day

I have been involved in the university system for more than 30 years. I used to interact with a large number of undergraduate students in the colleges and universities. I used to go to the colleges and universities to address students as a Vice Chancellor. Society has always been criticizing and doubting the purpose of education. What is the purpose of education in society? Dr. Radhakrishnan in his address today discussed the relevance of Gandhism and Buddhism in the cyber age. I used to talk in my lectures about the dehumanizing and alienating aspects of education. I used to tell students, particularly high-school and college-age students, about the dehumanizing aspect of the established types of education being offered.

In my lectures, I used to give an example of a highly educated brother and his almost illiterate brother. When something unpleasant happens, such as a fire or a bus accident, in the immediate vicinity of this illiterate brother and the highly sophisticated and educated brother, the moment the illiterate brother hears about this accident, he will run to that place as a sort of reflex action. The educated brother, he will ponder the situation and remark, "I will not go at any cost." He will even try to prevent his illiterate brother from going to that place and offering help to the victim. He will say, "Don't go there as there will be problems." The educated brother probably will not go to that place: He will wait to find out what happened the next day: Probably he will send a condolence message to the family of victim, or if he is one of the highly educated and sophisticated types of people, he will send a condolence message through the newspapers. That is an example of the type of education we are offering. Today, I will concentrate my remarks on Gandhi's views on education, with particular reference to India, and I will touch on some aspects of the Buddhist view on education.

This alienation, this dehumanization aspect of the established types of education is happening in India because we do not understand Gandhi's views on education. Dr. Radhakrishnan has also made passing remarks on the tension being created among the educated youth because of the established types of education and the over domination of science and technology. It is not the over domination of science, but it is probably the misinterpretation of science and technology that is the underlying cause for much of the tension.

We have heard about several of the educational reports contained in the UNESCO Report on Education that examines the different types of tension that are being created in educated individuals. The tension that exists between tradition and modernity is a very significant tension. This tension between tradition and modernity is not a new thing. Right from the start of the industrial revolution, this tension between tradition and modernity has been there. Not only in education, but also in the Arts, Literature, and our day-to-day dress, these tensions exist. Then there is the tension between materialism and spirituality, or you can call it the tension between science and religion. There is also a tension in the area of development, for example our view about long-term development and our short-term requirements. There is a feeling that science and technology can solve our problems immediately, and naturally, we resort to immediate, short-term solutions, neglecting the long-term views on development, thus, naturally causing concern in realms of the environment, ecology, and other areas.

If modern education is creating tension between these areas of concern, we definitely need to build consensus because of the way in which education is imparted. When people ask me about the purpose of education, or to define education, I refer to what Mahatma Gandhi said several decades ago. He said, "... education for life, education through life, and education throughout life."

Gandhi's Views on Education

These were the words he used. When I was working in the university in Kerala and I saw the different types of disturbances occurring on campuses. I used to say that literally we have taken life out of education. Everybody is doubting the purpose of education. Education is for life, life in its entirety and then education through life. This is not happening at all today. Education is only being provided through our so-called lectures and in the laboratory. Education throughout life is not happening at all. Of course, we are trying to supplement this education by using artificial means. Education throughout life: As teachers, we can say that once we get the qualifications, once we get our degree, we stop our education and do away with further study. I think nowadays we have several different types of education, whatever adjective we put before the word education, it is a different discipline altogether. This definition of Mahatma Gandhi would comprise everything that can be conceived under education.

Education for life, education through life, and education throughout life. That the concept of life has been taken away from education is precisely the reason for the dehumanizing, alienating aspect of education. I used to say that literally lives are taken away from the campuses because of the physical clashes among the members of the student body.

This is happening in India. Hence, when we give life in its entirety as part of education, Gandhiji's views on education are realized, and this act of instilling life into the education process is the solution for any kind of educational development for this country. I have just mentioned some random thoughts on his views of education and how these views are relevant for any society, any country for that matter.

To bring about a change in society, which is really a stupendous task, especially in a country where considerable disparities in income persist and ignorance and illiteracy widen the gulf between the elite and the masses. In a developing society like India, each one adopted a planned approach towards development, where education becomes a key agent of socioeconomic reform. As the famous education commission of 1964–66, the Radhakrishnan Commission, observed; "for achieving change on a grand scale the only effective instrument is education. Education does initiate changes in social institutions and sub-systems, and this affects the social situation of the country."

Gandhi's Scheme of Education

In the Gandhian constructive program, the most important element is '*Nai Taleem,*' or the new education, which in the words of Acharya Kriplani, "... is the coping stone of Gandhi's social and political edifice."

Gandhiji regarded his scheme of education as spearheading the silent social revolution and expected it to provide a healthy relationship between the city and the village, which would go a long way in eradicating the poisoned relationship between the classes. This view was affirmed by various other scholars and thinkers in the field of education.

Zakir Hussain once commented on Gandhi's views on education. He wrote, "... Gandhi socially considered the introduction of such practical productive work in education to be participated in by all." The children of the nation will tend to break down the existing barriers of prejudice between manual and intellectual workers and harmful elites to both. Such is the social significance of the so-called new educational concept of Gandhi, but it does not entail any sacrifice of the individual goal of education or its social goal. Gandhiji had said, "by education, I mean an overall all around drawing out of the best in child and man, in body, mind, and spirit." This concept of education serves both goals at the same time. The application of Gandhi's concept of education was first suggested for children between the ages of 7 and 14. This is called basic education. This was later on extended to all the stages. Gandhi felt that it should include the education of everybody, at every stage of life; including the university stage. The Sarvodaya thinkers accepted the whole idea underlying the new educational concept of Gandhi, including its social and individual aims.

Gandhi laid the foundation of a scheme of national education that was suited to our needs, requirements, genius, and aspirations for the future. It is left up to us to perfect it and extend it to cover the entire field of education. In this process, adjustment and adaptation may be necessary, but these actions must be undertaken in the spirit of the total philosophy of Gandhi, that is, for the individual and the society. Whatever may be its merits and demerits, we should not forget that education to Gandhi meant inspiring the children with a new ideology based upon personal purity and unselfish service, resulting in the creation of a society based upon truth and love. This is precisely the Buddha's concept also.

Basic education stands for a new outlook, a new approach. The fountainhead of all the conflicts in the world is that knowledge has been separated from work. They have been separated in thoughts by a faulty psychology. They have been separated in life by a faulty sociology. They have been assigned different market values by faulty economics. One of the basic principles of education is that work and knowledge must never be separated. Separation of learning from labour results in social injustices. In dynamic societies, education has to equip individuals with the skills and attitudes necessary for them to adapt to changing conditions, and for constructive participation in the task of social change. This is possible only through the adoption of a suitable educational system.

Gandhi believed that education should be intimately related with human experience, "what better book can be there than the book of humanity?" he asked. The convergence of ideas and action was the key note of his approach, which was national in scope, as he wanted to present an alternative to the system introduced by the British colonial system. He stressed that the educational system must be one in which the highest development of mind and soul is possible and which instills courage and self-reliance in the individual, while at the same time, helping them cultivate the highest intellectual scientific, moral, and ethical accomplishments.

Gandhiji aimed at developing a society, "a socially conscious 'man' dedicated to truth and nonviolence." His educational scheme was nationalist in setting, idealist in nature and pragmatic on one hand while social in purpose and spiritual in intent on the other hand. It was also an essential instrument for materializing his dream of *Sarvodaya Samaj*, in which the vertical and horizontal distance between people is reduced to a minimum. Gandhi formulated his scheme of basic education in the context of poverty, illiteracy, backwardness, frustration, and the degeneration of our masses, resulting from the disruption of traditional social institutions and the destruction of the small-scale cottage industry.

He says that we must draw out the best in adult and child, as I mentioned earlier. This radical scheme was geared up, checking the progressive decay of our villages, reviving the village economy, laying the foundations of a just social order, in which there is no unnatural division between the 'haves' and the 'have-nots' and everybody is assured of achieving acceptable standards. The basic educational scheme was an essential ingredient of Gandhi's plan to eliminate the rural-urban divide and redress the structural and socioeconomic imbalances that were abound in Indian society. Gandhi also addressed the issue of free education.

By free education, Gandhi did not mean an education fully supported and subsidized by the state or other outside agencies. Instead, he implied a system that had the maximum possible capacity of self-support from the people's work experience, which is both an instrument of education and a source of income. The Gandhian system was free in another sense also: It did not regard formal, full-time schooling of the pupil as essential. He had very specific views about secondary and higher education. There is a feeling that Gandhi was against research, higher education, etc.

He had very specific ideas about research, higher education and the accumulation of knowledge. In Gandhi's scheme, higher education performed the essential function of providing training and properly motivating human power for national needs and there was an urgent need for the purposive expansion of such education. I would like to conclude with a quote from Gandhi. He declared, "... under my scheme, there will be more and better libraries, more and better research institutes. Under, it we should have an army of chemists, engineers, and other experts who will be the real servants of the nation and answer the varied and growing requirements of the people who are becoming increasingly conscious other rights and wants."

Several critics say that Gandhi was only concerned with primary and basic education. This was not true. He had very specific views of higher education. Of course, I have a few more points to cover, which I will take them up with you later during the discussion session.

Gandhian Experiment in Primary Education

The Story of Taman Kanak-kanak 'Gandhi'

> *Nothing turns out right so long as there is no harmony between body, mind, and soul.* – *M.K. Gandhi*

'Taman kanak-kanak' is the Indonesian term for kindergarten, and in further references the letters TK will be used.

As background to TK 'Gandhi' in Candi Dasa should be mentioned the Bali Canti Sena Foundation, established in Denpasar, Bali, on 10 December 1970. Its objective was to meet the needs of the time, *i.e.*, to disseminate Gandhian ideas which would give the right orientation to our young generation and make them responsible citizens of the Republic of Indonesia. This, we believed, could only be done when the basis of our life and attitude was *ahimsa* and *satya*, the great twin principles of *Vedanta* successfully demonstrated by Mahatma Gandhi. We endeavoured to do this by starting a monthly that would bring out suitable articles to promote open minds, a spirit of enquiry and constructive activities. Holding camps and outdoor activities for students were part and parcel of this endeavour.

Several of such engagements, however, met with little success. It turned out that camps and outdoor activities were popular, but little was achieved in terms of sustained work. The Gandhian way required a more solid interaction.

Then with great trepidation we made bold to try out a Gandhian Ashram which we named 'Canti Dasa'—servants of peace—which, as if so ordained, was located at a beautiful spot at the foot of an ancient temple.

The urge to be of some service to our immediate community led to a concern for health. A modest dispensary was started, which brought in its wake a free lunch programme for our neighbour, the village school with its 300 or so pupils.

Hardly a year had this project been underway when we decided to suspend our activities due to strained relations with the provincial religious body, who were suspicious of the motives behind the lunch programme. In order to continue our feeding programme, we hit upon the idea of starting our own school. Our financial limitations compelled us to be modest and imposed severe economy in our approach. For this purpose a kindergarten seemed to be feasible, since our area had no kindergarten.

Candi Dasa derives its name from an ancient temple built around the year 800. It must have been some kind of retreat or hermitage, judging from the austere architectural style. It is an exceedingly beautiful spot: a strip of golden beach with hills as a backdrop, on top of which is perched this austere temple. A small freshwater lake fed by many springs on its banks runs into the ocean.

On the banks of the little lake is Ashram 'Canti Dasa', dedicated to the great soul of Mahatma Gandhi, whom we look upon as our guru, although he himself during his life emphatically refused to be anybody's guru. Such was his humility and honesty.

Looking back over the years we realize that, unknowingly, we started some pioneering work of the most difficult kind, *i.e.*, to change people's minds by using persuasion and personal example, the Gandhian way *par excellence*. And that, it should be added, in the teeth of opposition of vested interests.

With a kindergarten to be developed, our own objectives and goals began to take clearer shape. As a concrete manifestation of the Bali Canti Sena Foundation's aim, which has for its guiding principles *ahimsa* and *satya*, the objectives of TK 'Gandhi' are:

(a) To apply a holistic approach to the education of our pupils. The holistic approach, which is derived from the noble Vedantic dictum *tat tvam asi* – oneness of life – should be reflected in the methods and methodology of the school;

(b) To bring out and foster all the potential in the child and help it express these through *ahimsic* channels; and

(c) To make school a happy adventure of discovery for the child.

Candi Dasa cannot be properly called a village, as it consists of a score of hamlets sprawling across the beach area of the village of Bugbug. Its inhabitants number not more than 750 to 800 people. Their source of living is petty farming. Only coconut groves thrive in the locality. Cattle raising adds to their income, but in the dry season grass is scarce. Fishing is also taken up, but it seems that of late the catch has decreased due to superior methods of fishing by people with capital. Of the lime kilns that used to help a few families, some have had to be closed down due to the enforcement of laws supporting ecological balance. Even from colonial times this area has been a poor one and many of its people have over the years migrated to more prosperous parts of the island and of late also to other islands.

There used to be one village school only, our neighbour, but the new drive for education made Candi Dasa one school richer. However, now there is already the problem of filling the first grades of these schools with enough pupils. Apart from two or three carpenters and one blacksmith, no village industry can be discerned. These are only to be found in the adjacent village of Tenganan, which is famous because of its indigenous government and life-style that has remained intact for almost a hundred years. It has become one of the highlights of tourist interest. Although the tourist industry tries hard to sell this area it does not seem likely that hordes of tourist will come in the near future.

Experiment

In Indonesia even private schools have to follow the syllabus set by the government, with some concessions so long as there is no clash with the country's philosophy, *Panchashila.* In practice, thus, there is some leeway for teaching to depart from the government's dictates. In fact a good deal depends on the creativity and inventiveness of the teacher, who should know how to interpret the spirit of directives creatively. The teachers should be resourceful in integrating and weaving their own outlook and approach towards education into the government guidelines.

The ultimate objective of our educational approach being the attainment of true freedom of the individual, the immediate goal is how to foster those qualities and potential in the child that would help to bring about a peaceful, nonviolent human community where relationships are conducive to harmony and creativity.

The method of teaching emphasizes the self-activity of the child, in which the teacher participates and stimulates rather than teaches as understood generally. The main idea that a teacher should bear in mind is that whatever is done in class should be rooted in the children's environment. Whatever is artificial should be avoided; in other words, there should be harmony between life at home and in school.

The poverty prevailing in this area means that parents should be saved school expenses. Therefore the only money parents spend is on the few things absolutely needed in class, such as two or three cheap copybooks and a pencil every other month, while no fees or other expenses are charged.

It goes without saying that in our system the principle of *Swadeshi* is given prime importance. To make or produce whatever we need for our food or use is religiously practised in our school. This is possible because we grow our own food, have our own carpenter and tailor/dressmaker as well as musicians. The material we need also should be found in our environment.

Teachers

Ashram Canti Dasa, which runs the TK 'Gandhi', is truly a self-supporting community and receives no aid or subsidy from the government or other sources. Therefore our financial means are very limited and only the utmost economy enables us to survive. In such a situation there is no question of hiring teachers. When we opened the TK 'Gandhi' qualified kindergarten teachers were scarce anyway, while those who had been trained in government institutions were cut according to government taste. Luckily a teacher was found who due to political stigma had been jobless for a number of years. She was more than willing to accept our offer, even on a truly 'honorary' basis, her salary being of 'a basic need sufficiency'. The good luck was that she was a good singer and could teach the basics of Balinese dance as well.

After two years we drew the central government's attention and were then given by way of support a woman teacher to help out in our TK. However, as is usually the case with government employed people, she proved more of a liability than a real help. In effect all Ashram members get turns in assisting in the TK whenever they are free from their own duties in the Ashram.

For everyone of us knows something that could be put to good use in the TK class. One older woman is a master at making offerings and palm frond cuttings, so indispensable in Balinese ceremonies and decoration. Another knows how to play the flute and yet another girl teaches swimming. Thus our TK has quite a few different teachers in a week. This is how we make the most of our limitations. Finding the children to people our newly opened TK also presented a slight problem at first. As is well-known, in farming families children have to help out at home or in the field at an early age. For girls, from the age of four daily task could be from collecting firewood, minding younger siblings or just watching the new paddy harvest drying in the sun. Little boys are made to mind grazing cows or the ducks that are let loose in fields that have just been harvested, or perhaps simply watch the house while their mothers are fetching water.

With the cooperation of the village chief some kids were rounded up and within a month we had a class of 27 children. We considered ourselves fortunate that someone, and a woman at that, could be found willing to mind the children. To disseminate the ideas we nurse about education through this TK, all the members of the Ashram eventually became some sort of teachers according to their skills. Our children come from very poor backgrounds. Their parents struggle the whole day just to scrape a living. Therefore the principle of *Swadeshi*, aside from being an ideal – one that we try to follow faithfully, is pure necessity.

Teaching aids that seem to be a common sight in city or town kindergartens are conspicuous by their absence here. Thus, in this regard, the recourse taken to environment is a must. A real blessing for TK 'Gandhi' is its paradisiacal environment. We are, as it were, drenched in the gifts of nature: water, air, both pure and clear, plants in all shades of green, and healthy-looking animals and pets, the expanse of the blue ocean take our children daily in their happy embrace, stimulating in them free spontaneous movements, laughter and song. That our place is a veritable paradise is apparent from the fact that most of the children are already on the TK premises long before school starts. We can see them on the swing or the seesaw, running back and forth on the sandy beach, the little girls walking hand-in-hand while collecting edible berries and fruit that has dropped to the ground; or intently watching a newborn calf drink milk from its mother.

With the hills right behind us, as well as a freshwater lake, the Ashram's site indeed fulfils the three requirements mentioned in the *Veda*s to make it a fit spot for meditation and other noble pursuits.

Where the hills meet the ocean
And there are springs nearby.
Verily, that is the place for meditation.

The surrounding coconut groves offer plenty of yellow palm fronds for the children to practise on when weaving little mats to sit on, or when cutting decorative streamers and a variety of geometrical forms so indispensable in our celebrations.

The beautiful beach at the doorstep of our school can at any time be used as a vast sandbox in which the children can model, build castles of sand or simply draw and scribble to their hearts' content. Once the government supervisor of kindergartens came to inspect our school. His only remark was, 'The only pity is that there is no sandbox here for the children', to which our teacher replied: 'Sir, the whole ocean and its beach is the best sandbox one can think of '. What an apt remark to show how hidebound we often are, a result of our parrotlike education.

Twice a week the school goes for a walk in the nearby cluster of hamlets or in the hills, for the beach is their daily fare. This is the occasion to make them aware of the beauty of our surroundings and the industry of the villagers. For at any given time some activity is going on, be it feeding the pigs, pounding rice, weaving mats or a carpenter giving shape to the boat under his hands. Then all their senses can be stimulated, which is later reflected in the drawing class. Swimming is almost a daily feature of our curriculum. Simple exercises and postures, derived from yoga and Balinese dance, are integrated in their physical exercise hour, while indigenous children's games are promoted.

We do not follow the teaching of the three Rs too closely, for we believe that drawing, games and singing are more beneficial and anyway the primary school will offer enough opportunity for the three Rs. The managing of the garden's fruits, leaves, shells, stones, etc., more readily captures the children's attention. Singing and dancing are daily occurrences. The idea behind these two activities is to help preserve and promote the vernacular and local culture, since in the ethnic communities of Indonesia, of which there are many, vernaculars and their attending cultures run the danger of disappearing, the more so now, with the national language rapidly gaining ground and popularity due to its being identified with progress. Artistic Bali offers a wide range of local instruments which can be used in kindergartens and are inexpensive compared to instruments that are imported. In our TK we have a few wooden xylophones on which the kids can beat to their hearts' content.

Hygiene and Clean Habits

Holistic or integrated health is a supreme consideration in our approach. Consequently health of body, mind, and soul should be promoted whenever and wherever possible. But the stimulation should take place in a natural way. For instance the singing of *mantras* before starting the morning and when leaving the premises as well as before partaking of lunch is our way of getting involved in religion and a reverent attitude. *Mantras* promoting love for parents, teachers and guests, or for instilling a feeling for God as being the essence of life as so well expressed in '*tvameva mata, cha pita tvameva*', or for promoting friendship, fill the Ashram atmosphere at set times of the day.

Keeping the little hands busy at something useful and meaningful fosters healthy minds, whereas bodily health is taken care of by exercise, walks, swimming and games. In order to stimulate them in a natural way it is especially important that the teacher teaches by example and by personal participation in these activities.

An important feature of the hygiene and health concern is the free school lunch we offer our children. It is through the school lunch that many things are passed on, such as: (a) nutritious food for our lunches is so planned that the parents can make the most of whatever the environment offers in the way of greens, fats, protein, etc.; in fact their habit, dictated by poverty, of eating a variety of green leaves from hedges nearby proves to be most wholesome. It has been found that, for instance, the consumption of three different kinds of green leaves as mixed vegetables more than matches two carotene intake we get from carrots, which are alien to villagers anyway besides requiring 'sophisticated' methods for their cultivation; (b) fermented tapioca cake is an excellent way of taking in vitamins B-complex, while such cake is very cheap and thus considered a 'poor people's snack'; (c) *tempe*, a fermented soya bean item, contains the best and most easily digested vegetable protein. At first it was rejected by the children, as it originated in Java, where it is a 'people's food item. Persistent persuasion has now made *tempe* acceptable and popular.

Neat eating habits should be established and brushing teeth afterwards is to habituate the children to a clean feeling in the mouth. From remarks among the parents when they bring their kids to school we can conclude that our free lunch programme does not stop at lunchtime in our premises, as every newly introduced food item is heatedly discussed. The pros and cons are debated, but it is certain that there are always a few who adopt our novelties. Our dispensary, which serves the schoolchildren's health without excluding others from the village, has also helped in lessening the habit of smoking, for no smoker is served. Of late we have begun to offer acupuncture. The hardest fight was against the national habit of the Balinese of spitting. Luckily, this habit is dying out in our neighbour, the village school. A five-year campaign about plastic littering has yielded results, but not at the public level. That is, now people are careful about keeping their compounds plastic free, but this feeling of responsibility for public places is still very thinly spread.

The School's Interaction with Others

Interaction forms the basis of social intercourse of human society. It may be said that perhaps interaction beyond the family circle starts for the child in kindergarten. For the TK 'Gandhi' interaction has an added dimension. Naturally the children's interaction with Ashram members has its merits as well as a negative side. But an unusual opportunity is there due to our foreign guests' presence. Not a few of them took an interest in our TK kids and more often than not joined in by teaching simple songs and games from their own cultures.

Guests with small children loved to have their own offsprings join the kindergarten while they were holidaying with us. In the first year of the kindergarten children were afraid of our foreign guests, a few even immediately started crying at seeing a foreigner, but now we have to take care that they do not bother the guests, because of few of them like to spoil the children with all kinds of little presents, which can easily develop into some form of bribery. This aspect of interaction is conducive to developing the sense of 'one world' and the beginning of appreciation of cultures other than our own.

Instilling a sense of community is done through the children's participation in works of construction, repairs or building a new cottage. On such occasion the little kids can be seen joyfully carrying bricks or buckets on their heads and walking in single file to the site of construction. The weekly general cleaning-up of our premises always affords great hilarity as this gives them an occasion for running about everywhere, while not only collecting plastic rubbish but also firewood for the kitchen.

Interaction with nature at this tender age could be decisive for a child's later development. Our Ashram grounds and situation offer such interaction in abundance. Natural vegetation, stretches of green lawn, the beach and blue sea only a few metres away, the fresh pond bordering the Ashram grounds on one side, animals such as cows, calves, dogs, cats and a chicken or two, provide another living aspect of nature which may easily awaken a sense of wonder in the young child. And what is life worth without this sense of wonder?

Before school starts children take turns in tending the school garden, watering plants, pulling up dead parts; thus early they are trained to take an interest in whatever they do. Especially in gardening it is always an uplifting experience to watch a bean forcing up its way through the soil in a day or two and see it daily growing to full maturity, followed by the excitement of picking it and having it served as lunch afterwards.

The Place of Nature and Culture in Our School

Nature is divine for the Balinese. The primordial, deeply inbuilt respect and reverence for nature of the Balinese was a ready substratum for the *mahavakya* or great utterance in *Vedanta* introduced by the Hindus to Java and later Bali, in around the fourteenth century. This utterance *tat tvam asi* has even more strengthened our deeply-felt awe and reverence for nature, as is manifested on Plant Day, Animal Day, Tool Day, culminating in the feast of Sarasvati, the goddess of learning and the arts, and Earth Cleansing Day, which comes on the eve of our new year. These ceremonies, except for Earth Cleansing Day, come around every seven months, making Bali an island of daily festivals if individual birthdays and temple anniversaries are included. As a school we especially make much of Plant Day, Animal Day, Tool Day and Ganapati Day. The most festive is Sarasvati Day, celebrated by all schools and institutions or organizations engaged in artistic and literary pursuits.

On that day a priest is invited to lead the function of worship. Sweet and intimate is the celebration of Plant Day. On that occasion a good, fruit-bearing coconut tree in our garden is selected and decorated by the children. They come in their best dress to the school, each with a little offering of fruit and flowers. Sitting around the tree they sing devotional songs, glorifying and blessing the plants in the garden. After the prayer and *mantra*s the kids and the decorated tree are sprinkled with holy water. This and the partaking of fruit and cakes in the offering is enjoyed by all.

Days before a ceremony takes place one can feel the increased activity in the air, for everyone is up and doing something. So it is in our school, as the children have to make the decoration and offerings themselves while only for intricate designs do adults come in to assist. With frequent celebrations, hardly a week goes by in our Ashram without this joyous and busy atmosphere.

Thus reverence and identification with plants, animals, in short with the whole of creation, are fostered in the young child. Gradually through devotional songs, dignified language and a respectful attitude towards creation, culture is instilled in the young souls. Our school celebrations culminate in the commemoration of Gandhi Jayanti on 2 October each year. Then the whole day our place rings with laughter, chatter and the joyful shouts of some two hundred or so kindergarten kids coming from several schools of the region to celebrate with us. Competitions are held in drawing, singing local children's songs and reciting *mantra*s especially selected for young children, games and various skills such as cutting palm-leaf decorations, making little offerings, dancing and drawing. Viewing a whole year from this stance, indeed life for the Balinese is centred around celebrations. The whole of life in Bali is a celebration.

Daily Schedule of the School

The time children spend with us is from 7 in the morning till 11. During the four hours that they are under our care a general pattern as indicated by the timetable below is followed as much as possible:

07.00-07.30	arranging their tables and mats to sit on and sweeping the school garden
07.30-08.00	morning gathering with singing of *mantras* to start the day followed by local songs
08.00-08.30	outdoor physical activities such as games where bodily movements are emphasized.
08.30-09.00	swimming and bathing in the sea followed by rinsing in the freshwater lake and going for a walk in the hills or watching the daily village activities.
09.00-09.30	drawing or practising manual skills such as cutting palm-leaf fronds, mat weaving, moulding sand in various shapes and sizes.
09.30-10.00	serving lunch and washing up food bowls.
10.00-10.30	tooth brushing, as we cannot rely on parents to have their offsprings do this daily.
10.30-11.00	storytelling by teacher and children alternately.

However, this timetable is quite flexible, for whenever something special takes place that event or occasion is given priority. The children are most of the day outdoors and only drawing is done inside the classroom. Although in the curriculum prescribed by the government the time devoted to the three Rs is prominent, more importance is given by us to free drawing with chalk on blackboards cut to size or on the sand of our beach. This has been adopted to save on materials for which we would have to spend more money. Learning to discern letters from the alphabet is done by way of drawing enlarged letters, the arrangement of which should teach them to spell their own names and those of the most conspicuous objects in their environment. In this context the weekly walks in the hills and the neighbourhood serve to stimulate their imagination and power of observation, which afterwards finds expression in the drawing class.

Interaction with village institutions happens largely through the village chief, and it goes without saying that our channel to the island's government is the district supervisor. The parent-teacher association we formed at the beginning became inactive after a year due to the failure of parents to attend meetings. To make up for this, we have our teachers make home visits at least once a week in order to familiarize themselves with the home conditions of the children.

Most parents have such a struggling existence just to meet the family's daily needs that they are unable to get involved in school concerns. It is well-known that poor parents delegate all the responsibility for their children to the teachers and find a happy excuse for this by saying that they are ignorant and backward people who cannot be expected to think beyond scraping a living.

After 15 years of running TK 'Gandhi' the following observations can be made:

1. Running a kindergarten in our area also means endeavouring to change the parents' outlook on life.
2. How difficult it is and what a long time and patience it takes to break bad habits and establish new ones in their place.
3. How good and sensible eating habits, which includes some understanding of nutrition, ultimately trickle through to parents, be it at a snail's pace.
4. If at first it took some cajoling and persuasion to draw children to our school, now there is no need to do that. The real problem is how to cope with so many children with only two teachers available.

5. How hard it is to stem the tide of consumerism and to correct the idea of 'progress'. Especially the newly developing countries are dazzled by material progress as displayed by the West. Whereas our orientation is human progress, which is anchored in the spirit unanimously pronounced in all scriptures, such as the Bible's admonition: 'What profiteth it man to gain the world and thereby lose his soul?'
6. One particular phenomenon with poor people dies hard: as soon as they have a bit of money it is spent on status rather than on necessities. This has been driven home to us very clearly in the TK 'Gandhi'.

   We have tried very hard to stick to simplicity and truth. Thus we have never encouraged the wearing of shoes and socks, nor of a uniform. Instead a pair of thongs will do for the protection of the children's feet, while on our premises the children are encouraged to wear as little clothing as possible. When a different group of people came to settle down in our area, that is when it opened itself to tourism, the children of this group of clerks and hotel employees entered our school. That happened in 1986 and shoes, stockings and town clothing made their entry into our TK. Uniforms copied from other kindergartens appeared. Not long after, even the poor fishermen and farmer parents insisted on their children's wearing the same outfit, even though they had to borrow to meet the expense. We have not yet decided whether we should bar the wearing of uniforms in our school.
7. Another problem is the increase of 'snacking' in the Ashram grounds, and what annoys us most is the amount of fast food snacks the children bring with them from home. Naturally they are mainly the children connected with hotels, restaurants or shops. We are thinking of being more strict in this regard with the new school year by prohibiting the bringing of snacks into our premises.
8. A more optimistic note, luckily, can be sounded. When during the first three years we started school with giving the children baths, paring their nails and showing them

how to use the toilets, etc., this can now be dropped. Spitting and littering have almost disappeared, while whatever food is served at lunch is neatly finished and food bowls properly washed.

9. We started the school with 27 children, painfully gathered over three months. For three years this number remained more or less constant, then dropped to ten kids in 1983-84. Most likely this was a reflection of the fact that by that time family planning had already taken effect and small children were indeed scarce.

In 1986 the number picked up, for the children of tourism-employed parents flocked to TK 'Gandhi'. This changed the aspect of our school somewhat and the town image gained the upper hand. If the local children became somewhat naughtier after a year of school feeding, now their general behaviour became distinctly rougher, their language at times rude, while some among them have become downright cheeky. This year, with 40 kids to cope with, our two teachers have their hands full and two other Ashram members have had to be put on duty to maintain order and the general functioning of the school.

From the above it is clear that the reader should not be misled by the term 'kindergarten' evoking the picture of a well-furnished and well-equipped classroom with teaching aids and all the paraphernalia common in the West. All these we cannot afford. From that point of view perhaps our venture should be termed a 'child-minding' service. However, the spirit that moves our undertaking should be seen as part of an endeavour to free ourselves of foreign domination.

It is the spirit to hold on to our true self and identity, to preserve our mother tongue, songs, dance, crafts: in short, all that is our own and has in course of time given birth to our particular identity. Yet we must do this without being deaf or closed to what comes from outside. I must quote here Gandhiji's incisive remark: "I do not want my house to be walled in. Let the winds from all corners blow freely in my house, but I refuse to be blown off my feet." To enable us to stand firm on our own feet a start should be made in kindergartens when the mind is still tender and malleable and emotion still relatively free from self-interest and calculation. Pondering over this I realize what tremendous patience and devotion are required from kindergarten teachers. A kindergarten is, in my opinion, a place where *ahimsa* can be practised at its best. Again, as Gandhiji observed: 'He who has not in him the quality of infinite patience cannot observe nonviolence'.

For Gandhiji *ahimsa* and active, pure love were interchangeable terms. We are aware of the very tiny speck of progress all our fifteen years of existence have shown. Even to achieve this all our Ashram members — in all, some fifteen girls and women — and our many guests and student volunteers have been involved and have interacted with our TK kids. In view of the present global problems it is a most pressing need to provide sound and inexpensive education, at as little cost as possible, in order to remain within the reach of the masses. And another remark of Gandhiji's will help us to search unceasingly for the application of *Swadeshi* in establishing our own identity. He said lucidly and pithily: 'What the average person cannot have I should refuse to have'.

Plans for the Future

We have nursed the hope some day to have our own primary school, a follow-up to our efforts in the TK to lay the base for clean, healthy, and creative living. It is said that whatever good habits we managed to establish among our children during a year most likely will suffer abrasion after years of attending other schools later. One year is too short a time to achieve anything solid.

But circumstances and conditions make this hope a very distant dream. Apart from financial limitations, to start another primary school is also superfluous when the existing two now find it hard to fill their first grade classes. But we should and must continue improving and upgrading our present undertaking. Our present experience could be put to good use in what we plan to start next year. Our 1996 project is named 'Holistic health to our countryside'. In this project the upgrading of kindergartens will also be covered.

Having run our public reading room at Canti Dasa Ashram for three years we have found that it does not satisfactorily meet our expectations, *i.e.*, to promote and stimulate healthy reading habits among village youth and avail of the opportunity to offer a reading place to the adjoining village school of Candi Dasa. Therefore we have decided to try a somewhat different approach with our new project.

The main idea behind this project is to promote holistic health in the countryside, particularly addressing ourselves to the youth and adolescents. Holistic health will concentrate on offering classes, free of charge, of the following nature:

(a) Teaching *Hatha Yoga* for the promotion of bodily health in a manner, which requires no expenses.

(b) *Mantra* chanting, promoting mental peace and a desire to know those *mantra*s which strengthen willpower, solidarity, the shedding of fear, and in general promote a nonviolent attitude and turn of mind.

(c) Promoting familiarity with and desire to live up to Gandhian thought and life-style.

(d) Nutrition in conjunction with *rshi-kriti* or nonviolent farming and gardening.

(e) Revival of local nursery rhymes and children's songs.

A sizeable van manned by Ashram members to teach the above classes, also carrying edifying literature for young people to widen their horizons without upsetting them, will move from village to village according to a schedule. For three consecutive months two villages will be alternately dealt with, in the hope that in the course of five years 40 villages will have been exposed to our classes. The morning hours should be devoted by the Ashram team to gaining information on eating habits, hygiene in general, existing local skills, crafts and customs, since our classes will be held in the afternoons. This information should serve us well in carrying out our project. Socializing with established and influential village members should be given prime importance.

Every weekend the team will discuss the information gained and the week's experience in our Ashram, their base.

We believe that by faithfully carrying out this project for, say, five years, we will have reached enough young villagers to spread general knowledge regarding 'holistic health', which covers sustainable nutrition based on chemical-free food, nature cure supported by yoga, chanting and acupuncture and taking up handicrafts as the main cure for 'woolly' thinking and idleness.

All these activities should lead to greater self-esteem and self-reliance, because they are rooted in the sound faith of religion.

The first and indispensable requirements for our project are therefore a sturdy van and devoted, skilful teachers. To obtain these is now the focus of our effort and energy.

M.K. Gandhi (1869-1948) and Ki Hadjar Dewantoro (1889-1959)

If in India Gandhi was unanimously hailed as the Father of the Nation, in Indonesia Ki Hadjar Dewantoro is looked upon as the father of national education and culture. Gandhiji's life could be said to have been devoted to the welding of all the ethnic communities in India into one nation that could be likened to a huge tapestry of brilliant colours, a reflection of the many customs and cultures of its components.

Indigenous education in Indonesia were the *pesantren* for the Moslems and the *ashrams* for the Hindus. Both were largely occupied with religious instruction. With the advent of the Dutch, who introduced their own system of education, the Moslems retreated even more into their *pesantren*, making of them a stronghold for the education of their youngsters. But in Java, where the indigenous orientation called 'kebatinan' was deeply rooted, *pesantren* became strongly coloured by this ancient belief, which is a kind of mysticism. Ki Hadjar Dewantoro, a prince from a court in central Java, underwent the same agony as Gandhiji when noticing the suffering of his people under the Dutch heel.

After several years of political life and pamphleteering he arrived at the same wisdom as Mahatma Gandhi did: that the road to the real freedom of his country could only start with education. Without completely dropping his vocation as journalist and political activist, he translated his ideas on education into action and started his now well-known institution of education named Taman Siswa. It literally means 'a garden for children'; but the clear connotation is 'a place to learn how to live'.

Twenty years separated him from Gandhiji, but the same ideas, by and large, kept both men struggling and fighting foreign rule throughout their lives in a down-to-earth manner, through opening schools, starting cooperatives, encouraging all kinds of productive activities. Both suffered imprisonment. Ki Hadjar Dewantoro even was exiled to live in cold Holland far away from the 'field' which he wanted to cultivate. Living there in near penury with his wife and two small children, his fighting spirit or his political activities did not abate.

After six years of internment the Dutch, forced through circumstances, had to release him. With the financial help of friends he was able to return to his beloved Indonesia, where undauntedly he pursued his struggle and opposition to the Dutch colonial government. The Japanese occupation came, and according to the Japanese, now that the Dutch were gone there was no need any more to have 'national schools' side by side with government schools. However, in an unobtrusive way Taman Siswa education continued to be pursued, for Ki Hadjar Dewantoro, with his clear vision, saw that its spirit must be maintained and fostered in the teeth of the existing schools, which were fed on pseudo-nationalism while in fact preparing us for another yoke, this time the yellow yoke.

This is not the place to elaborate on Ki Hadjar Dewantoro's philosophy, which forms the basis of Taman Siswa education. Nevertheless a few outstanding ideas found in his philosophy should be mentioned to see how parallel Gandhiji's and Dewantoro's ideas run. This is not to be wondered at, because both selfless and patriotic men were passionate lovers of freedom, not only for themselves but for all the people they belonged to. Thus both were the embodiment of their peoples' aspirations and suffering. If the motives are the same, the outcome and method of the struggle must be the same. The more so, because both had an unshakeable faith in the power of God.

Freedom-fighter and author of national education and culture, Ki Hadjar Dewantoro's vision affected not only the world of education but also social life and society itself. The following points show clearly where both the great men, Ki Hadjar Dewantoro and Gandhiji, met:

(a) Cultural nationalism, a favourite term with Ki Hadjar Dewantoro, has been accorded a high place, which shows his ability to look to the future. For the many and varied ethnic communities of Indonesia must arrive at a kind of national culture to weld the country into one solid cultural region.

(b) He revived the phrase 'Tut Wuri Handayani', an ancient Javanese aphorism expressing an educational principle in teaching and bringing up children. It gives full freedom to the child's initiatives, while parents follow from behind ready to correct it when things tend to go wrong or cause harm. In a wider sense it applies also to the relationship between government and governed, or state and people.

(c) The Taman Siswa philosophy believes in the right of self-determination.

(d) Taman Siswa adheres also to democracy, but one with firm moral leadership which keeps it from deteriorating into unbridled freedom and anarchy.

(e) It upholds self-reliance which, consequently, imposes voluntary simplicity, planning and healthy discipline on Taman Siswa people.

(f) The extended family approach — so natural among Asians — should be observed and applied in economic, social and political spheres as well.

(g) Principles of concentricity, convergence and continuity should be honoured. These three Cs require some explanation, for Ki Hadjar Dewantoro attached a special meaning to them. Concentricity in the Dewantoro sense fully agrees with Gandhiji's idea of what he called 'concentric circles' as seen in the ocean. Thus a person, apart from being his personal self, is also part of the family and of mankind. The term 'convergence' as used by Ki Hadjar signifies the relationship that should exist between small, big and biggest communities. Finally, by continuity he referred to the unbroken nature of culture as it developed from the hoary past.

(h) Nature and her laws reign supreme in the Dewantoro worldview as they did for Gandhiji. We therefore go to nature and observe her, learn from her how to live in harmony with her and with ourselves.

These points require unceasing observance if we want to see their result. That Dewantoro's view was prophetic is supported by the fact that the Taman Siswa schools have multiplied, not only in Java, but also in Sumatra and other islands in Indonesia.

The democratic character of Ki Hadjar Dewantoro is patent. Born of an ancient noble family, without hesitation he dropped his title of nobility – no mean thing in those days (1913) when nobility was much sought after by Indonesians – and changed his name from Raden Mas Soewardi Soerjodiningrat, in England the equivalent of Lord Such-and-Such, into plain Ki Hadjar Dewantoro in order to prove his belief in a classless society. Whereupon the whole Taman Siswa world followed suit, adopting the term Ki for men, Nyi for married women, and Ni for unmarried girls. His view of nationalism should be made clear, now that here and there nationalism tends to narrow down to fanaticism and exclusivism. Nationalism to Ki Hadjar Dewantoro should not violate or go against the humanitarian universal values we find embedded in all world religions. Also, his rejection of idolizing human beings while they are still alive or putting them on pedestals is worth noting. He shared this belief with M.K. Gandhi, who was averse to any kind of human idols.

Ki Hadjar Dewantoro's spirit of dedication to the child is preserved in the vow every Taman Siswa Teacher has to take:

> *Free from any form of attachment, in the purity of my heart, I will approach the child entrusted to me. Without demanding any right or privilege instead, in all fullness I will dedicate myself and serve it to the best of my capacity.*

Is it to be wondered then that his birthday, 2 May, has been declared by law on 16 December 1959 as a national holiday under the name of National Education Day?

Words as Deeds: Gandhi and Language

A half century after Mahatma Gandhi's assassination at the hands of a member of an ideological movement dedicated to an anti-Muslim construction of the Indian nation, the political wing of that movement finally achieved sufficient electoral success to become the leading coalition partner of an Indian government and to bring South Asia to the threshold of nuclear holocaust. This may be an appropriate time to reflect, once again, on the figure of Gandhi, what he said and did as well as what people have made of him, as a way of understanding some of the central issues of modern South Asian history.

In recent years the relationship between what Gandhi said and what others understood him to say has been examined with considerable subtlety and imagination. Shahid Amin, first in his now classic *Subaltern Studies* article, then in his fine book on Chauri Chaura, finally gave substance to all the talk of Gandhi as a mobilizer of widespread popular resistance to British rule by showing how Gandhi's message of democratic empowerment was understood in ways that swept aside a good many of its finer nuances, such as nonviolence. That Gandhi's Satyagraha campaigns stimulated violence is nothing new: it was continually pointed out at the time, not only by British authorities and conservative Indians, but even more insistently by Gandhi himself. What Amin documents, however, is the perspective of people who found in Gandhi a liberation from established authority. In one vivid scene, Amin describes crowds of people in the middle of the night at the Kumshi railway station, eight miles from Chauri Chaura, demanding that Gandhi present himself, though he was fast asleep. What happened when they finally got him up was what Amin calls a "slanging match" with a very angry Mahatma.

The significance of such an event is not merely a matter of miscommunication, however; it is, in fact, the breakdown of established lines of dominance and maybe the beginning of a new self-conscious social collectivity. Amin doesn't tell us much about the "slanging match," but what he does tell us is enough to suggest that Gandhi and his unruly devotees, however much they differed, were able to speak something like the same language. And the crowd was not wholly wrong in perceiving in Gandhi the rejection of the established authority of the British regime and an affirmation of what they were: the rural, as we now say, "subaltern" the people of India.

Gandhi, however, had his own notions of authority; it was his task to educate, discipline and control what he freely called the "mob." That others were able to appropriate Gandhi's powerfully mobilizing presence for a far less radical project, as Partha Chatterjee argues, was also, for better and for worse, part of the making of the Indian nation-state. "My language is aphoristic, it lacks precision. It is therefore open to several interpretations." Chatterjee uses this quotation as the epigraph to his chapter on Gandhi in *Nationalist Thought and the Colonial World.* What I want to consider here, in a very preliminary way, are questions about Gandhi's language or languages as well as what Gandhi said about language. It is remarkable that questions of language—speaking, listening, reading and writing—have hardly ever been taken up in any detail in all the vast literature on Gandhi. For such questions, the problem of what language to use on what occasion, who should be authorized to speak, who was in a position to hear, were explicitly matters of long-standing concern in Gandhi's life and thought and have had, I would argue, a direct relevance to an evaluation of the significance of Gandhi's role in overturning British rule and in creating modern India.

Hind Swaraj, probably the central text in Gandhian thought, was written, it has been said—I am not qualified to judge—in a somewhat nonstandard Gujarati in 1908, when Gandhi was still an expatriate. It is a comprehensive rejection, as Chatterjee says, not only of industrial society but of civil society altogether, including newspapers, parliaments and the whole apparatus, as it existed then, of modern communications. The vision of society, particularly Indian society, which Gandhi presented in that work and which he held to throughout his life was one of strong local communities, a subsistence economy, and a weak state.

Yet as early as *Hind Swaraj* Gandhi sets out a notion of a national linguistic order consisting of "provincial languages" and "a universal language for India[,...] Hindi, with the option of writing it in Persian or Nagari characters." In later years, Gandhi spoke frequently of the need to enforce compulsory study of Hindi throughout India, to establish it as the *rashtra bhasha,* the state language of a united India, leaving English to a limited role in international communications. As a major formulator of India's national linguistic order, Gandhi seems to be making space for a surprisingly far-reaching measure of bureaucratic uniformity of the sort examined by the French anthropologist Pierre Bourdieu:

> *Only when the making of the 'nation', an entirely abstract group based on law, creates new usages does it become necessary to forge a standard language, impersonal and anonymous like the official uses it has to serve.... The normalized language is capable of functioning outside the constraints and without the assistance of the situation, and is suitable for transmitting and decoding by any sender and receiver, who may know nothing of one another. Hence it concurs with the demands of bureaucratic predictability.*

There is, then, a striking disjunction between Gandhi's decentralized, pre-industrial utopia and his insistence on a political structure of national and provincial languages, the basis, more or less, of what emerged after independence as India's linguistic states and so-called three language formula. But it couldn't have been otherwise because, as Bourdieu points out, any language that "makes itself heard by an entire group is an authorized language."

The business of Gandhi, after all, was to mobilize a population to break with established authority, and that, in Bourdieu's terms, was a matter of constructing a new language by means of "the labour of enunciation," "the labour of dramatization." By performing such labours, Gandhi was harnessing far-flung points of discontent and rebelliousness in a vast land to constitute new categories and social spaces for the exercise of authority. This is, of course, Chatterjee's argument about the role Gandhi played, for all his personal ambivalence, in constituting the Indian nation-state.

The context in *Hind Swaraj* of Gandhi's brief mention of Hindi and what he called provincial languages—at a time, of course, when no Indian province had been defined on the basis of language—was his rejection of the purported benefits of English education and the entire role of the English language in British India. Imperfectly educated in English, Indians had to continually defer to British authorities, British ideas and British institutions. That Indians communicated with each other in English and took their quarrels to British courts in English were marks of the humiliation of colonial rule and sources of organized social enmity, as between Hindus and Muslims. But it was not the British who were to blame. "It is we, the English-knowing Indians, that have enslaved India."

To break the bonds of British rule and, even more importantly, of British cultural and psychological domination, it was necessary to reject the English language as a language of the state, the schools and even private communication among Indians.

The central point of *Hind Swaraj* is that Indian self-rule must be more than what later came to be called a transfer of power from British to Indian officials or, as Gandhi put it, "English rule without the English."

Yet Gandhi seems to suggest here, as elsewhere, that Hindi or a combination of Hindi, Urdu, and "provincial languages" would occupy the public, official and educational niches already established for English. Indians would no longer have to defer to British rulers or British ideas, but Gandhi leaves open the possibility of a political order that would merely translate the colonial systems from one language to another.

I will try to sketch an outline, then, of Gandhi's role in the creation of the linguistic order of the modern Indian state by examining, first, Gandhi's own linguistic practice – his "enunciative labour," if you please – then his ideas about the languages of India, and finally the organizations and policies that he advocated and participated in.

Gandhi's Language

It is significant that Gandhi's major writings – *Hind Swaraj*, his autobiography, *Satyagraha in South Africa*, his lectures on the Gita – are all in Gujarati. He tells us in his autobiography that he studied in the English medium from the Fourth standard and there was little or no formal space in the curriculum for Gujarati after that. He did, however, study Sanskrit in school, though he was briefly tempted to switch to Persian because it would have been so much easier. But the bulk of his education was in English, and one of the repeated refrains in his writings on language was how difficult, time consuming and ultimately frustrating it was to learn that language. He came to realize the futility of perfecting his command of English when, along with his French and his dancing lessons, he studied English elocution in London with a Mr. Bell. "Mr. Bell rang my bell," he says in his autobiography. I suspect the phrase gains something in translation.

In any case, Gandhi's Gujarati was no doubt heavily influenced by his English. He used English texts as models, notably in his rendering of Ruskin's *Unto This Last*; often the English versions are pervaded with little knots of embedded quotations and idiomatic expressions—"a consummation devoutly to be wished," "the unkindest cut of all," or for that matter, "Mr. Bell rang my bell,"—that raise suspicions about what came first, the English or the Gujarati. But these are matters that others would have to study.

What is clear is that it was Gandhi's intention to break the spell of English on India. It was a theme he returned to again and again, even as he continued to use English for a significant portion of his own writings, publications, and speeches. When he returned to India from South Africa in 1915, his first address to a welcoming party was in Gujarati and it was primarily about why Gujaratis should not speak English to each other.

His first major public address after the year of silence that Gokhale had mandated for him, at the inauguration of Banaras Hindu University (BHU), denounced the language that it was delivered in, English, and called upon Indians to speak Indian languages.

In the course of his life, Gandhi spent a great deal of time trying to learn the rudiments of several Indian languages, including the scripts. It is not clear to me whether he had any significant multilingual exposure in his childhood in Porbhandar and Rajkot, though there are scattered references to Tulsidas's *Ramcaritmanas* and Surdas, texts in literary Avadhi and Braj respectively. On his return from London as well as in an interval during his South African period, Gandhi spent a number of months in Bombay, and it is reasonable to suspect that he picked up some colloquial Hindustani there. But Gandhi's major exposure to Indian languages was in South Africa. It was there that he started his career as a writer of Gujarati, and, he later said, that he learned to speak what he variously referred to as Hindi or Hindustani, if only in a rudimentary form, with others who knew it no better than he did. On shipboard between South Africa and India, he joined an Englishman in hiring an Urdu teacher from steerage, though the Englishman made more progress than he did.

He also worked on learning some Tamil from a British primer. Later at Tolstoy farm, he used this knowledge to teach Tamil and Urdu script to children in the school, though it should also be noted that he terminated the Tamil and Hindi editions of the *Indian Opinion,* when he became editor, continuing to publish it in Gujarati and English. In later years, Gandhi continued to study Hindi, Urdu and, to some extent, Tamil whenever he had a chance, mostly in jail.

On the basis of these experiences, Gandhi maintained that a North Indian could learn Hindi in just a few months. It would take a South Indian somewhat longer but, in any case, far less time than the many hard, laborious years it takes to learn English. In his speaking and correspondence, he attempted to use Gujarati with other Gujaratis – though probably not with Jinnah. Increasingly, he relied on Hindi-Hindustani whenever he could, and complained when circumstances required him to speak or write to Indians in English. When he spoke or wrote in Hindi, he often apologized for the imperfections it contained. He was well aware that there were standards of Urdu and Hindi, exemplified in speeches by such figures as Hasrat Mohani or Madan Mohan Malaviya, which were beyond him. He insisted that it was preferable to speak the language poorly than to speak English, but he still aspired to learning to speak the standard language. The criteria for defining the standard language was a matter he considered of central political importance.

Policies and Organizations

Soon after returning to India, Gandhi took up language issues with renewed attention. His BHU address in 1916 was preceded by one to the Nagarini Prachar Sabha, the organization which is the centrepiece of Christopher King's valuable book and which was at the forefront of promoting the use and official recognition of the *devanagari* rather than the Urdu script. In that brief speech, he apologized for his poor command of Hindi, learned in South Africa, but supported the cause of the organization. Two years later, in a presidential address to the other major Hindi organization, the Hindi Sahitiya Samelan, he was better prepared and more careful, arguing, as he had in *Hind Swaraj*, that the term "Hindi" must be conceived to include Urdu and that the Urdu script also deserved recognition. In these speeches, Gandhi argues that the work of national leadership requires people to speak Hindi rather than English, because, as he said in the BHU speech, only then could they "speak to the heart of the people."

One way of interpreting what Gandhi said in 1916 is that he was not calling for a universal knowledge of Hindi, but rather a trickle down of knowledge and political persuasion from English to Indian languages, a policy not really all that different from Macaulay's overly quoted "Minute on Education." The English language creates too great a barrier between an educated leadership and the public. Hindi is more accessible than English, he claimed, because its grammar and vocabulary are closer to the other languages of north India, and its vocabulary, if not its grammar, is closer to the languages of the south. Using Hindi rather than English, then, was a matter of efficiency: it was easier to learn. But Gandhi also argued that there was a cultural spirit in the languages of India that separated them from English: "Our languages is a reflection of ourselves, and if you tell me that our languages are too poor to express the best thought, then I say that the sooner we are wiped out of existence, the better for us." The argument for cultural self-sufficiency, for not deferring to Britain for authoritative speech, raises, however, the question of the sources of authority in an independent India.

In 1920, in the wake of the Rowlatt Satyagraha and the onset of the Khilafat Movement, Gandhi became the unquestioned leader of the Indian National Congress. At the Nagpur Congress, the discussion was all about noncooperation, but along with that, and without extensive discussion, came a new constitution for the organization that, among other things, reflected Gandhi's ideas about language. Although three years earlier the Congress had recognized provincial organizations for Andhra and Sind (neither of them political entities in British India) based, more or less, on linguistic criteria, the idea of linguistic provinces had not inspired widespread discussion or significant support. Now, however, the local and provincial subdivisions of the Congress, which were to be much more active and ongoing under Gandhi's leadership, were totally redefined along linguistic lines, virtually the same lines that were to become the basis for independent India many years later with the States Reorganization Act of 1956. Gandhi continued to reiterate his opposition to the role of English as a language of authority in India, as "a permanent bar between the masses and the English-educated classes." But, of course, English continued to be used in the deliberations of the Congress, and Gandhi himself published an English periodical, *Harijan,* alongside his Gujarati one, *Navajivan,* and the short-lived Hindi-Urdu *Harijansevak* – a three language formula operation in itself. In his 1935 speech, once again to the Hindi Sahitya Samelan (HSS), he stated the matter clearly: the ultimate linguistic order of India should be "to use the language of the province in the province, to use Hindi for all-India purposes and to use English for international purposes."

The recognition of linguistic provinces, reiterated in the Nehru Report of 1927, was consistent with Gandhi's own advocacy and devotion to Gujarati, even as he supported Hindi or Hindustani as the national language, the language that would take the place of English for communication among Indians of different linguistic backgrounds. In that spirit, Gandhi campaigned most vigorously for Hindi in the south, establishing in 1927 the Hindi Prachar Sabha, a network of teachers and a body of instructional materials aimed at teaching Hindi to speakers of Tamil, Telugu, Kannada and Malayalam, all in the name of patriotism and national service. Ignoring anti-Sanskrit sentiment in Tamil Nadu, Gandhi argued that the common Sanskrit vocabulary would serve to bind the languages of India together. At the same time, Gandhi advocated that all Indian languages be written in the same script, *devanagari,* in order to make them easier to learn.

The one exception to Gandhi's notion of the unity of Indian languages and the desirability of a common script was his consistent concession to the legitimacy of Urdu's separate script and, to some extent, its Persian and Arabic vocabulary. Gandhi's definition of Hindi, Hindustani and Urdu and their interrelatedness varied from time to time and from setting to setting, and is closely bound up with his abiding concern about the relationship of Muslims to the Indian nation. In *Hindi Swaraj*, he appears to think of Hindi as a single language that can be written in either *devanagari* or Persian script, the latter a concession to Muslim sensitivities.

In 1917 Gandhi defined Hindi as "that language which Hindus and Muslims in the North speak and which is written either in the Devanagari or Urdu script." The difference between Hindi and Urdu, he then said, was merely a matter of the script. He dismissed the distinctions of lexicon—Hindi as "Sanskritized" and Urdu as "Persianized"—as trivial, of interest only to a few among "the educated classes," not to the "masses." Some years later, in 1937, Nehru, in an essay on language written with Gandhi's guidance elaborated this argument as follows:

> *Most of our present troubles are due to highly artificial literary languages cut off from the masses. [But if writers] think in terms of a mass audience, [t]his will result automatically in a simplification of language.... Language which is to make appeal to the masses must deal with the problems of those masses.*

There is no recognition here that there might exist significant linguistic variation aside from class or religion, or that "simplification" might also restrict the range of what people might want to say—when they are not speaking English. As for script, Gandhi conceded in his 1917 speech that "for the present, Muslims will certainly use the Urdu script and Hindus will mostly write in Devanagari." He recognizes here that among Hindus there was some significant identification with Urdu. He says, however, that once there is mutual trust and harmony among Hindus and Muslims, the matter of selecting an appropriate script will be decided on practical and scientific grounds.

In fact, Gandhi believed that ultimately *devanagari* would become the universal Indian script, but he was careful to mute that idea in most of his public statements on the issue. In his presidential address to the (HSS) in 1918, Gandhi stated that the term Hindi subsumed Urdu and that those who advocate the advance of the language should welcome the enrichment that Urdu might bring to it. By the mid 1930's Gandhi had formulated an idea of Hindi vs. Hindustani as the difference between a literary standard language and a language for oral communication, thus alienating a significant constituency of Urdu supporters. Then he shifted to the term "Hindi-Hindustani" to indicate that he advocated a language that freely used words of Persian or Arabic or, for that matter, any other origin, and to disassociate himself from those in the HSS who sought to purge Hindi of any marked Urdu words while opening the language freely to unmodified Sanskrit ones.

Finally, in 1942, Gandhi decided that the term Hindi had become irretrievably bound up with hostility to Urdu, so he shifted entirely to "Hindustani," forming a new organization, the Hindustani Prachar Sabha (HPS), and resigning, after much private and public negotiation, from the HSS. The HPS devoted itself to preparing teaching materials in a "Basic Hindustani," a concept first put forward by Nehru in his 1937 essay. It was to be modeled on something called "Basic English," an 800 word package that C.K. Ogden and I.A. Richards had devised as a universal language. The Quit India Campaign and subsequent imprisonment of the Congress leadership interrupted the project, but it was briefly revived in 1945 before being swept away by the partition.

The purpose of Gandhi's campaign for Hindustani was to stop what he claimed was an increasing differentiation between Hindi and Urdu, both of which he defined as "diseases" of the cities. As before, Gandhi claimed that there was a single unified "dehati," that is, rural, language, spoken by both Hindus and Muslims. As a national language, Hindustani should be learned in both scripts, though now he suggested that the language could also be learned in the scripts of other regions. Gandhi's position on script and Hindustani was entirely motivated by his concerns about Muslim-Hindu relations. Here he was torn between a desire to recognize the otherness of Muslims in a plural India and a desire to incorporate them into his vision of a monolithic India. In 1920, Gandhi had made a huge personal commitment to the Khilafat Movement entirely on the basis of its religious importance to Muslims. If it is important to our brothers and fellow countrymen, he argued, that in itself is sufficient reason to support the cause. His attitude toward Urdu script was similar: it was a matter of religious importance to Muslims and should be respected and nurtured for that reason. Hindus should learn Urdu in order to appreciate the culture of their Muslim neighbours.

Eventually, however, the two streams, Hindi and Urdu, would flow together, restored to what Gandhi claimed was their prior unity: "The source of the river of language lies in the Himalayas of the people." "Ultimately, when our hearts have become one, ... we shall reach a common language with a common script, whilst we shall retain provincial languages for provincial use."

I have argued that Gandhi sought to establish a new linguistic order to eliminate the dominance of English. Robert King has shown how Nehru handled the language issues, holding back for a time and then conceding on the issue of provincial languages, keeping the door open for the continued use of English but basically resisting the more vociferous attempts to impose compulsory language regimes upon India. Now, on reflection, fifty years after independence, the grand disputes about language have largely died down and the result has been something fairly close to what both Gandhi and Nehru had in mind. The standardized regional languages of India are in place at the state levels. What of Hindi-Urdu-Hindustani? If the guardians of a more Hindustani *shudh* Hindi are somewhat more relaxed now, it is because Urdu has virtually no official function and little educational recognition in contemporary India. In old Delhi's Urdu bazaar, on the steps of the Jumma Masjid, in the *maktab* at the Fatehpuri *masjid*, even Islamic texts are increasingly being sold and studied in *devanagari*. And English? You don't have to read the *New Yorker* to know that it is still there and not going away, and that it is the mark of class privilege. At least it isn't British anymore. Nor is it, by the way, American. "It is not that I am making a fetish of language," Gandhi said in 1937. "It is not that I would refuse to have Swaraj if I could have it at the cost of our language, as indeed I should refuse to have it at the cost of Truth and Non-Violence." He would not be pleased at the continued hegemony of English in significant sectors of Indian life, but then there is much in contemporary India that he would find far more appalling.

11

Legacy of Gandhian Education

Like many Indian philosophers, Gandhi subsumed freedom under truth. Only the free man, that is, one able to make his choices and decisions himself was able to discover, develop and live by his unique ontological truth. Freedom was thus the necessary basis and precondition of one's ability to be true to oneself. To deny, a man freedom was to force him to be untrue to himself and to live by someone else's truth. For Gandhi the case for freedom was simple, and the same as that for truthfulness. Respect for truth implied respect for human beings as they were constituted at a given point in time, and for their desire to live by their truth. Love of truth involved love of one's fellow-men as they were constituted, and not as one would like them to be. It could never therefore justify 'forcing them to be free' or sacrificing them at the altar of an abstract and impersonal ideal.

Even as Gandhi radically redefined the concept of freedom, he redefined the concept of equality. In much of the liberal and socialist literature on the subject, equality is defined in comparative, contractual, competitive and individualist terms. As we saw earlier, for Gandhi men were necessarily interdependent, rose and fell together, and were born subject to non-repayable debts. He located the idea of equality in this context. Relations between human beings were mediated by their membership of the social whole, and thus non-atomic and noncontractual in nature. Human beings grew and fell together, and hence their relations were necessarily noncompetitive and non-conflictual. And since they were uniquely constituted and had different needs and capacities, they were inherently non-comparable and could not be treated according to a uniform standard.

Since society was necessarily a fellowship of unique and interdependent beings, the concept of equality had to be defined in non-comparative, noncompetitive and non-atomic terms. For Gandhi, it basically consisted in each individual enjoying full access to his community's economic, political, moral and cultural resources in order to realise *his* unique potential; that is, not an abstract human potential as determined by a philosophical conception of human nature or by an arbitrary moral standard, but his potential *as an uniquely constituted being.* As a progressive and reflecting being each individual 'grew from truth to truth' and strove to enrich, deepen and reconstitute his being. Equality of human beings consisted in all alike being able to do so. It did not mean that I should get what others get, but rather that I should get what I need for my development as I define it. It was not only in my interest but that of all others that they should treat me equally, for in degrading and demeaning me they degraded and demeaned themselves and deprived themselves of the contribution I would make as a rich human being. Equality thus was not a mechanical concept or a synonym for uniformity. It was at bottom a relationship of mutuality and fellowship.

Gandhi also redefined the concept of citizenship. As a political activist he knew that not consent, nor will, nor fear, but cooperation was the basis of the state. Every state, democratic or otherwise, depended on the cooperation of its citizens, be it silent or vocal, passive or active, willing or unwilling. Since the state was an agency of action, their cooperation consisted in rendering it such specific services as carrying out its orders, paying taxes, and obeying the law. The state did not exist independently of its citizens, and was ultimately nothing more than a system of institutionalized cooperation between them. Since the state was a vast and complex organisation, they did not notice that it was their acts of daily cooperation that sustained it and that they were morally responsible for all it said and did. Every government was tempted to misuse its power, and the democratic government was in that respect no better than the autocratic.

What distinguished the two was the fact that one did and the other did not succumb to the temptation. And that was so because a democratic government knew that if it did, its citizens would refuse to cooperate with it. Notwithstanding all its institutional checks and balances, a democratic government could easily turn evil if its citizens became apathetic, vulnerable to corruption and manipulation, or lost their sense of moral responsibility. For Gandhi the virtues and vices of a government were not inherent in it but derived from those of its people. It was the coward who created the bully, the worm which encouraged others to trample on it, the morally irresponsible citizen who created a tyrant.

As a moral being the citizen had a duty to decide whom to give his loyalty and support and under what conditions. His self-respect and dignity required that his loyalty should not be unconditional or taken for granted. When a law was just, he had a 'sacred duty' to give it his 'willing and spontaneous obedience'. The duty had a dual basis. As a moral being he had a general duty to do or support the good. And as a citizen he had a specific moral duty to the community into which he was born and rooted, by which he was profoundly shaped, whose benefits he had enjoyed, and to whose members he was bound by the ties of loyalty and mutual expectation. If a law was unjust or morally unacceptable, he had a duty to protest against and even to disobey it.

To obey an unjust law was to 'participate in evil' and to incur moral responsibility for its immoral consequences. In Gandhi's view it was a 'mere superstition' and an attitude worthy of a 'slave' to believe that a citizen should uncritically obey all laws. To be a citizen was to be co-responsible for the activities of the government. And to obey a law was necessarily to support the government. Citizenship was not an autonomous and discrete role, but a mode of expressing and realizing one's wholeness and humanity through the medium of the state. No human being could extend uncritical and absolute support to the state without forfeiting his humanity.

I have so far concentrated on Gandhi's thought, and that is only a small and ultimately perhaps not the most important part of his remarkable life. Unlike men of thought whose ideas can be detached from and examined in isolation from their lives, Gandhi's thought, like that of Jesus and the Buddha, is deeply embedded in and of a piece with his way of life. His ideas grew out of his reflections on his experiences, even as his life represented a determined attempt to live out the ideals he espoused. The two formed a unity such that his ideas are best articulated not in the books and articles he wrote but in the kind of life he lived. His life was his greatest book and provides the most reliable clue to his writings.

For the first thirty odd years of his life, Gandhi was a *Grihasthi* who, in dutiful obedience to the conventions of his society, married, raised children, and discharged his social obligations. After that he felt free to disregard the social conventions and to write the script of his life as he thought proper. His central moral passion from now onwards was to attain *moksha*" a Hindu concept which had exercised him greatly for the past few years and which he radically redefined in the light of his understanding of his own religious tradition as well as Christianity and Judaism. In this redefinition *moksha* meant three things: first, total mastery of all ' the senses including sexuality; second, a mind freed of fear, jealousy, pettiness, meanness, vanity, and so on; and third, total dissolution of the sense of selfhood and the consequent identification-with all living beings in a spirit of universal love and dedication to the cause of 'wiping away every tear from every eye'. The first two primarily related to the personal, and the third to the social and political areas of life. Gandhi carried on an intense struggle at all three levels and sought to forge a pure and beautiful soul. The struggle was fierce and uncompromising and marked by moments of doubts and despair, but the overall result was a life of rare moral and spiritual grandeur.

A few random incidents of his remarkable life tell the story. During one of his many periods of incarceration, a black warder was bitten by a scorpion. When Gandhi heard his screams, he rushed to the spot, called for a doctor, and in the meantime started sucking out the poisoned blood, without the slightest thought for his life and in utter disregard of his own bleeding teeth. He went on spitting out the sucked blood until the victim felt relief, and quietly left the place as if nothing had happened.

Indulal Yajnik, his one-time close colleague, turned against him and wrote a vicious attack on him. He regretted this later and went to Gandhi to apolozise. It was Gandhi's day of silence. He saw Yajnik among his visitors and, before the latter could say anything greeted him with a reassuring smile and sent him a hastily scribbled note complementing him for changing sides only once whereas he, Gandhi, had done so more often. The poor Yajnik was in tears.

Maulana Azad, the Congress President, had without Gandhi's knowledge and against his wishes sent Stafford Cripps, the visiting British minister, a confidential note saying that he and the Congress had an open mind on the partition of India. When Cripps called on Gandhi, he was surprised to find that Gandhi knew nothing about the note and left it with him to mull over. When Azad went to see Gandhi the next day, the latter asked him if there was any communication between him and Cripps. Azad lied. Although his note to Cripps was lying on Gandhi's desk, Gandhi kept quiet. After Maulana's departure Gandhi's secretary suggested that the note should be copied and kept for a future occasion. Gandhi rebuked him, asked him to return the original to Cripps, and blamed himself for being unworthy of Azad's trust.

At one of his prayer meetings in 1947, a bomb exploded. As the frightened crowd began to scatter, Gandhi rebuked it for being frightened of a 'mere bomb', and continued to pray unperturbed. When the Government of India insisted that he should henceforth curtail his activities or at least accept protection, he rejoined that both courses of action compromised his commitment to nonviolence and were unacceptable to him. When Indian independence was drawing near, there was extensive inter-communal violence. Gandhi was deeply distressed and thought his entire life a failure. Not given to despair and defeat, he decided to fight the wave of violence single-handed.

Disregarding their physical safety, he and his followers fanned out into remote trouble spots and strove to create inter-communal peace. Believing, wrongly in my view, that he would be able to end the violence only if he eliminated all traces of violence and aggressiveness in himself, he embarked upon the daredevil experiments of sleeping naked with his female associates to achieve total purity Although attacked and shunned by his colleagues, he stuck to his guns. Just because they had made him a Mahatma, he was not prepared to confirm to their expectations of him. His life was his and it had to be based on *his* truth. If that meant losing his Mahatmahood, he was only too happy to shed the burden, and if it involved public criticism, he was prepared to brave it so long as he was convinced after deepest reflection that his action was right. Such an uncompromising spirit of moral independence is rare in any society; in a largely conventional India, it stood out as an enduring public symbol of dissent and defiance.

It is difficult to say whether or not and which of Gandhi's ideas would prove of lasting value. However there is little doubt that his life had a rare grandeur about it. His uncompromising commitments to truth and justice, his courage to write the script of his life himself, his relentless search for coherence and wholeness, his total lack of fear, his constant experiments with the possibilities of human existence, and so on are lasting sources of inspiration. As Gandhi said in 1937, 'My writings should be cremated with my body. What I have done will endure, not what I have said or written'. His life is surely his greatest legacy. And since it was a carefully crafted text, his thought too shares in its permanence.

Bibliography

Abbasayulu, Y.B.: *Scheduled Caste Elite: a Study of Scheduled Caste Elite in Andhra Pradesh*, Osmania University, Hyderabad, 1978.

Agarwal, L.B.: *The Harijans in Rebellion*, Taraporewala, Bombay, 1934.

Ahir, D.C.: *Dr B.R. Ambedkar: Buddhist Revolution and Counter-Revolution in Ancient India*, B.R. Publishing, Delhi, 1996.

__________: *Gandhi and Ambedkar: A Comparative Study*, Blumoon, New Delhi, 1995.

Ahluwalia, B. K.: *Netaji and Gandhi*, Indian Academic Publishers, New Delhi, 1982.

Ainapur, L. S.: *Dynamics of Caste Relations in Rural India*, Rawat Publications, Jaipur, 1986.

Aiyappan, A.: *Social and Physical Anthropology of the Nayadis of Malabar*, Bulletin of the Madras Government Museum, Madras, 1937.

__________: *Social Revolution in a Kerala Village: a Study in Culture Change*, Asia Press, Bombay, 1965.

Alter, Joseph S.: *Gandhi's Body: Sex, Diet, and the Politics of Nationalism*, University of Pennsylvania Press, Philadelphia, 2000.

Aluwalia, B.K. & Shashi B.R.: *Ambedkar and Human Rights*, KK Publishers, New Delhi, 1981.

Ambedkar, B. R.: *Annihilation of Caste: An Undelivered Speech*, Arnold Publishers, New Delhi, 1990.

__________: *Mr. Gandhi and the Emancipation of the Untouchables*, Thacker & Co., Bombay, 1943.

__________: *What Congress and Gandhi Have Done to the Untouchables*, Thacker & Co., Bombay, 1925.

__________: *Annihilation of Caste, with a reply to 'Mahatma' Gandhi*, Dalit Sahitya Akademi, Bangalore, 1987.

__________: *What Congress and Gandhi Have Done to the Untouchables*, Thacker, Bombay, 1945.

Anand, J. H.: *Dalit Literature is the Literature of Protest*, Dalit Solidarity, Delhi, 1995.

Anandhi, S. *Contending Identities: Dalits and Secular Politics in Madras Slums*, Indian Social Institute, New Delhi, 1995.

Arnold, David: *Gandhi, Harlow*, Longman, New York, 2001.

Atal, Yogesh: *The Changing Frontiers of Caste*, National Publishing House, Delhi, 1968.

Attenborough, Richard: *In Search of Gandhi*, Bodley Head, London, 1982.

Bailey, F. G.: *Caste and the Economic Frontier: A Village in Highland Orissa*, University of Manchester, Manchester, 1957.

Bakshi, S. R.: *Gandhi and Champaran Satyagraha*, Akashdeep Pub. House, Delhi, 1988.

Bamfield, J.A.M.: *Thoughts on Dr. Ambedkar*, Bheem Patrika Publications, Jaladhar, 1972.

Bandyopadhyaya, Jayantanuja: *Social and Political thought of Gandhi*, Allied Publishers, Bombay, 1969.

Bari, S.A.: *Gandhi's Doctrine of Civil Resistance*, Kalamkar Prakashan, New Delhi, 1971.

Barill, C.: *Social and Political Ideas of B.R. Ambedkar*, Aalekh Publishers, Jaipur, 1977.

Benjamin, Joseph: *Scheduled Castes in Indian Politics and Society*, Ess Ess Publications, New Delhi, 1989.

Beteille, Andre.: *Caste: Old and New*, Asia Publishing House, Bombay, 1969.

Bharti, Brahm Datt: *Gandhi and Gandhism Unmasked: Was Gandhi a Traitor?*, India: Erabooks, New Delhi, 1992.

Bhatt, Anil: *Caste and Political Mobilisation in Gujarat District*, Orient

Longman, Delhi, 1970.

Bhatt, V.: *The Harijans of Maharashtra,* All India Harijan Sevak Sangh, Delhi, 1941.

Bhattacharya, Bhabani: *Mahatma Gandhi,* Arnold Heinemann Publishers (India), New Delhi, 1977.

Blunt, E. A. H.: *Caste System of Northern India,* Oxford University Press, London, 1931.

Bondurant, Joan: *Conquest of Violence: The Gandhian Philosophy of Conflict,* University of California Press, Berkeley, 1971.

Borale, P.T.: *Segregation Desegregation in India: a Socio-legal Study,* Manaktala, Bombay, 1968.

Borman, William: *Gandhi and Non-Violence,* State University of New York Press, New York, 1986.

Bose, Anima: *Mahatma Gandhi: A Contemporary Perspective,* B.R. Pub. Corp., Delhi, 1977.

Brown, Judith M.: *Gandhi and Civil Disobedience,* Cambridge University Press, London, 1977.

Chadha, Yogesh: *Rediscovering Gandhi,* Century, London, 1997.

Chakravartty, Gargi: *Gandhi, a Challenge to Communalism: A Study of Gandhi and the Hindu-Muslim Problem, 1919-1929,* Eastern Book Centre, New Delhi, 1987.

Chatterjee, Partha: *Caste and Subaltern Consciousness,* Oxford University Press, Delhi, 1994.

Clark, S.: *Dalits and Christianity: Subaltern Religions and Liberation Theology in India,* OUP, New Delhi, 1998.

Cohn, Bernard S.: *The Changing Status of a Depressed Caste,* The University of Chicago Press, Chicago, 1955.

Dalala, Candulala Bhagubhai: *Gandhi: 1915-1948: A Detailed Chronology,* Gandhi Peace Foundation, New Delhi, 1971.

Danda, A.K.: *Weaker Sections in Indian Villages,* Inter-India, New Delhi, 1993.

Dangle, Arjun: *Poisoned Bread: Translations from Modern Marathi Dalit Literature,* Orient Longman, New Delhi, 1992.

Desai, I. P.: *Anti-reservation Agitation and Struggle of Gujarat Society,* Adjanta Publications, Delhi, 1985.

Index

□□□